DIVERSITY CHALLENGED

DIVERSITY CHALLENGED

Evidence on the
Impact of Affirmative Action

Edited by **GARY ORFIELD**
with Michal Kurlaender

The Civil Rights Project, Harvard University
Harvard Education Publishing Group

Library of Congress Card Number 00-136370
ISBN 1-891792-02-4

Harvard Educational Review
8 Story Street
5th Floor
Cambridge, MA 02138

Cover Design: Kate Canfield
Cover Photograph: Susie Fitzhugh
Editorial Production: Dody Riggs
Typography: Sheila Walsh

Contents

107827

Acknowledgements

We are grateful for the support provided to The Civil Rights Project by the John D. and Catherine T. MacArthur Foundation, Charles Stewart Mott Foundation, Ford Foundation, and Spencer Foundation. Christopher Edley, Jr., codirector of The Civil Rights Project, has been a strong and consistent supporter of this work. We also express our appreciation to the staff at The Civil Rights Project who contributed to various aspects of this enterprise, in particular Suenita Lawrence, Marilyn Byrne, Johanna Wald, and Christina Safiya Tobias-Nahi.

We are indebted to the Harvard Education Publishing Group, especially Dody Riggs, without whose extraordinary work this book could not have been completed. We also extend our appreciation to Susan Kenyon, Edward Miller, and Joel Vargas, who contributed at different stages of the editing process.

Most importantly we want to thank the authors, who put other work aside to answer our call for new research on this subject and who have been responsive and patient throughout a long editing process.

Introduction

GARY ORFIELD

In the courts and in referenda campaigns, affirmative action in college admissions is under full-scale attack. Though it was designed to help resolve a variety of serious racial problems, affirmative action's survival may turn on just one question—whether or not the educational value of diversity is sufficiently compelling to justify consideration of race as a factor in deciding whom to admit to colleges and universities. This book is designed to address that question.

Concerns about racial justice, about training leaders for the future of communities and the professions, about purging campuses of racist attitudes, worries about excluding large sectors of the tax-paying population—all these have influenced university admissions policy but have been largely ignored by the courts. For almost a quarter century, affirmative admissions policy has rested precariously on a one-vote majority in a U.S. Supreme Court decision that turned on the educational benefits of diversity on campus. Future decisions may well turn on whether researchers find evidence strong enough to convince skeptical judges that schools with very few minority students offer a more limited education and an intellectually weaker campus environment.

In *Regents of the University of Califormia v. Bakke*, the Supreme Court's closely divided 1978 decision upholding a limited form of affirmative admissions policy, Justice Lewis Powell, who cast the deciding vote, recognized only one legitimate justification for considering race as a factor in a multidimensional process of selecting students—that diverse student bodies produce better education and more stimulating campus communities. This was, he said, the reason why universities had traditionally been given broad latitude in selecting their students and why they sought to reflect many forms of diversity on campus. He quoted with approval Harvard College's justification for its affirmative action policy as a critical ele-

1

ment in providing a good education. Ironically, it has now become necessary to prove that white students and all other students gain something vital educationally to justify policies intended to offset the history and traditions of white preference.

Affirmative action is rooted in the civil rights revolution of the 1960s, which produced the most important civil rights laws of the twentieth century and led to conclusions both by enforcement agencies and the courts that race-conscious civil rights policies were necessary in a number of areas of entrenched racial inequality. After many years of trying voluntary and case-by-case solutions, judges and other officials concluded that the only way to achieve equal opportunity was to plan for it, to explicitly consider race when necessary to break segregation and exclusion, and to measure the results. After years of civil rights policies that created equal opportunity on paper but left the basic structures of inequality virtually untouched, the law required policies strong enough to actually change the outcomes.

Policies taking race into account to break the effects of long-term discrimination were not merely tolerated but often required by courts and civil rights agencies. School desegregation remedies by the late 1960s had explicit racial goals and required prompt reassignment of students and teachers on a racial basis to produce truly desegregated schools. Fifteen years of frustrating choices and transfer policies had left the basic segregation system almost untouched.[1] The Voting Rights Act's powers were triggered, in good part, by statistics showing a history of exclusion and conditions likely to perpetuate those differences in a state or community.[2] Trying to prove discrimination against minority voters in every community had proved to be ineffectual. Affirmative action in employment and minority contracting came out of the failure of case-by-case prosecution of job discrimination and a recognition of the difficulties of starting businesses able to compete with long-established firms whose decisive advantages grew out of the history of discrimination. In housing, the Supreme Court approved a remedy in the Chicago *Gautreaux* decision[3] that called for policies to move segregated public housing families to subsidized private apartments in white suburbs.

Affirmative action in college admissions was part of this movement. Until there were explicit plans, very little integration occurred on selective campuses. Elite campuses outside the South went into the civil rights period with no significant integration. The basic idea of the new policies was that the effects of a history of racial exclusion were deeply embedded and could not be altered without a serious plan to change them. Nineteen U.S. states had a history of setting up separate black public colleges and universities. Few selective campuses in any part of the country had significant numbers of blacks, Latinos, or Native Americans before affirmative action.[4]

Though segregation by law was ruled unconstitutional in the 1950s, enforcement in higher education was desultory for decades. The 1964 Civil Rights Act required federal action against discrimination, including cutting off federal aid when colleges did not comply with civil rights requirements. In 1973, however, in *Adams v. Richardson*, a federal court found that the government had failed to enforce the law. It found continuing failure of enforcement in subsequent years. The resulting 1978 federal regulations led states with historically segregated colleges to adopt explicit plans with statistical goals, targeted scholarships, and other policies to break down the continuing racial separation and to ensure that students from each race would have equal access to public colleges. Federal sanctions were never used, however, against any state failing to meet its goals. The Reagan administration announced that the goals did not need to be met.

The peak of the movement for diversity on campuses came in the mid-1970s, when minority high school graduates had about the same chance as whites to start college the next fall. The Supreme Court's decision in the 1978 *Bakke* case, which limited affirmative action and opened up campuses to suits by whites, slowed change, as did major cutbacks in financial aid and the increased use of entrance examinations during the 1980s.

The Hopwood Shock

The pendulum of civil rights policy began to swing clearly in the other direction after many new judicial appointments during the Reagan-Bush era. For almost two decades after *Bakke* there had been no serious challenges to the limited university affirmative action policies, and little research was conducted to prove its benefits, which seemed obvious to many in higher education. In retrospect, there was a clear failure of the higher education community to foresee the implications as the courts were restructured by hundreds of conservative appointments. These judges became increasingly hostile to all forms of race-based policies in other areas of civil rights.[5]

Academic leaders, however, were stunned by the 1996 Texas decision prohibiting affirmative action and the California state referendum that made it clear that no consensus existed on the benefits of diversity, and by the fact that the academic world, whose leaders were overwhelmingly committed to maintaining diverse campuses, had not done its homework. The research had not been done to prove the academic benefits and the necessity of affirmative action admissions policies.

The higher education and civil rights communities have been struggling to recover ever since. Besieged by threats of lawsuits, political attacks, and claims that their policies are not necessary, university leaders must have good evidence. There is a serious risk that some judges will rule against universities unless they can prove that affirmative action is essential for compelling educational needs that cannot be met well without considering race in admissions. This is, of course, a question that can be researched and thought about within a number of disciplines and research traditions. Though it might seem a simple question—does having more minority students on campus produce educational gains?—the truth is that universities are complex institutions and the knowledge of what impact change has on students is limited. It is important to know not only the impact on students' coursework, but also on their understanding and capacity to think and work within a complex and rapidly changing society. To evaluate this we need to know what to look for, how the institutions evolved, and how to think about, measure, and interpret the impact of diversity. Philosophy, history, economics, law, sociology, education, political science, and public policy are some of the disciplines that have been brought to bear on these questions.

The basic intellectual challenge posed by the current legal situation is to demonstrate clear relationships between more diversity in campus enrollment and enriched intellectual experiences for students and professors. The first step is to consider theories of how the expected benefits work. This is difficult for many reasons, one being that little relevant data is collected at colleges. In the ideal research world we would have students of each race studied before their education, again near the completion their studies, and afterward to see how things changed for them. We would have students attending schools with widely varied racial compositions and, if we wanted to control all the selection bias issues, assign them to diverse or segregated campuses and classrooms on a randomized basis. In reality, most colleges collect substantial data about achievement before students enroll but very little systematic information afterward—little more than grades and graduation statistics. In the real world it is unlikely that we will ever have randomized experiments on college enrollment, and it would be a number of years before any major new longitudinal data could be collected. To inform the current debates, we focus first on what can be learned from existing data and from studies that can be carried out in a limited period of time.

In 1996, at a time when some federal courts began to shift the burden of proof to those who wished to maintain affirmative action and California voters outlawed affirmative action through a public referenda, no major research addressing these issues had been done. There had been substantial research on the impact of desegregation in elementary and secondary education, which is summarized in Janet Schofield's chapter in this book. That research was mostly about the impact of diversity on black students, and most of it studied little more than short-term test scores. Little is known about what white students learned from interacting with blacks and Latinos, though we know that they did not suffer academically. Desegregation research does, however, provide important starting points for thinking about higher education issues. It showed that the scope of the gains depended on how the desegregation was handled, and that some of the most important effects were not about easily measurable academic skills but about how the students' future education, jobs, and adult relationships worked out. These findings suggested that assessing diversity in higher education would not be simple or one-dimensional. The effects of diversity are likely to be multiple, to be played out over time, and to be influenced by issues of climate, leadership, and policies. Putting all these variables into a research design for colleges would be extremely complex, expensive, and time-consuming. Little baseline data has been collected so far.

Good research requires good theory to help decide which relationships should be measured, to either prove or disprove the theory. Good theory is also needed to help interpret results and explain their meaning. Fortunately there had been serious thought about the theories of the educational impact of diversity on colleges by faculty committees and administrators, by researchers, and by the courts in *Bakke* and earlier decisions on college segregation. An elegant and wide-ranging expression of the theory in the context of Harvard University, whose policies were relied upon by the Supreme Court in *Bakke,* is presented in this volume in the chapter by Harvard president Neil Rudenstine. Rudenstine argues that diversity is indeed a central and compelling interest of the college, and he lays out many of the issues explored in the research reported in later chapters. His essay fleshes out the assumptions of *Bakke* and contains a number of propositions, offered as logical deductions, that research in other chapters shows to be true.

Ultimately, judgment about the evidence on the impact of diversity will be made in the courts and the issues will be shaped by legal considerations embodied in the most important judicial pronouncements on this and related civil rights issues. The courts are shifting the burden of proof to affirmative action supporters and have gone a long way to define the questions that the researchers must answer if their work is to help shape the outcome of these challenges. Researchers may object to the assumptions and to the way the questions are framed, but answers are nevertheless needed to a set of questions within a context of assumptions about history and the society. Researchers must try to find the best evidence on the questions as they are posed. At the same time, of course, researchers can explain why some questions are, in principle, unanswerable, and draw on both empirical research and theory to explain why other issues should be added to the analysis. Scott Palmer's chapters provide a valuable research guideline by trying to translate the court decisions into empirical questions and to outline the most relevant research questions. His essays show how narrow the path is for the defense of affirmative action under the Rehnquist Court and how much work must be done.

Facing important national policy questions that cannot be answered fully for a long time, we decided to take the more modest steps feasible now to move the debate from one of pure ideology and supposition to one using information from the best available sources that could answer elements of the large questions. Our first step was to contact researchers, college officials, legal scholars, civil rights lawyers, government officials, and others to ask them to help to define the key immediate and longer-term research questions and to identify data sources that could help answer them. This was done through three national conferences, widespread correspondence and discussions with researchers across the country, and extensive review of published research. These steps led to commissioning a series of scholarly studies for our national conference on diversity, and to a strong collaboration with the American Council of Education and other organizations in defining research goals. In addition to our work, the American Educational Research Association sponsored a related project at Stanford University, which produced another series of studies,[6] and national surveys of general faculty and law school faculty were implemented. In mid-2000, the American Council of Education and the American Association of University Professors released the first studies from the faculty surveys growing out of the consortium working on research priorities.[7]

Five years after the 1996 crisis, the chapters in this book show that a great deal has been learned. One of the first steps was to try to extract whatever might be learned from large surveys that happened to contain information that could illuminate some of the important issues. Large surveys of college students and faculty by UCLA and the American Council of Education, for example, contained a few questions that addressed some of the theories of educational impact. The chapters by Mitchell Chang, Sylvia Hurtado, and Jeffrey Milem are derived from such survey datasets and were the first empirical work on the subject that the project was able to commission. Each of these chapters uses a few questions from large surveys designed for other purposes to obtain some findings on the issues. Chang shows that more diversity promotes more interaction and that socialization across racial lines, and is associated with more discussion of issues, better retention in college, and higher satisfaction with the college experience. Milem shows that faculty on campuses with more diversity are more likely to use different teaching styles and to deal with diversity in their teaching. Hurtado finds evidence of benefits in terms of leadership, awareness of other cultures, and ability to work collaboratively. The basic results of these studies are that diversity does make a difference, but that the differences are neither automatic nor uniform.

Another creative use of existing data is presented in the chapter by three economists, Kermit Daniel, Dan Black, and Jeffrey Smith, who use existing longitudinal data collected for other purposes to explore the relationship between college diversity and earnings, defining as one of the compelling interests of the institutions and society the production of maximum added economic benefits for the economy from higher education. If minority students get far bigger benefits than whites from access to competitive colleges, a finding strongly confirmed in Bowen and Bok's *The Shape of the River*, increasing minority enrollment increases net benefits. Even more interesting is the finding that whites also gain economically from attending diverse campuses. These researchers find that increased campus diversity increases economic productivity for both groups, perhaps through creating economically valuable skills that are not measured in conventional research but are clearly valued in the market, such as the ability to understand diverse markets.

There are many limits to what can be learned from data collected for other purposes. Explicit tests of theories through new research are much more difficult and time-consuming. Discussions among researchers concluded that new surveys of faculty and students examining the impact of diversity in much greater depth than existing studies would make a difference. It is much easier to reach conclusions on specific effects if direct and indirect questions can be designed into the surveys, and if they can be asked to appropriate samples in a variety of ways rather than inferred from a few general survey questions designed for very different purposes. This book contains several essays from a growing wave of new research. Roxane Gudeman's study of faculty attitudes toward diversity is both an important case study of the beliefs of the faculty about the impact of diversity on education in a highly ranked liberal arts college in the Midwest, and was also the first test of a faculty survey developed by the research consortium. Subsequently this survey was administered to a sample of campuses.[8]

The study by Gary Orfield and Dean Whitla is a 1999 survey of students at two of the nation's leading law schools about the ways in which diversity shapes the educational experience at these extremely selective and competitive schools. The data speak directly to the theories set out a half century ago, in the Supreme Court's early decisions on desegregation of law schools in the South and on the right of universities to select their own student bodies to realize their educational goals. The survey produced strong positive findings about the intellectual impact of diversity, very consistent across the campuses and across the racial and ethnic groups on campus. Students saw a positive impact by very large margins, and many believed that more should be done to fully realize the possibilities. The results tended to confirm both Justice Powell's theory in *Bakke* and Rudenstine's philosophical analysis.

The Louisville (Kentucky) study of juniors in high school by Michal Kurlaender and John Yun provides another look at the impact of diversity on student development. This study, developed in collaboration with researchers across the nation and the National School Boards Association's Council of Urban Boards of Education, surveyed students during the 1999–2000 school year. Though not a study of higher education, these students were near the end of public school education and thinking seriously about the upcoming transition into college. Metropolitan Louisville, where the city and suburban school systems were combined by a court order a quarter century ago and where all of the students have attended desegregated schools for many years, offers an unusual opportunity to explore the issues in schools with much higher levels of integration than have been achieved so far in most selective colleges. Most of these students had consistently attended substantially desegregated schools. On a number of the outcomes, as many as 90 percent of the students (in virtually identical results for both blacks and whites) express large or significant benefits from their educational experiences. The students believe that they are ready to work and live in a multiracial community and are confident that they have learned how to discuss complex issues constructively across racial lines. If the existence of effective crossracial democracy and successful collaboration at work within our profoundly multiracial society that will have no racial majority in a half century are compelling interests, these data suggest that they can be furthered by diverse educational experiences.

The surveys of the law students and the high school juniors show that students at both levels believe they have achieved an understanding of racial differences and of ways of living and working together successfully. These beliefs could, of course, be mere rhetoric or expressions of hope. In this respect, the important work done by Patricia Gurin at the University of Michigan and some of the longitudinal studies of the effects of school desegregation offer important confirming evidence. At Michigan, students who were studied years after their experiences with diversity on campus actually showed the ability to think about issues in a more complex way than those without such experiences.[9]

School desegregation research has, in a number of studies, reported "perpetuation effects" suggesting that students who learn in a desegregated way lead desegregated lives, enjoy greater success in college, and work in different jobs, and that white and minority students are more likely to live in integrated neighborhoods as adults (studies summarized in Wells and Crain).[10] Susan Eaton's study of black students bused to suburban schools in Boston shows that their multiracial experience had a large impact on their ability to move successfully across racial lines in professional positions as adults.[11]

This book also presents two other ways of thinking about the issue of diversity. One, in the chapter by Tim Ready, explores the importance to the medical profession of training a diverse group of medical practitioners in a diverse setting. Since the best efforts of a number of medical schools with strong outreach efforts have not succeeded in maintaining diversity after the end of affirmative action, these are very important issues; a failure to resolve them may block not only the judgment of the professionals in the schools about their mission for the state, but also the provision of basic and essential health services for populations already poorly served in racially stratified communities where few whites ever set up practice.

A final perspective comes from a scholar who has watched the transformation of his own university throughout the struggle over desegregation and affirmative action. The University of Virginia, founded by Thomas Jefferson and one of the nation's leading public institutions, was almost totally segregated until the late 1960s and is now under pressure to end affirmative action. Paul Gaston, a professor emeritus and an eminent historian of the South, offers a historical perspective and personal observations of the change, reflecting on the fact that a university cannot really effectively teach about the realities of American history and society without reflecting the diversity within. Since so much of the analysis by the courts and by researchers is without historical perspective, this is an important corrective. Gaston argues that the pre-affirmative action university was neither neutral nor benign, but dominated by attitudes of white supremacy and without a significant challenge in classes. He reflects on the ways the coming of significant integration profoundly improved discussions of the region's own history and produced not only a greatly improved discussion, but also circumstances under which students became much more able to think across the racial line and understand and seriously consider the perspectives from the other side.

Before considering the rich and diverse perspectives in this book, I will briefly discuss two general issues that affect the entire discussion. The first is the way history is treated in reshaping the legal framework of affirmative action. The second is a specific finding in the most important decision forbidding affirmative action—*Hopwood v. Texas*, which concluded that there were no differences that made an intellectual contribution to universities that came from admitting students of other races and, therefore, there could, of course, be no compelling interest in continuing this policy.

The first of these issues is tilting the legal battle in a serious way. The assumption is that discrimination ended when civil rights laws were enacted and that the history of discrimination in all aspects of public policy for many generations has no continuing effects that the courts need to consider today, unless someone can directly and precisely prove the contrary. I believe this conclusion is simply indefensible and betrays a profound misunderstanding of the overwhelming social science evidence on the situation of minorities and whites in American society.

The basic assumption is that there was discrimination and exclusion long ago but that active discrimination ended with the enactment of civil rights laws between 1964 and 1968. These historic laws, the assumption goes, changed contemporary practices and substantially ended discrimination, and the impact of previous discrimination gradually dissolved. Therefore the inequalities observed today must result from nonracial causes and are not the responsibility of government. Even in a state like Texas, which has generations of de jure segregation of higher education, it can be assumed that the effects of that history no longer matter, even if the basic pattern of segregated campuses never fundamentally changed, and even if the state has fallen far short of its 1978 higher education desegregation plan for equitable college access for minority high school graduates, and even if the federal courts repeatedly found that enforcement of higher education civil rights regulations had fallen far short in the 1970s and 1980s (no sanctions had been imposed on any institution or state government that failed to meet the diversity goals it submitted to the Office for Civil Rights of the U.S. Education Department). The historical assumptions are that the long-established racial identities of the campuses do not matter, that the alumni connections to segregated campuses do not matter, that the differences of wealth growing out of unequal college education in the past have no continuing effects, that the continuing pattern of segregated and unequal public schools has no relationship to history, that the absence of a significant presence of minority faculty and administrators throughout the history of many campuses has no continuing effect, and that on-campus isolation and discrimination today is not linked with the state's past. I think that these assumptions are not credible.

No one disputes that race was terribly relevant for a very long time. The history of apartheid laws and practices in Texas, for example, enforced segregation in many aspects of life until well into the 1960s. The first president from Texas, Lyndon Johnson, often discussed his personal experience with segregation in his state and recalled teaching Mexican American children in painfully unequal schools.[12] Though civil rights laws have prohibited the use of law to require segregation or unequal treatment, giving formal equality of opportunity in a society where the history meant that the various races had profoundly unequal resources, contacts, and information, and where private discrimination was still commonplace, does not produce genuine equity. Unequal situations and the institutions and attitudes developed around race tend to perpetuate themselves unless there are effective interventions that actually overcome the vestiges of historic discrimination. The enactment of civil rights laws did not transform the views of those who were prejudiced or end the temptation to exploit racial fear and polarize communities on racial lines with "wedge issues" intended to win elections. This was, in fact, the basic policy of the first president elected after the civil rights era, Richard Nixon, whose chief of staff has described in detail the president's own beliefs in minority inferiority and his continual directives to use civil rights issues to polarize white voters.[13] Laws do not enforce themselves and attitudes about difficult social issues tend to last and to have a continuing impact. The court decisions assuming that the burden of history has been lifted and that race no longer matters in American society assume a kind of sudden and irreversible change for which our history of race relations offers little support.

If one accepts the assumptions about the end of discrimination and starts with the premise that all existing conditions are disconnected from the institution's and the state's history, and that the institutions have fully met their constitutional obligation to overcome the damage caused by segregation, then it would be reasonable to require that supporters of affirmative action prove that the disparities in student admissions are caused by discrimination today. Under this policy the mere fact that few minority students were admitted would have no significance. One would have to have either a confession by officials that their policies were intentionally designed to discriminate or proof of the way specific problems were related to particular historical "vestiges of discrimination." Since discrimination works on many levels and its effects are often internalized in the actions of the victims, and since its influence is mixed with many other influences on students and many of the factors that are used as "controls" in measuring discrimination (such as income and social and educational status) are often themselves products of the history of differential treatment, the analysis becomes impossibly complex. Anyone demanding precise proof of such relationships is demanding something that is not possible and is, in effect, denying the right.

If all these assumptions were true it would, of course, be appropriate to be concerned that continuing civil rights remedies would be unfair to whites and that whites should be the principal protected class, and that policies producing the result of unequal treatment of a white student with a higher test score could be presumed to be discriminatory. This is the kind of intellectual universe within which anti–civil rights decisions are being framed. Most of these propositions cite no evidence. They are simply asserted. The nature of these assumptions should be kept in mind as readers consider the evidence in this book.

Are We All the Same?

The second issue is that there are no real differences among the black and white and Latino experiences in contemporary American society and culture, and therefore there are now no grounds to legitimately treat all members of a race as the members of a disadvantaged group since few if any characteristics are reliably linked to race. The Court of Appeals decision in *Hopwood* argued that it was irrational to believe that achieving diversity actually brought to campus students with different perspectives and experiences:

> The use of race, in and of itself, to choose students simply achieves a student body that looks different. Such a criterion is no more rational on its own terms than would be choices based upon the physical size or blood type of applicants. . . .

> A university may properly favor one applicant over another because of his ability to play the cello, make a downfield tackle, or understand

chaos theory. An admissions process may also consider an applicant's home state or relationship to school alumni. . . .

The assumption is that a certain individual possess characteristics by virtue of being a member of a certain racial group. . . .

To believe that a person's race controls his point of view is to stereotype him . . .

The court holds that there is no rational basis to predict that minority students will bring different views or perspectives to campus. Yet one of the most consistent findings of social research and government statistics and reports in the United States is that race does make a difference and the differences are often profound.

Before considering some of the evidence on these questions, we need to think about both the implicit and the explicit premises of the court's reasoning. The decision states, quite accurately, that race does not automatically or always determine perspectives and that there is a good deal of individual difference within races and overlap among the views of blacks, whites, and Latinos. From this truism, the argument leaps ahead to claim that, because everything is not different, there are no important differences among the groups or even any racial differences deserving recognition. It is like saying, for example, that there is no difference that it would be legitimate to recognize in assigning military personnel to combat duty because there are some women who are much tougher and more eager for combat than some men. That is true, but there are still very important differences, and the law recognizes the legitimacy of recognizing them in policy.

There is a deep internal contradiction within the *Hopwood* decision. It concludes that diversity arguments that depend on the probability, not the absolute certainty, that students of difference races will bring different perspectives and experiences to the student body are not permissible, in part because all minority students do not have such views; on the other hand, the probability, which is far from a certainty, that a student with a particular test score will perform better than a student with a lower score can be considered a fair measure of absolute merit in making decisions about individuals. The court assumes that tests can do much more than is actually possible and that minority admissions can do much less, treating one as a clear and specific measure of individual merit and the other as having no value for predicting intellectual contribution. In fact, both have real but limited predictive power, but the predictions cannot be applied to any individual with any certainty. Admissions decisions are judgments about probabilities; no one ever knows just how any individual student will perform. The best admissions tests only explain part of the average performance in the first year at college of a *group* of students within a certain test score range. On average a group of students with an SAT in the 700 range will get higher grades than a group of students with around 550, but some of the 700s will fail and some of the 550s will end up with A's. In fact, a given administration of a test cannot even tell with confidence whether or not the student is really a 700. There are measurement errors and inconsistencies of scores by the same student.

The court in *Hopwood* displays a serious misunderstanding of both the race-based and the "objective" measures of merit and of the nature of admissions decisions. It incorrectly assumes that some differences it does believe should be recognized in admissions, such as test scores, are absolute individual measures of merit and legitimate grounds for decisions in their own right. In fact, tests are no such thing. They are neither designed to nor do they accurately predict individual achievement. In fact, the same individual often gets quite different scores on different administrations of the same test. Anyone who has served on college admissions committees has seen many cases of large differences of this sort, and we know that scores can be raised by paid tutoring. Any faculty member who has served on an admissions committee has seen many files where the SAT scores of the same student differ by more than 100 points between one testing and the next. More important, the testing organizations recognize a large margin of error in their predictions and claim relative accuracy of prediction not for individuals but for groups of people with the same scores. Thus, what appears to be a very specific and accurate individual prediction of academic merit is actually a very imperfect statistical prediction of early course grades for groups of people with similar test scores. All of the major factors that admissions committees consider, such as grades and recommendations, share similar limits—they are rough predictors of probabilities of success, not highly reliable and accurate predictors of the individual student's career.

Thus what we are doing in admissions is making general assessments of students, estimating on the basis of probabilities what they will bring to the campus community. Students with very high test scores are more likely to receive very high grades, students who have strong high school athletic achievement are more likely to contribute to college teams, and high school debaters may well become better political science students, but none of these predictions is highly accurate in all cases. In spite of the uncertainty, it is well worth considering these factors in admissions. By the same token, it is well worth considering race if the goal is to bring into the classroom students with a broader range of experience and perspectives.

There is powerful evidence to show that admitting minority students is likely to bring onto the campus students with different worldviews and experiences that can enrich the discussions and exchanges in and out of class that are so important to a good college education. In spite of shared values, there is a strong probability that most blacks and Latinos in American society will have a different view of many important issues from that held by most whites. There is abundant data showing that deep racial and ethnic differences persist.

Students from different races and ethnicities grow up in a highly segregated society, one in which minority segregation tends to be related to many interacting differences of opportunity, and where millions of blacks and Latinos understand and speak at home languages or dialects that are difficult or impossible for most whites to fully understand and are not valued in schools, where people listen to different music on different radio stations and attend highly segregated and often different churches on the weekends. There are extraordinary differences in the prevailing views of government, of the legal system, of discrimination, of the causes and cures of poverty, and of many other aspects of life. The minority communities have and use media of mass communication that few whites are familiar with, though many minority members are very familiar with white media. Whites are by far the most segregated group of students in American public schools and thus are likely to have the least knowledge of effective intergroup skills. There are important differences in the political and ideological orientations of members of different groups. The middle-class suburban communities in which most whites live are different in many respects from the central city and declining suburban communities where the great majority of blacks and Latinos live. There is clear evidence that blacks and Latinos are treated differently and often experience discrimination in important aspects of life, even decades after the enactment of civil rights laws.

In other words, contrary to the *Hopwood* premise that it is simply irrational to think of what students bring in terms of race, there are reasonable grounds, backed by massive social research, to predict that admitting a substantially larger group of minority students will bring to campus students whose experiences, perspectives, community connections, and ideologies will broaden and deepen the discussion of many issues on campus, both in class and in informal settings. This does not means that these possibilities are always realized, but minority admissions will make representation of these perspectives much more likely. Colleges are perfectly justified in assuming that considering race is likely to increase the diversity of experience and perspective within the student community.

It was apparent to Justice Powell that racial diversity added something to the educational experience of members of the university community, as it had been to the Supreme Court a generation earlier in ruling against segregated law schools, holding that the experience of preparation for the profession under such circumstances could not be equal.[14]

To most social scientists familiar with basic data on racial differences in American society, the factual claims about racial differences in the *Hopwood* ruling seem bizarre. In the academic world, in government, in the mass media, and in politics, race is extremely salient. In a wide variety of scholarly studies, race, social and economic status, and gender are the most frequently examined variables. Race and ethnicity appear as critical categories in all kinds of U.S. government reports—including the *Census and the Statistical Abstract of the United States*. Even in conservative periods when there was no intention to implement social change, statistics on race were collected. Race is used so frequently as a basic category, generation after generation, century after century, because the United States has always had profound racial divisions and the experiences of the various races have been very different. Data reported by race often show large differences; data omitting racial breakdowns are often difficult to interpret because they combine fundamentally different distributions of opinions or experiences. The argument about diversity of students assumes that the differences students bring with them to college could contribute not only to on-campus education but also to the university's missions of creating new knowledge through research, serving the community, and training professionals and leaders of public and private life, all through exposing students of one racial or ethnic group to the experience and perspectives of others.

The argument about diversity is only about probabilities. There are, of course, blacks and Latinos who are richer and more conservative than the great majority of whites, just as there are many whites whose incomes are lower than middle-class minority families. But average white income and wealth far exceed those of blacks, Native Americans, and Latinos. Moreover, even wealthy, successful minorities often experience discrimination; they tend to have close contact with the broader minority community and empathy for its needs, and their close relatives often experience severe need.

Middle-class minorities still tend to face residential segregation and discrimination, and their children often must attend segregated schools with classmates much less prepared than the classmates of similar white children. White students of the same income are likely to get better educations in more competitive schools with more qualified teachers and better prepared peers. Minority children are much more likely than white children to be placed outside the academic track and to be in schools that do not offer advanced or AP courses.

The typical experiences, beliefs, and ideologies of Americans differ substantially. To name just a few of these dimensions of difference: blacks, Latinos, and Native Americans are much more likely than whites and Asians to live in poverty, to live in rented rather than their own housing, to have little or no personal wealth, to attend low-achieving segregated schools, to have been poor for long periods, to live in areas of concentrated poverty even if they are not poor, to face more prosecution and conviction for crimes than whites do in the same circumstances, to be liberals, to vote Democratic, to be victims of violent crime, to die younger, and not to speak or write standard academic English. They are likely to have different views of American history. Their expectations about the future of their communities and the nation differ significantly from those of whites. They have a much more positive and expansive view of government than most whites. There are differing views about bilingualism, particularly between Latinos and non-Hispanic whites. The differences are particularly sharp in their attitudes toward controversial racial policies. Most whites express the view that enough or too much has already been done for civil rights; blacks and Latinos strongly disagree.

Blacks have distinct life experiences in many ways. In 1994, for example, the life expectancy of black males at birth had not increased in sixteen years and was about one-eighth lower than that for white males.[15] The black birth rate in 1994 was more than one-third higher than the white rate.[16]

Black children are four times as likely as whites to be born into a single-parent household. A study following families over fifteen years showed that 72 percent of black children lived in a single-parent home for at least part of their childhoods, compared to 30 percent of white children. Seventy-four percent of white children lived in families that never dipped below the poverty line, compared to 21 percent of blacks. About nine-tenths of the children living in persistent poverty in the early 1990s were black.[17]

Black and Latino families living below the poverty line are also far more likely than whites to live in extreme poverty. In 1995, 20 percent of blacks and 16 percent of Latino children—but only 3 percent of whites—were living in families whose incomes were less than half the poverty level.[18] Black children are substantially more likely than whites to be abused and neglected.[19]

Blacks and Latinos are far more likely to live in cities and in neighbor-hoods of concentrated poverty. Black and Latino children are vastly more likely to be educated in the schools of the largest cities. In 1994–1995, for example, 17.8 percent of black students and 22.7 percent of Latino students, but only 1.7 percent of white students, went to public schools in the nation's ten largest central city districts. In other words, black students were ten times more likely to have this experience, and Latino students thirteen times more likely.[20] It would be very uncommon for a white student on a university campus to have direct knowledge of inner-city schools, and many times more likely that a black or Latino student would.

A substantial share of Native American students, but almost none from other groups, are educated in Bureau of Indian Affairs and tribally controlled schools on reservations—an extremely different experience from that of the white students concentrated in middle-class suburbs. Seventy-four percent of Latinos and 67 percent of blacks attended schools with nonwhite majorities in the 1994–1995 school year. Seven-eighths of the schools that were 90 to 100 percent black or Latino that year had more than half of their students living in poverty. Of the schools with less than 10 percent black or Latino students, on the other hand, only one out of twenty had more than half the students living in poverty.[21] Within their schools, black, Latino, and Native American students were less likely than white or Asian students to be in a college preparatory program.[22]

Language is obviously fundamental for understanding other societies and their cultures. Most American students have no working knowledge of a second language, even though such knowledge has long been considered one of the goals of a good education. Ninety-six percent of blacks and 98 percent of whites graduating from high school in 1992 spoke English as their native language, compared to 46 percent of Asians and 45 percent of Latinos.[23] Language, particularly when developed to a high level, carries with it understanding of cultural differences that add to campus diversity. In a more tangible way, since language learning is far more effective when interacting with native speakers outside of class, ethnic diversity can produce a more positive setting for acquiring a second language.

Experiences with crime and views of the justice system differ significantly by race. Blacks are much more likely than whites to be victims of handgun crimes. During the years from 1987 to 1992, black males were about four times as likely as whites to be victims of such crimes, and black females were almost three times as likely as whites to be victims.[24] An ex-

traordinary 40 percent of black males ages sixteen to nineteen were victims of gun crimes.

Blacks are also greatly overrepresented in criminal arrests, accounting
for 31 percent of all arrests in 1993 and 62 percent of those arrested for
robbery.[25] Blacks are very disproportionately represented among the
prison population. In 1991, for example, they accounted for 47.3 percent
of all those in state prisons.[26] In some states blacks are twelve times as
likely to be incarcerated as whites. Blacks are much more likely to be convicted and imprisoned than whites charged with the same offense.

By the mid-1990s, nearly three-fourths of new admissions to prisons
in the United States were African Americans and Latinos. Between 1980
and 1993, according to the U.S. Department of Justice, the number of
prison inmates in the United States soared from 500,000 to 1.5 million;
the percentage of black inmates went from 47 to 51 percent, while the Latino share jumped from 8 percent to 14 percent.[27] By the early 1990s it
was estimated that more than one-fourth of all young black men were either incarcerated or on parole or probation. A 1997 Justice Department report shows that, if the existing trends continue, 28.5 percent of black
men, 16.0 percent of Latino men, and just 2.5 percent of white men can
expect to find themselves in a state or federal prison during their lives.
Black men are thus eleven times more likely than whites to be imprisoned, Latino men six times more likely. Although few women are imprisoned, black women are seven times more likely than their white counterparts to be behind bars.[28]

Released prisoners, who often resume their criminal activities, usually return to their old neighborhoods where so many minority families
are victimized by crime. Black students are, on average, much more likely
to come to college with personal or family experience as crime victims
and of the workings of the justice system. It is not surprising that minority communities have intense and sometimes highly divergent views of
that system.

Public discussion and media images often reflect a gulf between popular perception and fact. The drug problem is a good example. Suburban
youth are substantially more likely than city kids to use drugs, but city
kids are much more likely to be prosecuted for drug offenses and incarcerated if convicted. Children in affluent suburbs are usually protected from
serious consequences by local authorities.[29]

Blacks, Latinos, and Native Americans are vastly more likely to experience the kind of poverty that dramatically affects life chances. Among
those Americans who have experienced poverty are many millions for

whom it poverty involved a temporary loss of employment and income, and a much smaller number for whom it was a long-term condition. The two kinds of experience are fundamentally different. Being a poor child in a middle-class community is not at all like growing up in a community where poverty is the norm, where the schools and services are what we typically provide to the poor, and where there are few if any successful adult role models. Those living in such conditions of concentrated poverty are very disproportionately black and Latino.

A 1994 report on longitudinal research conducted for the U.S. Office of Juvenile Justice and Delinquency Prevention summarized the way that conditions of isolation, poverty, and negative neighborhood influences tend to interact and lead to seriously deviant behavior. The report concluded that the risk factors include "birth trauma, child abuse and neglect, ineffective parental discipline, family disruptions, conduct disorder and hyperactivity in children, school failure, learning disabilities, negative peer influences, limited employment opportunities, inadequate housing, and residence in high-crime neighborhoods."[30] There are few such white communities in metropolitan America. The impoverishment and isolation of black and Latino communities create a syndrome of forces that lead to serious social pathology, a set of conditions few whites have directly experienced.

There are similarly dramatic differences in employment and earnings by race in the United States, but blacks and whites have divergent views of the situation. A 1995 survey showed that 58 percent of whites believed that blacks were "as well off or better off than the average white person," but only 23 percent of blacks agreed with the statement. Forty-five percent of whites also believed that Latinos had equal or better jobs.[31] When asked to select among possible causes of "the economic and social problems African Americans face today," 37 percent of whites, compared to 74 percent of blacks, chose "lack of jobs."[32] In 1995, median black family income was $22,393, about three-fifths of the median white income of $35,766.[33] The difference was a result of blacks' higher unemployment, lower wages, and more single-parent families—all related to race or the effects of previous racial discrimination and inequality.

Economic and Political Differences

One can go back generations without finding significant exceptions to the rule that black men will have at least twice the unemployment rate of whites, in spite of great increases in black high school and college completion and gains in black achievement test scores. Employment and wage

TABLE 1   *Percent Employed, 1996 High School Graduates and Dropouts, by Race*

	Whites	Blacks	Latinos
Graduates not in college			
Employed	64.7%	40.8%	41.7%
Unemployed	35.3%	59.2%	58.3%
Dropouts during year			
Employed	48.8%	20.7%	54.3%
Unemployed	51.2%	79.3%	45.7%

Source: Bureau of Labor Statistics, "College Enrollment and Work Activity of 1996 High School Graduates," USDL 97-240 (Washington, DC: U.S. Department of Labor, July 23, 1997).

rates of blacks are lower at virtually every level of education, especially for men. In the fall of 1996, for example, 35 percent of white high school dropouts were jobless, but 59 percent of black dropouts had no work (see Table 1). Only one-fifth of the young blacks who had dropped out during the previous school year had jobs, compared to about half the whites.

Looking back over twenty-five years of unemployment statistics for black and white males from 1972 to 1997, it is apparent that huge discrepancies persist even as the economy moves up and down. Black male joblessness is usually two to two-and-a-half times that of whites (see Table 2). At the peak of economic expansions, black men experience higher unemployment rates than whites do at the worst points of most recessions. In April 1997, when the jobless rate fell to its lowest level in twenty-four years, 4.1 percent of the total white labor force was unemployed, compared to 8.1 percent of Latinos and 9.8 percent of African Americans.[34]

There are major racial differences in participation in civic life and the democratic system. The Census Bureau reports that in the 1996 elections, for example, 68 percent of voting-age whites and 64 percent of blacks, but only 36 percent of Latinos, were registered to vote. Fifty-six percent of whites, 51 percent of blacks, and 27 percent of Latinos actually voted. Since the mid-1970s the Latino voting rate has been about half the white rate and far below the black rate.[35] The youth and the immigration status of Latinos explain some of these differences, but the differences create divergent political understandings. Whites are more than twice as likely as Latinos to be involved in political organizations, but blacks are about twice as likely as whites and Latinos to take part in protest demonstrations.

TABLE 2   *Unemployment Rate for Black and White Males, 1972–1997*

	Whites	Blacks	Ratio of Black to White Level
1972	3.6%	7.0%	194%
1974	3.6%	7.9%	219%
1976	5.5%	10.8%	196%
1978	3.6%	8.5%	236%
1980	5.8%	14.0%	241%
1982	8.5%	19.2%	226%
1984	5.6%	13.5%	241%
1986	5.4%	13.7%	254%
1988	4.1%	9.1%	222%
1990	4.4%	11.5%	261%
1992	6.4%	13.1%	205%
1994	4.5%	9.4%	209%
1996	3.9%	9.7%	249%
1997	3.6%	7.8%	217%

Source: Bureau of Labor Statistics September survey data for each year, seasonally adjusted, adults twenty years and older.

The country's electorate arranged itself along racial lines in the 1960s. Beginning in 1964, African Americans turned overwhelmingly to the Democratic party and in a number of elections the percentage of whites voting Republican was five times or more the percentage of blacks voting Republican. In some elections the gap was much larger. In several national elections fewer than one black in twenty voted Republican. Clearly, race was much more salient than socioeconomic status in these choices, although income is normally strongly related to party affiliation in the United States.[36] Minority students admitted to college are likely to bring different perspectives on politics and public issues, enriching the civic discussion on campus and in class.[37]

The most formative influences on life experience and opportunity—family, community, work, education, safety, and health care—are available to different racial groups in different ways that are still strongly related to race and ethnicity. The American dream consists of a good job, a home in a nice community, and higher education for the children. Home ownership, in particular, has long been considered one of the most powerful influences and probably the most important source of wealth for most families. Housing determines peer groups for children and access to schools. The federal government provides massive tax breaks to encourage home ownership because of its belief in these values. But housing opportunities in the United States are very unevenly distributed by race.

The tax subsidies for home ownership far exceed the money spent for subsidizing housing for the poor. Seventy-one percent of whites are homeowners, compared to 47 percent of blacks and 45 percent of Latinos. In other words, 55 percent of Latinos live in rental housing compared to only 29 percent of whites.[38] In many areas with the most high-achieving schools, however, there is little or no rental housing for families because of restrictive local zoning and land-use policies that make it difficult or impossible to build these units. Not being a homeowner may mean exclusion from schools that would train a family's children for college most effectively.

Studies of housing markets in the 1990s have shown the continuing impact of discrimination in rental and sales patterns, and major continuing inequalities in mortgage financing by race. Research sponsored by the Department of Housing and Urban Development showed a continuing high probability of different treatment for blacks and Hispanics when matched pairs of minority and white home-seekers applied for housing.[39] And the practice of most developing suburban communities of excluding both rental and affordably priced housing for families continues with few limitations in many areas.

The attitudes of whites and minorities on racial issues often differ dramatically, especially on current, unresolved matters. There are also wide differences on many nonracial issues. Surveys have focused mainly on differences between whites and blacks, but important differences are emerging between Hispanics and the other three major groups on the role of government, the provision of health care, the fairness of the police, and other issues. These subjects are, of course, related to many questions discussed in university classrooms.

Blacks typically have a more positive view of the federal government than whites do. In surveys from 1964 to 1992, at least one-third and sometimes more than half of the white public believed that the federal government was "too powerful." Only about one-fifth of blacks, and sometimes as few as 5 percent, typically shared this view. In surveys between 1982 and 1994, whites were always more than twice as likely as blacks to favor cutting back services and government spending. Surveys between 1956 and 1968 found that whites were more than eight times as likely as blacks to say that government should stay out of health-care provision. During the same period whites were several times more likely to endorse an approach to economic security emphasizing self-reliance.[40]

On civil rights and related issues, the differences in opinion by race are dramatic. A national *New York Times*/CBS News poll in December 1997 found that 35 percent of whites but 80 percent of blacks thought that affirmative action should be "continued for the foreseeable future." Fifty-two percent of whites compared to 14 percent of blacks thought that such programs should simply "be abolished." Asked about "laws to protect minorities against discrimination in hiring and promotion" (rather than "affirmative action"), 31 percent of whites compared to 9 percent of blacks said that they were "not necessary."[41] A 1997 Gallup poll reported that 53 percent of blacks believed that affirmative action programs should be increased, compared to only 22 percent of whites. Forty-five percent of blacks reported having experienced racial discrimination within the previous month.[42] In a 1997 California survey, less than one-third of Californians said that qualified black and Latino students had less opportunity than whites to get a college education; 22 percent said that middle-class students had less opportunity than others.[43]

A 1997 *Time*/CNN national poll of teenagers showed that just 17 percent of whites believed that standardized tests were biased, compared to 40 percent of black teens. Seventy-six percent of young whites but only 55 percent of young blacks thought that U.S. race relations would "ever get better."[44]

Blacks were much less likely than others to say that their local public schools were excellent. Only 6 percent of blacks reported that their schools were excellent; nationwide, for all groups, the figure was 19 percent.[45] Fifty-nine percent of whites described race relations in their community as excellent or good, compared to 31 percent of blacks and 44 percent of Latinos. When asked "how much discrimination and prejudice exist against blacks in the United States today," 21 percent of whites and 43 percent of blacks said "a lot."[46]

Latino, black, and white adults tend to have very different opinions on language-related issues. A 1994 survey in southern California found that 72 percent of whites and 69 percent of blacks but only 30 percent of Latinos favored the designation of English as the "official language." Latinos were almost twice as likely as whites to favor some kind of bilingual education. Eighty-three percent of Latinos but only 47 percent of whites favored printing ballots in non-English languages.[47]

To the extent that we are a culture in which self-image is shaped by mass media, students of various racial and ethnic groups tend to bring significantly different experiences to higher education. Minority students who reach college almost inevitably have had a great deal of contact with white culture and institutions. The same is not true for white students. Only Native Americans are likely to be familiar with the nation's oldest cultural traditions—those of the hundreds of tribal communities. Few non-Natives know the story of how the land in their area was seized from local tribes and what has become of the treaties that were negotiated. Only Spanish-speaking students are likely to be familiar with the information conveyed in the vast Spanish-language media. Few nonblacks are familiar with the quite distinctive news coverage in the nation's African American press.

Three decades after the enactment of the federal fair housing law, whites and minorities have profoundly different views of the housing market. A survey released in 1997 showed that only 17 percent of whites in the Boston metropolitan area thought that there was discrimination against blacks in housing; only 16 percent thought there was mortgage discrimination by banks. Yet 47 percent of blacks perceived housing discrimination and 64 percent thought there was discrimination in home finance. Many minority home-seekers still confront easily detectable discrimination, but most whites believe that the problem has been largely solved by civil rights laws.[48]

How Differences May Affect Teaching and Learning

Differences in experience and attitude cited above are, of course, not equally relevant to all aspects of the college curriculum. Their relevance to training in sociology, law, education, literature, political science, history, criminology, journalism, urban planning, public policy, international affairs, Spanish and Asian languages and cultures, and anthropology should be immediately apparent. Less obvious, perhaps, but nevertheless clear is their impact on business studies—such as marketing, personnel, management, and advertising—in a society that is rapidly growing more ethnically diverse. Students preparing for careers in medicine, nursing, and public health similarly need to understand and communicate with diverse clients and to understand their communities and their cultures. Indeed, the same can be said for a wide range of professions, from accounting to the clergy.

Students preparing for many of these professions need to understand the dimensions of racial differences. First, they need the facts: what is known about differences among groups and what aspects of their traditions and cultures may be important to successful relationships and treatments. Second, students need to understand how to work effectively in multiracial settings—especially where they are among the minority. White students are the most segregated in U.S. public schools. They especially need the experience of diversity, including encounters with the full range of views among major social groups, if they are to understand the realities of a multiracial society. Universities themselves need to foster good working relationships in minority communities, which provide training sites and future employment for students. Such relationships are facilitated when those seeking training and jobs include significant numbers of students who share the racial or ethnic background dominant in those communities.

Some critics of race-conscious affirmative action point out that many black, Latino, and Native American students are poor, and ask whether their different experiences and beliefs aren't largely a product of poverty. Can't colleges then achieve diversity by admitting more poor students, without considering race? This is a logical and important question and one on which there is great confusion in the public debate. The answer is that race is related to poverty but is different in key respects. Poverty affects the various racial groups differently, and many racial problems have a serious impact on people who are not poor. As a result, admitting poor students through race-blind affirmative action would not produce the kind of diversity we have been describing, though it might add some other important dimensions to the diversity of the campus. Middle-class blacks are actually more likely to perceive discrimination in their lives than are poor blacks, perhaps because they have more interaction with the white world, and the most wealthy group of blacks is as likely to be segregated residentially as the poorest group. Douglas Massey and Nancy Denton's research found that, across all levels of income for blacks, "black segregation does not differ by affluence." Comparing thirty metropolitan areas, they found that very poor families experienced high levels of segregation but that they were not statistically different from the most wealthy group of black families, who could well afford to purchase homes in most white areas and did not prefer all-black communities.[49] A virtual caste system persists preventing marriage between whites and blacks. Admitting poor people does not address race problems. In fact, if admissions is carried out in a way that uses poverty plus test scores, it is likely to produce students from families that are temporarily poor but well educated, such as recent Asian immigrants or children of recently divorced suburban households. Race is not class and class is not race, through there are obvious and important relationships.

Summary

The assault on affirmative action assumes that problems growing out of the organization of American society and its institutions on racial lines have been largely solved and that race no longer makes any significant difference. If these propositions were true, affirmative action would be unnecessary and of little educational value. In fact, however, deep racial differences remain, and this book explores what is known about how increasing minority enrollment changes and enriches the educational process. This book shows that the academic world is far better prepared to support the central proposition of *Bakke* now than when the challenge was raised in 1996. Much has been learned and additional important research is in progress. In spite of the fact that no large national studies have been funded, substantial evidence is developing around a set of conclusions that show that diversity of students can and usually does produce a broader educational experience, both in traditional learning and in preparing for jobs, professions, and effective citizenship in a multiracial democracy. The evidence also suggests that such benefits can be significantly increased by appropriate leadership and support on campus.

This does not mean that further research is not urgently needed, including major new data collection. The longitudinal studies at the University of Michigan look not only at students' perception of the value of diverse experiences, but also at the actual long-term impact of such experiences on the thinking of the former students years afterward. Institutional and national studies of this sort are strongly needed, including sections on the efficacy of various interventions. We need much more work on the ways that diversity on campus is actually linked to understanding and successful collaboration and interracial living as adults, and how the campus composition and climate influence the development of courses and research subjects for faculty members. We should explore the reasons for the economic benefits that come with personal experience in diversity by job candidates and how to maximize those benefits. This book moves the debate, but there is much more to be learned. If universities are to protect their right to pursue diversity as a legitimate and educationally necessary goal, part of their work must be documenting what their students and faculty have accomplished in building a more diverse and intellectually powerful learning community that would be damaged by policies that would slash minority enrollment.

Notes

1. For an analysis of the history of desegregation enforcement and the impact of moving to outcome-related standards, see Gary Orfield, "Why It Worked in Dixie: Southern School Desegregation and Its Implications for the North," in *Race and Schooling in the City*, ed. Adam Yarmolinsky, Lance Liebman, and Corinne S. Schelling (Cambridge, MA: Harvard University Press, 1981), pp. 24–44.

2. U.S. Commission on Civil Rights, *Political Participation* (Washington, DC: Government Printing Office, 1968).

3. *Hills v. Gautreaux*, 425 U.S. 284 (1976).

4. William G. Bowen and Derek Bok, *The Shape of the River: Long-Term Consequences of Considering Race in College and University Admissions* (Princeton, NJ: Princeton University Press, 1998).

5. Steven A. Shull, *American Civil Rights Policy from Truman to Clinton* (Armonk, NY: M. E. Sharpe, 1999), pp. 183–192.

6. Mitchell Chang, Daria Witt-Sandis, James Jones, and Kenji Hakuta, eds., *The Dynamics of Race in Higher Education: An Examination of the Evidence* (Palo Alto, CA: American Educational Research Association and the Stanford University Center for Comparative Studies in Race and Ethnicity, 1999).

7. *Does Diversity Make a Difference? Three Research Studies on Diversity in College Classrooms* (Washington, DC: American Council on Education and American Association of University Professors, 2000).

8. Geoffrey Maruyama and Jose Moreno, "University Faculty Views about the Value of Diversity on Campus and in the Classroom," in *Does Diversity Make a Difference?* pp. 8–36.

9. Patricia Gurin, "The Compelling Need for Diversity in Higher Education," expert testimony in *Gratz et al. v. Bollinger et al.*, No. 97-75928(E.D.Mich, 1997).

10. Amy Stuart Wells and Robert L. Crain, "Perpetuation Theory and the Long-Term Effects of School Desegregation," *Review of Educational Research, 64* (1994), 531–555.

11. Susan E. Eaton, *Blurring the Race Boundary: Black Adults Raised in Urban Neighborhoods and Schooled in White Suburbia* (New Haven, CT: Yale University Press, 2001)

12. Johnson started teaching in a segregated Mexican American school and encountered students "mired in the slums . . . lashed by prejudice . . . buried half alive in illiteracy." Johnson remembered children feeling, "Why don't people like me? Why do they hate me because I am brown." Robert Dalek, *Lone Star Rising: Lyndon Johnson and His Times, 1908–1960* (New York: Oxford University Press, 1991), p. 78. Johnson described "an America that accepted distinctions between blacks and whites as part and parcel of life." Lyndon B. Johnson, *Vantage Point: Perspectives of the Presidency, 1963–1969* (New York: Holt, Rinehart & Winston, 1971), p. 155.

13. H. R. Haldeman, *The Haldeman Diaries: Inside the Nixon White House* (New York: G. P. Putnam's Sons, 1994).

14. *Sweatt v. Painter*, 339 U.S. 629 (1950).

15. The difference is 11.5 percent, National Center for Health Statistics, *Monthly Vital Statistics Report, 45,* No. 3 (1996).

16. National Center for Health Statistics, *Monthly Vital Statistics Report, 44,* No. 11 (1996).

17. Mary E. Corcoran and Ajay Chaudry, "The Dynamics of Childhood Poverty," *The Future of Children, 7,* No. 2 (Summer/Fall 1997), 40–54.

18. U.S. Bureau of the Census, Current Population Reports, Series P-60, No. 194, reported in *Federal Interagency Forum on Child and Family Statistics* (Washington, DC: Government Printing Office, 1997), p. 66.

19. *Statistical Abstract of the United States* (Washington, DC: Government Printing Office, 1995), p. 215.
20. Gary Orfield, Mark Bachmeier, David R. James, and Tamela Eitle, *Deepening Segregation in American Public Schools* (Cambridge, MA: The Civil Rights Project, Harvard University, 1997).
21. Orfield, Bachmeier, James, and Eitle, *Deepening Segregation,* tables 4, 9, 11.
22. National Center for Education Statistics, *Understanding Racial-Ethnic Differences in Secondary School Science and Mathematics Achievement* (Washington, DC: Government Printing Office), table 2.18.
23. U.S. Department of Education, National Center for Education Statistics, NELS 1988: Second Follow-Up, 1992.
24. *Statistical Abstract of the United States,* p. 205.
25. *Statistical Abstract of the United States,* p. 206.
26. *Statistical Abstract of the United States,* p. 217.
27. Fox Butterfield, "More in U.S. Are in Prisons, Report Says," *New York Times,* August 10, 1995, p. A14.
28. Thomas P. Bonczar and Allen J. Beck, *Lifetime Likelihood of Going to State or Federal Prison,* NCJ-160092 (Washington, DC: Office of Justice Programs, March 1997), p. 2.
29. Sean Fitzpatrick Reardon, "Social Class and the Community Ecology of Adolescent Drug Use: A Study of Two Communities," Diss., Harvard Graduate School of Education, 1997.
30. David Huizinga, Rolf Loeber, and Terence P. Thornberry, *Urban Delinquency and Substance Abuse, Initial Findings* (Washington, DC: U.S. Office of Juvenile Justice and Delinquency Prevention, 1994), p. 1.
31. *Washington Post/*Kaiser Family Foundation/Harvard University Survey on Race, October 1995.
32. *Washington Post/*Kaiser Family Foundation/Harvard University Survey on Race, October 1995.
33. *New York Times,* January 30, 1997.
34. *New York Times,* May 3, 1997, p. 30.
35. U.S. Bureau of the Census, "Percent Reported Voted and Registered by Race, Hispanic Origin and Gender: November 1964 to the Present," Internet release date, October 17, 1997.
36. The National Election Studies, University of Michigan, table 9A.1.1, generated May 2, 1996.
37. Sidney Verba, Kay Lehman Schlozman, and Henry Brady, in *Classifying by Race,* ed. Paul E. Peterson (Princeton, NJ: Princeton University Press, 1995), figure 15.4.
38. U.S. Census Bureau, "Housing Vacancies and Home Ownership, Second Quarter 2000" (Washington, DC: U.S. Department of Commerce, July 26, 2000).
39. John Ginger, *Closed Doors, Opportunities Lost: The Continuing Costs of Housing* (New York: Russell Sage Foundation, 1995).
40. The National Election Studies, University of Michigan, tables 4A.4a.1, 4A.1.1, 4A.2.1, 4A5.1, generated May 2, 1996.
41. Sam Howe Verhovek, "In Poll, Americans Reject Means but Not Ends of Racial Diversity," *New York Times,* December 14, 1997, pp. 1, 34.
42. Gallup Poll data, *Buffalo News,* June 11, 1977, A6.
43. John Immerwahr, "Enduring Values, Changing Concerns: What Californians Expect from Their Higher Education System" (San Jose, CA: California Higher Education Policy Center, March 1997), table 2.
44. Christopher John Farley, "Kids and Race," *Time,* November 24, 1997, p. 90.

45. David Bositis, "Joint Center for Political and Economic Studies 1997 National Opinion Poll: Children's' Issues," June 1997, p. 6.

46. David Bositis, "Joint Center for Political and Economic Studies 1997 National Opinion Poll: Race Relations," June 1997, tables 1 and 4.

47. Los Angeles County Social Survey, 1994, reported in Sherwaine Videnago, C. van Laar, and David O. Sears, *Becoming an American: The Political Socialization of Latinos,* Paper presented at the annual meeting of the American Political Science Association, San Francisco, 1994.

48. Charles Stein, "Economic Divide of Races Is Cited," *Boston Globe,* October 26, 1997, p. A27.

49. Douglas S. Massey and Nancy A. Denton, *American Apartheid: Segregation and the Making of the Underclass* (Cambridge, MA: Harvard University Press, 1993), pp. 85–87.

CHAPTER 1

Student Diversity and Higher Learning

NEIL L. RUDENSTINE

Introduction

Few issues have aroused more contentious debate over the past decade than those surrounding the importance of diversity in higher education, and the related use of affirmative action in admissions decisions. The controversy swirling around these topics has intensified significantly since 1996, when the U.S. Court of Appeals for the Fifth Circuit ruled that the University of Texas could not consider race as a factor in its law-school admissions in *Hopwood v. State of Texas*. A series of subsequent legal decisions and public referenda outlawing the use of race-conscious admissions policies has created a climate of ferment and uncertainty within the higher education community.

In a debate that is too often framed by the competing interests of different groups, it is all the more important that we remember the most fundamental rationale for student diversity in higher education: its educational value. Students benefit in countless ways from the opportunity to live and learn among peers whose perspectives and experiences differ from their own. A diverse educational environment challenges them to explore ideas and arguments at a deeper level—to see issues from various sides, to rethink their own premises, and to achieve the kind of understanding that comes only from testing their own hypotheses against those of people with opposing views.

In the pages that follow, I briefly trace the evolution of the concept of diversity in higher education in this country, and the very real—if slow and uneven—progress that has been made in achieving greater inclusion, drawing in particular on the experiences at Harvard. My intention in doing so is to demonstrate why the goal of diversity remains so important to the actual quality and breadth of education for all our students, and why our existing policies continue to offer the most effective and promising pathway to the future.

Early Origins of the Notion of Diversity

Contrary to popular belief, the deliberate, conscious effort to achieve greater student diversity on our campuses was not born in the 1960s. In fact, it reaches back to the mid-nineteenth century, when issues of racial, ethnic, and other forms of diversity were no less volatile in American life than they are today. At Harvard, the coming of the Civil War prompted some of the earliest comments on the subject. President Cornelius C. Felton recognized an urgent need for universities to reach out more consciously to students from different parts of the country because gathering such students "must tend powerfully to remove prejudices by bringing them into friendly relations."

During the latter part of the nineteenth century, Harvard president Charles W. Eliot expanded the concept of diversity, which he believed to be a defining feature of American democratic society. He sought to attract students from a variety of "nations, states, schools, families, sects and conditions of life" so they could experience "the wholesome influence that comes from observation of and contact with people different from themselves." Eliot identified the "great diversity in the population of the United States as regards racial origins" as a critical element in America's heterogeneous society.

While the goals of Felton, Eliot, and other educators may strike many as irrelevant to our present circumstances, the essential principles they espoused helped to pry open the doors of Harvard, along with many other higher education institutions, to children of new immigrants, to members of religious minorities, and, in smaller numbers, to African Americans. One black student, W. E. B. Du Bois, class of 1890, wrote that Harvard "was no longer simply a place where rich and learned New England gave its accolade to the social elite. It had broken its shell and reached to the West and to the South, to yellow students and to black."

In reality, however, African Americans, Jews, Latinos, Native Americans, and others continued to find only limited ports of entry into excellent educational institutions during most of the first half of the twentieth century. This situation began to shift dramatically in the aftermath of World War II, with the introduction of the GI bill and the initiation of active efforts at Harvard to recruit students from rural, urban, and suburban areas across the country, and with a wide array of talents. By the 1950s and 1960s, student diversity came to be seen as a value in its own right, enhancing the experiences of an entire educational community. At Harvard, student diversity was seen as "stimulating to the Faculty" and "more relevant to liberal education."[1] Moreover, each new class was viewed increasingly as an ensemble, rather than as a simple aggregation of individuals chosen without any significant reference to the pattern produced by the whole. The Harvard admissions policy statement of that era wrote of the student body as an "educational resource of coordinate importance with our faculty and our library, laboratory and housing arrangements."[2] It suggested that the "measure of a class" consists largely in "how much its members are likely to learn from each other—the real beginning of learning, both intellectually and emotionally."[3]

Civil Rights Legislation and the *Bakke* Case

During the 1960s, lingering social, ethnic, and racial barriers to higher education were shattered at an unprecedented speed. The Civil Rights Act of 1964 (and related initiatives) represented a major attempt by the federal government to promote equal opportunity for all Americans. Under this act, admissions (and other specific activities) in colleges and universities that received federal funding became subject to requirements of nondiscrimination. The legislative history of the act reveals deep and passionate divisions in both the Congress and the country. Proponents argued that government had a special responsibility to make certain that programs and activities supported by federal funds were free of discrimination. Opponents foresaw a future in which controversies about race or ethnicity—and later about gender—would create continuing unrest, discontent, and litigation.

As in the case of any genuine dilemma, the real issues were beyond immediate resolution, and they contained the seeds of ongoing disagreement. In higher education, a variety of programs related to affirmative action were designed during the late 1960s and 1970s. Some of these programs soon met with legal challenges. Perhaps the most conspicuous involved the University of California, in a case brought by Allan Bakke. In 1978, the Supreme Court issued in *Regents of the University of California v. Bakke* what remains its most significant statement concerning questions of race and admissions in higher education.

At issue in this case was the policy employed by the Medical School of the University of California at Davis of reserving sixteen of the one hundred places in each class for members of certain minority groups.

Candidates for these spaces were considered separately from others, and were held to a different standard of admissions. The process was largely quantitative in nature, involving the use of precise "benchmark" scores and "cutoff" points. Bakke contended that, as a white student, he had been unfairly excluded from competing for one of the sixteen places reserved for minorities, even though his test scores and other indices were stronger than those of students admitted under the special admissions program.

The *Bakke* case set a precedent because it directly addressed both the legality of quotas, or set-asides, in admissions, and the use of race or ethnicity as factors in admissions decisions. The Court decided, in a 5-4 vote, that the clear separation of eighty-four "regular" admissions places from sixteen "special" places for minorities, together with the use of different numerical cutoff points for the two groups, was unlawful.

Several of the justices' opinions[4] restated the view that racial categories and preferences—even if "benign" in purpose—are problematic, given the broad and unqualified language of the equal protection clause of the Fourteenth Amendment. While the original initiative that led to the Amendment's adoption in 1868—and ultimately to the Civil Rights Act of 1964—was clearly intended to break systematic patterns of discrimination against African Americans, the basic constitutional and legislative goals involved equal protection for *all* persons, whatever their race.

In his pivotal opinion in *Bakke*, Justice Lewis Powell concluded that "racial and ethnic distinctions of any sort are inherently suspect and thus call for the most exacting judicial examination."[5] However, he also wrote—and a majority of the Court concurred—that it was permissible to take race explicitly into account as one factor in making university admissions decisions, provided that the institution can show that the practice is necessary to promote a substantial interest.[6]

This particular aspect of Justice Powell's opinion was, of course, extraordinarily significant. The California Superior Court and the Supreme Court of California (both of which had previously decided in favor of Bakke) had specifically declared racial considerations to be impermissible in admissions decisions. By contrast, Justice Powell stated clearly that conscious consideration of race or ethnicity in decisionmaking is not intrinsically unconstitutional, even though its use must be strictly circumscribed:

> In enjoining petitioner [the University of California] from ever considering the race of any applicant, the courts below failed to recognize that the State has a substantial interest that may legitimately be served

by a properly devised admissions program involving the competitive consideration of race and ethnic origin.[7]

In addressing the question of what constitutes a sufficiently substantial interest, Justice Powell rejected several arguments advanced by the University of California.[8] The only rationale that he found persuasive was based directly on educational grounds: the presence of minority students contributed—along with the presence and contributions of other students—to diversity, and therefore to the total educational environment of an institution, as well as to the education of all its members. In short, he judged some consideration of racial and ethnic characteristics to be appropriate, because "the interest of diversity is compelling in the context of a university's admissions program."[9]

Justice Powell grounded this conclusion in part on the longstanding definition of academic freedom used by Justice Frankfurter in *Sweezy v. New Hampshire*:

> It is the business of a university to provide that atmosphere which is most conducive to speculation, experiment and creation. It is an atmosphere in which there prevail "the four essential freedoms" of a university—to determine for itself on academic grounds who may teach, what may be taught, how it shall be taught, and who may be admitted to study.[10]

In his discussion of these issues, Justice Powell emphasized both the "robust exchange of ideas"[11] of special concern to the First Amendment, and the broader concept of student exposure to the "mores"—the customs, habits, and outlooks—of fellow students who are "as diverse as this Nation of many peoples."[12] While the educational benefits of such exposure may appear to be most striking during a student's university years, their long-term significance was held to be equally valuable: "The Nation's future depends upon leaders trained" in this way,[13] and the results of such training can have a lasting effect on individuals, and therefore on the society of which they are a part.

If it is permissible to take race and ethnicity into account as one factor in an admissions process, but generally not permissible to "set aside" places (or to use a set of differently defined standards) exclusively for members of a particular ethnic or racial group (or groups), how can one design and administer an appropriate process? In *Bakke*, the Justices devoted considerable attention to this issue.

Justice Powell quoted Harvard College's policy statement on admissions extensively in his opinion and included it in full as an appendix.

This policy carried the strong endorsement of President Derek Bok, whose constant efforts on behalf of diversity and affirmative action helped to determine Harvard's goals and extend its progress throughout the 1970s and 1980s. Two passages from the Harvard statement are particularly pertinent. The first concerns the way in which different criteria can be weighed simultaneously in making admissions decisions; the second concerns the question of so-called critical mass, including the issue of quotas as contrasted to approximate (and flexible) goals:

> When the Committee on Admissions reviews the large middle group of applicants who are "admissible" and deemed capable of doing good work in their courses, the race of an applicant may tip the balance in his favor just as geographic origin or a life spent on a farm may tip the balance in other candidates' cases. . . .
>
> In Harvard College admissions the [Admissions] Committee has not set target-quotas for the number of blacks, or of musicians, football players, physicists or Californians to be admitted in a given year. At the same time the Committee is aware that if Harvard College is to provide a truly heterog[e]neous environment that reflects the rich diversity of the United States, it cannot be provided without some attention to numbers. It would not make sense, for example, to have 10 or 20 students out of 1,100 whose homes are west of the Mississippi. Comparably, 10 or 20 black students could not begin to bring to their classmates and to each other the variety of points of view, backgrounds and experiences of blacks in the United States. . . . Consequently, when making its decisions, the Committee on Admissions is aware that there is some relationship between numbers and achieving the benefits to be derived from a diverse student body, and between numbers and providing a reasonable environment for those students admitted.[14]

Distinctions between the Harvard College program and the University of California at Davis program were discussed in some detail in *Bakke*. Justice Harry Blackmun wrote that, while he saw the advantages of the Harvard program, he was not convinced that the difference between the two was "very profound or constitutionally significant." He concluded that the Harvard program was "better formulated than Davis' two-track system," but added:

> The cynical, of course, may say that under a program such as Harvard's one may accomplish covertly what Davis concedes it does openly. I need not go that far, for despite its two-track aspect, the Davis program, for me, is within constitutional bounds, though perhaps barely so.[15]

In his opinion, however, Justice Powell insisted on the fundamental difference between a two-track process involving set-asides and a unitary process that judged all candidates by the same set of criteria:

> In such an admissions program, race or ethnic background may be deemed a "plus" in a particular applicant's file, yet it does not insulate the individual from comparison with all other candidates for the available seats. The file of a particular black applicant may be examined for his potential contribution to diversity without the factor of race being decisive when compared, for example, with that of an applicant identified as an Italian-American if the latter is thought to exhibit qualities more likely to promote beneficial educational pluralism. Such qualities could include exceptional personal talents, unique work or service experience, leadership potential, maturity, demonstrated compassion, [or] a history of overcoming disadvantage. . . . Indeed, the weight attributed to a particular quality may vary from year to year depending upon the "mix" both of the student body and the applicants for the incoming class.

Finally, it is important to note that Justice Powell considered the contribution of diversity to education at the graduate as well as the undergraduate level. He viewed law schools, for example, not only as academic institutions, but as "the proving ground for legal learning and practice"—places that "cannot be effective in isolation from the individuals and institutions with which the law interacts. Few students and no one who has practiced law would choose to study in an academic vacuum."[16]

A similar perspective was relevant to medicine. "Physicians serve a heterogeneous population," wrote Justice Powell, and

> an otherwise qualified medical student with a particular background —whether it be ethnic, geographic, culturally advantaged or disadvantaged—may bring to a professional school of medicine experiences, outlooks, and ideas that enrich the training of its student body and better equip its graduates to render with understanding their vital service to humanity.[17]

This important issue—of graduate and professional school admissions—deserves at least some additional discussion. Generalizing about admissions criteria across very different disciplines is obviously difficult, because programs vary widely in the nature of the required preparation. A Ph.D. program in statistics or plasma fusion, for instance, will undoubtedly have technical requirements for admission that would ordinarily not have clear parallels in a program in English literature or European history.

Nonetheless, if we want a society in which our lawyers, physicians, teachers, architects, public servants, and other professionals possess a developed sense of vocation and calling; if we want them to appreciate and understand the variety of human beings with whom they will work, and whom they will serve; if we want them to think imaginatively and to act effectively in relation to the needs and values of their communities, then we shall have to take diversity into account as one among many significant factors in graduate and professional school admissions and education. Relevant academic training and expertise, while indispensable, can take one only so far in many of the situations that are now the substance of everyday professional life, and the realities of our time require forms of education that are broad in their human dimensions as well as powerful in their intellectual content.

Admissions: Alternatives in a Post-*Bakke* Era

As we move further into the post-*Bakke* era, we must consider various policy alternatives concerning student diversity and admissions. We can continue with admissions policies that take many individual qualities and factors into careful account (including a person's ethnicity, race, or gender). These policies have served us extremely well for a very long time, and have enhanced the educational mission of our universities.

Alternatively, institutions may choose on their own to take less account of race, ethnicity, and gender in admissions; or they may find themselves prohibited from doing so by legislative or judicial actions at either the state or federal level—referenda in California and Washington have banned the use of affirmative action at public institutions of higher education in those states. The University of Michigan currently faces two separate court challenges to its admissions policies. It is entirely possible that the Supreme Court will soon accept a challenge to affirmative action that could determine the legality of using race-conscious measures in every public institution of higher education in the country.[18]

My own view—as suggested throughout these pages—is that the main question to be addressed in this context is not so much affirmative action itself, but the broader matter of diversity as it relates to the quality, breadth, and texture of student learning. The primary purpose of diversity in university admissions, moreover, is neither to achieve abstract goals nor to compensate for patterns of past societal discrimination. It represents now, as it has since the mid-nineteenth century, positive educational values that are fundamental to the basic mission of colleges and universities. It is also, as I have emphasized, extremely important to the development of civic virtues—and of future leaders—vital to the health and effective functioning of our democracy.

The most constructive and well-conceived admissions programs are those that view affirmative action in relation to the educational benefits of diversity. They may take various characteristics such as race, ethnicity, or gender into account as potential "plus" factors (among many others) when evaluating candidates, but they do not assign such characteristics an overriding or determinative value. Nor do they aim to achieve specific numerical targets, either through the use of set-asides or quotas. They involve energetic efforts in outreach, but not mandated outcomes. Programs of this kind, when they are carefully designed and implemented, preserve an institution's capacity—with considerable flexibility—to make its own determinations in admissions. This capacity and flexibility have been critical in the past, and will continue to be so in the future.

With these general considerations in mind, let me comment briefly on some of the main arguments that have recently been advanced by thoughtful critics of affirmative action in university admissions:

1. *Affirmative action programs were important during an interim stage as a step toward greater equality of opportunity and the creation of a "level playing field"; but we have now reached a point where discrimination has been so significantly reduced that African Americans (or other historically underrepresented groups) no longer face serious obstacles of this kind.*

There have clearly been increased opportunities for members of historically underrepresented groups in colleges and universities during the past quarter century. Positive steps of this kind, however, are very recent and are far from secure. Twenty-five to thirty years of improved access to higher education is a very brief time span. It is scarcely one generation—barely long enough for graduates of the late 1960s to raise children who are now reaching college age.

To understand more precisely what has been achieved, it is helpful to consider some of the data concerning (for example) African Americans in higher education programs during the past two to three decades. While the focus must remain on the broad concept of diversity as it relates to learning—as distinct from any narrowly quantitative search for "equal outcomes"—such data are useful in assessing the extent of actual progress in achieving diversity during an era when intensified efforts have been made to enhance opportunities for historically underrepresented groups in both undergraduate and graduate education.

- In 1964, only 4 percent of African Americans twenty-five years or older had completed at least four years of college, compared to 10 percent of whites in the same age group. By 1998, the figures had risen to 14.7 percent for African Americans, 25 percent for whites, 11 percent for Hispanics, and 42 percent for Asians—indicating a significant advance by all groups, but also a persistent gap.[19]

  In 1975, African Americans received about 1,000 (3.8%) of the roughly 26,000 doctoral degrees awarded by American universities to U.S. citizens of known race or ethnicity. After periods of modest increase and decline in that percentage, African Americans received about 1,600 (3.7%) of the roughly 45,000 such degrees awarded in 1996. Hispanics received 999 (2.2%). (During this period, the percentage of blacks and Hispanics in the population grew rapidly.)
- If attention is confined to doctorates in the basic arts and sciences disciplines (excluding business, communications, education, and certain other fields), the percentages are smaller—roughly 2 percent in 1975 and 3 percent in 1995. Indeed, in 1995 a total of roughly 850 doctorates were awarded to African Americans (or black permanent residents) in the basic arts and sciences nationwide.[20]
- In the field of law, blacks received 6.7 percent of first professional degrees awarded by American universities in 1994–1995, compared to 4.0 percent in 1976–1977. In medicine, the comparable figure was 5.9 percent in 1994–1995, up from 5.3 percent in 1976–1977. In business, blacks received 5.3 percent of the master's degrees awarded in 1994–1995, up from 3.8 percent in 1976–1977.[21]

However we interpret these statistics—and there are many considerations that must be taken into account—two main conclusions seem to me to be clear.

First, since the advent of affirmative action programs at colleges and universities in the late 1960s and 1970s, there has been marked improvement in the participation of African Americans (as well as other historically underrepresented minorities) in higher education. This is particularly true at the undergraduate level, but there have also been modest gains at some advanced levels.

Second, in spite of these gains, the figures show that we are still very much "in process." There is substantial unrealized potential in each of the different degree programs and fields of study just cited. In addition, the gaps in certain areas are startling, and they highlight critical shortages that are exceptionally troubling from a national point of view. The doctoral situation in the arts and sciences shows only glacial change—from a very low baseline—over time. While the data for professional education are more encouraging, the overall numbers are not robust, and the representation of African Americans in some fields remains very modest. Successes to date are strongly dependent upon affirmative action. The situation illustrates the need for continued and focused attention in the years ahead.

We need to remember that progress in advanced education depends directly on the gains achieved at previous stages. This is a classic "pipeline" problem, where the linkages in the entire system are crucial, and where a weakening or breakdown at any juncture along the way has major implications for the possibilities at every successive phase. With the outlawing of affirmative action in our two largest states, parts of the pipeline are threatened. Hence, we cannot expect to find in two or three decades noticeably more African Americans (or members of other underrepresented groups) in Ph.D. programs or in professional schools, unless access to excellent undergraduate education remains very strong—and indeed expands.

If the achievements to date are real, they remain too recent, too fragile, and too incomplete for any relaxation of effort. Far from having reached a point where we can feel confident about the gains that have been made since the 1960s, we are still very much in the process of creating the conditions necessary for continuous long-range sustainability. At times in our past, there has been a temptation to believe we had moved beyond the point where continued attention to the particular problems and available opportunities of different racial or ethnic groups was necessary to make further progress in economic and educational areas, but the judgment proved premature.[22] At this moment in our history, we should be mindful of the progress that has been made, but we should not mistake that progress for the full realization of a durable success.

2. Affirmative action programs, while well-intentioned, are focused on the wrong target. Instead, our attention and resources should be devoted to solving more basic social and economic difficulties, by investing in children's health, improved schools, better housing, and school-to-work transitional programs.

Large-scale social investments intended to solve social and economic (and educational) problems might well make a significant difference. But I do not see evidence that such investments, on a major scale, are likely to be forthcoming in the near future. Even if they were to be developed, we would need to monitor them over a considerable span of years in order to make certain that they were having a real impact, and that they would be continued.

The question, therefore, is not whether appropriate forms of affirmative action in higher education represent an adequate response to large-scale social problems. Instead, it is whether well-designed and -administered programs can be helpful as one part of a more general approach.

Moreover, to appreciate the full contribution of these programs, we should remember that they have several far-reaching effects beyond any results that can be measured simply in terms of admissions decisions or their ability to contribute to diversity and learning. They stimulate, for example, national outreach efforts that identify talented candidates and expand the pool of qualified applicants from underrepresented groups. Teachers, guidance counselors, and alumni volunteers (among others) participate in this process, which makes clear to young students that increased educational opportunities do in fact exist—in hundreds of institutions, not just a few. This signal itself becomes a powerful catalyst; mobilizing thousands of students who previously saw far less reason for hope.

As we evaluate the effects of affirmative action in higher education, therefore, we should not underestimate the role it plays in launching an entire cycle of activity involving outreach, advice, and professional guidance. It helps to foster aspiration and to convince talented and determined young people that they can in fact find opportunities in higher education.

3. Affirmative action programs run the risk of stigmatizing and thus injuring the very people they are designed to assist and protect.

The concern about stigmatization is serious and troubling. Some of the Justices in *Bakke* considered this issue, but clearly did not give it decisive weight. I would place greater importance on this point if it were supported by credible evidence.

In fact, however, there is not a strong consensus, especially among those who have been assisted by affirmative action programs, that the difficulties resulting from stigmatization are sufficiently clear and substantial as to outweigh the increased opportunities and protections. Although opinion is to some extent divided, my own observation suggests that the greater weight of informed views—particularly from members of underrepresented groups—remains substantially in favor of well-designed and carefully administered affirmative action initiatives in admissions, because of their demonstrated positive effects.

The findings of Derek Bok and William Bowen, based on their exhaustive analysis of the undergraduate admissions process and subsequent experience of 45,000 students of all races who entered twenty-eight selective colleges in 1976 and 1989, confirms this view. The Bok/Bowen data explode the notion that black students who enter selective colleges and universities with lower high school grades and SAT scores than many of their classmates suffer academically and psychologically because they are "mismatched" with their surroundings. On the contrary, Bok and Bowen found that black students who attended the more selective institutions in their study were more likely to graduate, to earn advanced degrees, to earn high salaries, and to be satisfied with their college experience than black students with similar test scores at less selective institutions. According to Bok and Bowen, "It's time to abandon the idea that well-intentioned college and university admissions officers have somehow sacrificed the interests of the black students whom they have admitted." [23]

4. Affirmative action programs are inherently unfair because they deny admissions to students with high test scores (or grades) in favor of students with less impressive "objective" records.

The potential for unfairness exists, and needs to be taken scrupulously into account. That, of course, was the main reason for the Supreme Court's insistence in *Bakke* that any use of racial or ethnic categories must be subject to exacting judicial scrutiny. At the same time, at least two other considerations are important to bear in mind.

First, any definition of qualifications or merit that does not give considerable weight to a wide range of human qualities and capacities will not serve the goal of fairness to individual candidates (quite apart from groups) in admissions. Nor will it serve the fundamental purposes of education. The more narrow and numerical the definition of qualifications, the more likely we are to pass over (or discount) applicants—of many different backgrounds—who possess exceptional talents, attributes, and evidence of promise that are not well measured by standardized tests.

Second, a college or university is responsible first and foremost to the applicants it chooses to admit. This means it must create the best possible educational environment for them. A major consideration in the achievement of this goal is the composition of an entering class—and the entire student body. Admissions decisions are not isolated, atomistic events. They focus on individuals, but each decision is made in the context of others, where the pattern of the whole is also taken into account. This pattern contributes significantly to student diversity—and diversity, as we have seen, is strongly linked to the quality of learning.

The way to proceed in the future is not to introduce absolute prohibitions on the consideration of race (or other factors) in admissions, but to treat such characteristics with the same care and scrupulousness that we have historically given to so many aspects of diversity. That is what we are doing now. That is what we have done in the past—well before the advent of affirmative action programs in the late 1960s.

Conclusion: Assessment of Diversity in the Full Light of Our History

To sustain our policies in the future will require the same kind of care that we have traditionally devoted to them. It should be recognized at the outset that there is—regrettably—no ideal, friction-free way to arrive at decisions regarding admissions, and no effective way to explain such decisions to the thousands of individuals who are affected by them.

This situation is a direct outgrowth of the post–World War II boom in higher education, and in our collective national expectations concerning full access to educational opportunities. During the past half-century there have been far more applicants than anyone would once have imagined possible. Even if the total number of places in our higher educational system were equal to the number of potential students, many individual colleges and universities would still remain oversubscribed and would have to turn away qualified applicants. Therefore, with or without consideration of race, ethnicity, gender, geographic location, income level, or various other factors, there will be thousands of disappointed candidates.

When such a large proportion of applicants is barely distinguishable on statistical grounds, the admissions process must remain essentially human. It must depend on informed judgment rather than numerical indices. And it will be subject to all the inevitable pressures and possible misconceptions that any exceptionally competitive selection process involves.

In order to sustain a balanced, consistent, and highly attentive process, long-established basic principles continue to offer the best guidance.

- Our commitment to excellence means that we will continue to admit students as individuals, based on their merits: on what they have achieved academically, and what they promise to achieve; on their character, and their energy and curiosity and determination; on their willingness to engage in discussion and debate, to entertain the idea that tolerance, understanding, and mutual respect are goals worthy of persons who have been truly educated.

In assessing individual merit, we will—as we have in the past—take a number of criteria into account. Grades, test scores, and class rank will be viewed in the context of each applicant's full set of capabilities, qualities, and potential for future growth and effectiveness.

- Our commitment to excellence also means that we will seek out—in all corners of the nation, and indeed the world—a diversity of talented and promising students.

Such diversity is the substance from which much human learning, understanding, and wisdom derive. It offers one of the most powerful ways of creating the intellectual energy and robustness that lead to greater knowledge, and to the tolerance and mutual respect so essential to the maintenance of our civic society.

In our world today, it is not enough for us and our students to acknowledge, in an abstract sense, that other kinds of people, with other modes of thought and feeling and action, exist somewhere—unseen, unheard, unvisited, and unknown. We must interact directly with a substantial portion of that larger universe. There must be opportunities to hear different views directly—face to face—from people who embody them. No formal academic study can replace continued association with others who are different from ourselves, and who challenge our preconceptions, prejudices, and assumptions, even as we challenge theirs.

- In selecting those students who will be offered places, the whole must be seen as genuinely greater than the sum of the parts.

When an individual student is admitted, the decision is rarely if ever the result of a circumscribed choice between two—or three, or a very few—applicants who are competing for a single place. Once a standard of high quality has been assured, the central question becomes how to admit a collective class capable of teaching and learning from one another.

Such a selection process involves the conscious consideration of different forms of diversity. In this process—as I stated earlier—quotas or set-asides in admissions are not acceptable. By the same token, efforts to prohibit, categorically and absolutely, the consideration of particular characteristics or criteria are no less arbitrary than to accord such factors a completely sheltered, insulated form of protection or status.

In closing, we should not romanticize diversity as we assess its values. But we do need to remember that the character of American society, from its very beginnings, has been shaped by our collective willingness to carry forward an unprecedented experiment in diversity, the benefits of which have seldom come without friction and strain.

The extent of our nation's success in dealing with diversity can be measured only in the full light of our entire history. Without such a long-term view, as well as an informed awareness of what can be achieved in a heterogeneous society (and at what speed), we will almost certainly undervalue all that has been accomplished so far and be tempted to over-dramatize the shock effect of periodic incidents: incidents that can easily be interpreted as evidence of crisis or failure, when in fact they are often no more than signs of the inescapable if unsettling stresses that exist in a large and complex democratic society such as ours.

As we try to assess the progress made to date on our campuses, we ought to ask whether there are ways to evaluate more systematically the degree of success that has so far been realized. Are there concrete lessons that can be learned from the experience of the past quarter century? Are there certain kinds of institutional arrangements, norms, and stated expectations that enhance the experience of diversity and learning for students and others—and are there some that affect it more negatively?

Clearly, we have much more institutional knowledge and experience now than even a decade ago, and far more than we had in 1970. We also have a growing body of alumni (still relatively young) who have graduated since the late 1960s, when Harvard and many other institutions became gradually more inclusive.

The study by Derek Bok and William Bowen provides by far the most comprehensive and data-intensive analysis to date of the experience of this group of students and alumni. The study found that black students at selective institutions are far more likely to graduate from college than either their black or white counterparts nationwide: 75 percent of black students entering selective colleges graduate, as compared with a 40 percent graduation rate for all black college students and a 59 percent rate for white college students. Furthermore, black graduates of selective institutions are far more likely to obtain graduate degrees than blacks nationwide, earn much higher salaries, and are more likely than their white classmates to hold leadership positions in civic and community activities.

The findings of Bok and Bowen are equally strong with respect to qualitative measures of diversity as a dimension of the college experience. Large numbers of both white and black graduates believe that their college experience contributed substantially to their ability to get along and work with members of other races. And almost 80 percent of white graduates feel that their college or university should continue to place as much or more emphasis as it currently does on achieving a diverse student body. Of the many thousand of students surveyed, Bok and Bowen found that "the vast majority believe that going to college with a diverse body of students made a valuable contribution to their education and personal development."[24] Their qualitative inquiry led them to conclude: "There is overwhelming support for the proposition that the progress made over the last thirty years in achieving greater diversity is to be prized, not devalued."[25]

This kind of data should reinforce the commitment of colleges and universities to sustaining and improving our ongoing national experiment in diversity. Furthermore, as I look at the present situation on many of our campuses, I believe that the achieved level of tolerance and respect among thousands and thousands of students is extraordinary. How many of us would have predicted, in 1950 or 1960, that so great a number of talented and dissimilar students would be studying together and learning from one another after so brief a passage of time? No similar transformation has ever before taken place in the long history of higher education, either in this country or elsewhere.

These achievements have their roots, as we have seen, in ideas and actions that reach back more than a century in our history. The record is impressive. The progress, however imperfect, is inspiring. That is why it is so imperative, at this juncture in our history, that higher education's commitment to diversity be sustained and strengthened. To change course now would be to retreat from decades of difficult but steady hope and fulfillment, to follow pathways far less bright, and far less full of promise.

Notes

1. Admission Committee Report, 1966–1967, *Official Register of Harvard University*, p. 114.
2. Admission Committee Report, 1964–1965, pp. 100–101.
3. Admission Committee Report, 1963–1964, p. 92.
4. No single opinion represented the views of a majority of the Court, although brief passages of Justice Lewis Powell's pivotal opinion stated the judgment of the Court on the key issues in dispute.
5. *Regents of the University of California v. Bakke,* 438 U.S. 265, 291 (1978) (opinion of Powell, J.); see also ibid., 356–362 (opinion of Brennan, J., et al.).
6. Ibid., 320 (opinion of Powell, J.); see also ibid., 356–362 (opinion of Brennan, J., et al.).
7. Ibid., 320; see also ibid., 355–356 (opinion of Brennan, J., et al.).
8. An attempt, for instance, to compensate for previous general "societal discrimination" against minorities was judged by Justice Powell not to be an adequate reason for giving special consideration to minority candidates in admissions, because there had been no determination that the University of California at Davis had itself engaged in discriminatory practices requiring remedial effort. Ibid., 307–310.

Four justices of the Court—those who along with Justice Powell formed the majority concluding that race could be used as a "plus factor" in university admissions—took a different view of the "societal discrimination" issue. Ibid., 362 (opinion of Brennan, J., et al.) ("remedying the effects of past societal discrimination is . . . sufficiently important to justify the use of race-conscious admissions programs where there is a sound basis for concluding that minority underrepresentation is substantial and chronic, and that the handicap of past discrimination is impeding access of minorities" to the university).

9. Ibid., 314.
10. Ibid., 312 (quoting 354 U.S. 234, 263 (1957) (concurring in result)).
11. Ibid., 312 (quoting *Keyishian v. Board of Regents*, 385 U.S. 589, 603 (1967)).
12. Ibid., 313.
13. Ibid., 312 (quoting *Keyishian v. Board of Regents*, 385 U.S. 589, 603 (1967)).
14. Ibid., 316.
15. Ibid., 406.
16. Ibid., 314 (quoting *Sweatt v. Painter*, 339 U.S. 629, 634 (1950)).
17. Ibid., 314.
18. Private colleges and universities may well be affected by the decisions in any such cases through provisions of the Civil Rights Act linked to the receipt of federal funds.
19. U.S. Department of Commerce, Bureau of the Census, *Statistical Abstract of the United States* (Washington, DC: Government Printing Office, 1999), table 263, p. 169.
20. U.S. Department of Education, National Center for Education Statistics, Integrated Postsecondary Education Data System, "Completions" Survey, 1994–1995, and "Consolidated" Survey, 1995, table 4d.
21. Ibid., table 4e; *Digest of Education Statistics 1980* (Washington, DC: Government Printing Office), tables 111, 112. Degrees awarded to nonresident aliens are not included.
22. See, for example, part III.2 above.
23. Derek Bok and William G. Bowen, press release regarding publication of *The Shape of the River*, Princeton University Press, p. 4.
24. William G. Bowen and Derek Bok, *The Shape of the River: Long-Term Consequences of Considering Race in College and University Admissions* (Princeton, NJ: Princeton University Press, 1998), p. 255.
25. Ibid., p. 255.

CHAPTER 2

A Policy Framework for Reconceptualizing the Legal Debate Concerning Affirmative Action in Higher Education

SCOTT R. PALMER

Introduction

The U.S. Supreme Court has established that all race-based affirmative action programs are subject to "strict scrutiny" and will be upheld only where there is a sufficient "basis in evidence" to support the belief that the given program serves a "compelling interest" and is "narrowly tailored" to achieve that interest.[1] Based on Justice Lewis Powell's opinion in *Regents of the University of California v. Bakke*,[2] a number of colleges and universities are currently implementing affirmative action programs to serve, in whole or part, their interest in promoting the educational benefits of diversity.[3] However, several key issues remain unsettled regarding the application of the strict-scrutiny standard to the case of nonremedial affirmative action in higher education.[4] For example: Can a university's interest in promoting educational diversity constitute a compelling interest? What does a narrowly tailored affirmative action program look like? What evidence is necessary and sufficient to justify nonremedial affirmative action?

This chapter asserts that in order to evaluate and make the case for affirmative action in higher education based on the diversity rationale, it is essential first to reconceptualize the legal debate into a policy-oriented framework. The model presented here is simple: "Policy development" can be divided into four interrelated parts—goals, objectives, strategy, and design, each of which is linked to the next by evidence and analytical presumptions.[5] As used here:

- Goals are the broad, non-operational interests that drive policy choices;
- Objectives are concrete, operational aims that promote the broader goal(s);
- A strategy is a general plan of action designed to achieve the desired objective(s) and thereby promote the broader goal(s); and
- Design is a detailed statement of the strategy.

Understood in these terms, promoting racial diversity in higher education is not an end in itself; rather, it is an objective designed to further various goals of higher education. It is those goals that a court must examine to determine if they are sufficiently "compelling" to justify affirmative action. In order to achieve the objective of racial diversity, a university may institute a given strategy, such as race-based affirmative action in student admissions, which in turn has a certain design, such as a "plus-factor" design in which race is considered as one factor among many in the admissions process.

Using this policy framework to reconceptualize the legal debate concerning nonremedial affirmative action in higher education can help clearly identify the arguments in support of affirmative action based on the diversity rationale and highlight what needs to be done to make those arguments most effectively.[6] In particular, the framework can help clarify the legal issues on which social science and other evidence regarding the benefits of diversity would be most valuable.

This chapter applies the policy framework described above to the issue of affirmative action in university admissions designed to promote the educational benefits of diversity. The chart below summarizes the analysis that follows. Based on that analysis, I conclude that there is a strong case to be made for affirmative action in higher education based on the diversity rationale, but more needs to be done by the higher education community both to use the resource of educational diversity more effectively and to evaluate it more rigorously.

The Goals of Higher Education

In the Supreme Court's 1978 decision in *Regents of the University of California v. Bakke*,[7] Justice Powell's opinion declared that a university's interest in securing the educational benefits of diversity is sufficiently compelling to support affirmative action in university admissions.[8] Nearly twenty years later, in *Hopwood v. Texas*,[9] the U.S. Court of Appeals for the Fifth Circuit rejected *Bakke*'s diversity rationale, without fully considering the

A Policy Framework for Conceptualizing the Case for Nonremedial Affirmative Action in Higher Education Admissions Based on *Bakke*'s Diversity Rationale

The Model	I	II	III
Goals of Higher Education • Which goals, if any, are likely compelling, alone or in combination?	Improve student learning	Enhance students' civic values	Promote students' preparation for employment
Evidentiary Links • What evidence is likely necessary to link the objective to the goal?	Evidence showing that racial diversity can improve learning outcomes, including broader and deeper understanding of substantive issues and/or enhanced critical thinking and problem-solving skills	Evidence showing that racial diversity can improve civic outcomes, including improved racial attitudes (e.g., reduced stereotypes, increased tolerance) and/or improved intergroup relations (e.g., openness toward integration)	Evidence showing that racial diversity can enhance economic outcomes, including improved ability to work effectively in diverse environments and/or to understand the value of diverse perspectives
Objective • What level of racial diversity is likely necessary?	Racial diversity in the student body, including a critical mass of students from different racial backgrounds	Racial diversity in the student body, including a critical mass of students from different racial backgrounds	Racial diversity in the student body, including a critical mass of students from different racial backgrounds
Strategy • Are race-based strategies necessary?	Race-based affirmative action in admissions	Race-based affirmative action in admissions	Race-based affirmative action in admissions
Design • Are individualistic values being upheld?	Race used as "plus factor" in admissions process	Race used as "plus factor" in admissions process	Race used as "plus factor" in admissions process

relevance of racial diversity to the various goals of higher education. The *Hopwood* court often seemed to consider all nonremedial uses of affirmative action to be equivalent to the use of race for race's sake. Thus the court said, "[W]e see the case law as sufficiently established that the use of ethnic diversity simply to achieve racial heterogeneity, even as part of a number of factors, is unconstitutional."[10]

Clearly, a university's use of affirmative action to foster racial diversity must serve some goal beyond the achievement of diversity itself. That much was clear from *Bakke*. [11] Racial diversity in the student body is not an end in itself; it is an objective that is sought because it is believed to serve several core goals of higher education, including goals related to improving educational outcomes for all students. Once again, it is those goals that a court must judge to determine if they are sufficiently compelling to justify affirmative action.

Several potentially compelling nonremedial goals of higher education may be enhanced by promoting racial diversity in a university's student body. Per Justice Powell's opinion in *Bakke*, the primary nonremedial justification for affirmative action in higher education is the interest in promoting the educational benefits of diversity, which can be divided into three potentially compelling goals:[12]

1. Improving student learning—enriching the learning environment by providing diverse perspectives that can improve students' understanding of substantive issues and/or enhance students' critical thinking and problem-solving skills;
2. Enhancing students' civic values—bringing students together in ways that can improve racial attitudes, strengthen intergroup relations, and prepare students to function as good citizens and leaders in our multicultural, democratic society; and
3. Promoting students' preparation for employment—improving students' professional development by teaching them the value of diverse perspectives and how to function effectively in diverse business settings and the expanding global marketplace.

Other potentially compelling nonremedial goals also exist and are discussed briefly below, but they are not the primary focus of this chapter. For example, racial diversity may, in some cases, promote the goal of remedying the lack of essential-service providers in society—producing well-educated professionals to practice in underserved communities—and/or the goal of remedying racial stratification in society—producing well-educated minority graduates to serve at advanced levels of society. These goals are somewhat different than the three educational goals itemized above, which emanate directly from *Bakke*'s diversity rationale. These last two benefits do not flow from students' interactions with persons from different racial and ethnic backgrounds per se, but generally from the inclusion of minority students at selective universities.

Whether any or some combination of these goals is sufficiently compelling to justify affirmative action logically depends, in part, on the importance of the goal(s) to the mission of the given institution of higher education and to society. However, even if one or more of the above goals is potentially compelling, courts will likely uphold affirmative action only where there is a sufficient "basis in evidence" linking the objective of promoting racial diversity to the goal(s). This evidentiary requirement likely serves the related purposes of demonstrating that affirmative action is legitimately necessary to promote the articulated, potentially compelling goal(s) and ensuring that the articulated goal(s) is not merely a pretext for discrimination.[13]

It is unclear how much and what kind of evidence is necessary to meet this evidentiary requirement. Nonetheless, several factors arguably weigh in favor of universities in their efforts to present sufficient evidence of the educational value of diversity. For example:

- The First Amendment concept of academic freedom recognizes that it is chiefly the university's place "to determine for itself on academic grounds who may teach, what may be taught, how it shall be taught, and who may be admitted to study."[14] Educators are appropriately due some deference in their educational judgments regarding the value of diversity.
- While universities must present evidence of the value of diversity, the ultimate burden of proof remains with the plaintiff(s) challenging a university's affirmative action program to prove that it violates his/her equal protection rights.[15]
- How much and what kind of evidence is required under the strict-scrutiny standard may depend, in part, on what evidence is available.[16]

The higher education community has long believed that diversity in a university's student body, including racial diversity, is a vital tool for providing students with a complete educational experience,[17] but, until recently, comparatively little had been done to prove the value of diversity. Several recent studies and other efforts show meaningful, positive results, and others are under way. To strengthen the case for nonremedial affirmative action, however, the higher education community likely must develop additional evidence that racial diversity can, when used effectively, promote the potentially compelling educational benefits identified

above. Several types of research may provide valuable evidence of the educational benefits of diversity, including opinion evidence (e.g., testimony from education leaders and survey evidence from students and faculty regarding the benefits of diversity), programmatic evidence (e.g.,
qualitative descriptions of promising practices that institutions are implementing to promote the benefits of diversity), and outcome evidence (i.e.,
studies showing the educational outcomes that can result from learning
in diverse versus homogeneous environments).

The remainder of this section explores in greater detail each of the
above goals of higher education and its evidentiary link to the objective
of promoting racial diversity. The section also references some examples
of evidence supporting each link, including the studies presented in this
volume, but it is not intended to be a comprehensive review of the research literature.[18] Finally, this section considers which, if any, of the
above goals are likely to be considered "compelling" by the Supreme
Court. The Court has offered little guidance concerning precisely what
the term "compelling interest" means.[19] Nonetheless, it is possible to
glean some general principles from the Court's jurisprudence and to reach
tentative conclusions with regard to the goals identified above.

1. Improving Student Learning

One core goal of higher education that may be served by promoting racial diversity in student admissions is the goal of improving student
learning. As Justice Powell recognized in *Bakke*, "People do not learn very
much when they are surrounded only by the likes of themselves."[20] Diversity in a university's student body, including racial diversity, can promote substantive teaching and learning, both in and out of the classroom, by exposing students to a variety of perspectives on many subjects,
thereby increasing their breadth and depth of knowledge on those subjects, and by challenging students' existing perspectives, thereby enhancing their critical-thinking and problem-solving skills. Racial diversity,
therefore, benefits all students by providing them with a more complete
educational experience.[21]

The most common criticism levied against this interest in the affirmative action context is that it equates race with viewpoint: As the Fifth
Circuit asserted in *Hopwood*, "To believe that a person's race controls his
point of view is to stereotype him."[22] But this criticism misses the point.
The belief here is not that a person's race controls his/her viewpoint, but
rather that a person's race may affect his/her background and life experience and, in turn, his/her perspective on certain issues.[23] This does not
stereotype a person any more than the belief that where a person was

born and raised may have a similar effect. In a sense, what is at issue is not racial diversity at all, but experiential diversity: "The variety of viewpoints that the University seeks to foster does not come from any innate difference between the races themselves, but rather from the varying life experiences of the individual, due in large part to their racial backgrounds."[24] And this experiential diversity can enrich the learning environment. "Students 'come to "understand" primarily on the basis of their own reflecting experience, into which they seek to incorporate the new ideas they encounter in their courses.' Because their experiences determine their frame of reference, minority students bring the influence of these experiences to assignments and discussions."[25]

The Fifth Circuit in *Hopwood* seems to deny the role of race in society—stating that race is no more relevant than blood type.[26] But blood type, unlike race, is in no way correlated with such factors as educational opportunity, socioeconomic status, or the nature of interpersonal relations in our country.[27] The Fifth Circuit may wish that there were not racial differences in society, but it cannot deny reality: "One must be careful to distinguish between issues of is and ought."[28] And if the court's goal is to delegitimize racial differences in society,[29] the question from the perspective of university admissions is, what is more likely to facilitate that goal—allowing students of different races to interact in the university marketplace of ideas or limiting such interaction by disallowing affirmative action in student admissions?

A second criticism that may be lodged against the use of affirmative action to further the interest in improving student learning is that it relies on a faulty pedagogical premise: The university is a place where faculty teach students, not where students teach students.[30] But this criticism, too, is flawed. First, substantial evidence indicates that teaching and learning at universities occurs not only between faculty and students but also among students themselves.[31] Second, the role of faculty is to constantly discover as well as to share knowledge, and "[these] functions of discovering and sharing knowledge are intimately related."[32] Third, apart from teaching and learning in the classroom, "[a] great deal of learning occurs informally."[33] Finally, even if it were true that only faculty teach students, it is widely believed that student-centered teaching (e.g., discussion sections in college, the Socratic method in law school, the case method in business school) can improve the overall educational experience. "In the classroom, professors can use the backgrounds and experiences of other students as a learning tool."[34]

To sustain affirmative action based on this potentially compelling goal of improving student learning, institutions will likely be required to produce evidence linking racial diversity in a university's student body to enhanced learning outcomes. This evidence would likely include studies showing that greater learning, including greater breadth and depth of knowledge on substantive issues and/or improved critical-thinking and problem-solving skills, can be achieved in racially diverse environments compared to racially homogeneous environments. Studies showing a direct link between racial diversity and improved teaching and learning are likely hard to produce. Nonetheless, several recent and encouraging attempts have been made. These studies illustrate that racial diversity, when used effectively, can promote positive learning outcomes.

For example, several recent longitudinal studies based on institutional and nationwide student survey data show positive correlations between increased cross-racial student interactions and various learning outcomes. For example, a study by Patricia Gurin found, "Students who experienced the most racial and ethnic diversity in classroom settings and in informal interactions with peers showed the greatest engagement in active thinking processes, growth in intellectual engagement and motivation, and growth in intellectual and academic skills."[35] In addition, Mitchell Chang's study, published in this volume, finds that increased cross-racial student interactions have direct and/or indirect positive effects on such educational outcomes as student retention, satisfaction with college, and intellectual and social self-concept.[36] Other longitudinal studies have shown similar results.[37]

Other forms of testimonial and survey evidence are also probative, including surveys of faculty and students. Many education leaders have spoken in support of the educational benefits of diversity.[38] For example, Neil Rudenstine, president of Harvard University, in an essay that appears in this volume, said:

> [I]t is . . . important that we remember the most fundamental rationale for student diversity in higher education: its educational value. Students benefit in countless ways from the opportunity to live and learn among peers whose perspectives and experiences differ from their own. A diverse educational environment challenges them to explore ideas and arguments at a deeper level—to see issues from various sides, to rethink their own premises, and to achieve the kind of understanding that comes only from testing their own hypotheses against those of people with opposing views.[39]

In addition, several recent surveys of university faculty indicate strong support for the belief that racial diversity is important to the mission of their institutions and that diversity promotes various learning opportunities and outcomes, such as broadening the variety of experiences shared in class and encouraging students to examine their own perspectives.[40] For example, in a recent case study regarding faculty attitudes toward diversity at Macalester College, reported in this volume, Roxane Harvey Gudeman found that more than 60 percent of faculty agree that racial diversity promotes such learning benefits as broadening the issues and perspectives discussed in class (though opinions were strongest among faculty that focused on or taught about race or ethnicity).[41] Furthermore, in a recent survey of students at Harvard Law School and the University of Michigan Law School, reported in this volume, Gary Orfield and Dean Whitla found that the vast majority of students believe that racial diversity has enhanced learning experiences, such as "how you and others think about problems and solutions in classes."[42] Moreover, approximately 90 percent of students surveyed consider racial diversity to be either a moderately or clearly positive element in their educational experience.[43]

Some studies have measured the effects of diversity on teaching and learning at a more micro-level. For example, a study by Maurianne Adams and Yu-hui Zhou-McGovern found that participation in an undergraduate social diversity course with a racially diverse student enrollment had a statistically significant, positive effect on students' cognitive development based on tests administered before and after the semester.[44]

Furthermore, the premise that racial diversity in the student body improves student learning can perhaps also be established by analogy through existing research related to the benefits of diverse work groups. "Studies have shown that work team heterogeneity promotes critical strategic analysis, creativity, innovation, and high-quality decisions."[45] Therefore, it can be argued that racial diversity in the higher education context can enhance group analysis and thereby improve teaching and learning on many issues, at least in student-centered learning environments.

Finally, there is the question of whether this interest in promoting teaching and learning, which is a central part of the educational diversity endorsed by Justice Powell in *Bakke*, is likely to be found "compelling" by the Supreme Court today. This issue can perhaps best be examined by considering the likely view of each Justice. Justices Antonin Scalia and Clarence Thomas and Chief Justice William Rehnquist are unlikely to find this interest to be compelling. Justices Scalia and Thomas have indicated that they favor full race neutrality,[46] and Chief Justice Rehnquist shows no signs of favoring the diversity rationale.[47] Justice John Paul Stevens, however, clearly supports educational diversity as a compelling interest.[48] Furthermore, while the views of Justices David Souter, Stephen Breyer, and Ruth Bader Ginsburg are somewhat less known, their dissents in *Adarand v. Pena* and other writings clearly evidence a rejection of strict race neutrality and potential support for educational diversity as a compelling interest.[49]

The apparent swing votes, therefore, on the Court in 2000, are Justice Sandra Day O'Connor and, to a lesser extent, Justice Anthony Kennedy, whose views are somewhat difficult to discern. Both justices have on occasion advocated race neutrality.[50] Justice O'Connor, joined by Justice Kennedy and others, authored the main dissent in *Metro Broadcasting, Inc. v. FCC*, which suggested that only the remedial interest in overcoming the present effects of past discrimination could ever constitute a compelling interest.[51] Nonetheless, there are clear differences between the broadcast diversity at issue in *Metro* and the interest in improving student learning in the higher education context, which might cause Justice O'Connor to reach a different result in the latter context.[52] Furthermore, Justice O'Connor's prior opinions indicate some level of support for educational diversity.[53] Finally, in *Adarand*, Justice O'Connor avoided repudiating *Bakke*, indicated that strict scrutiny is not "fatal in fact," and, joined only by Justice Kennedy, reaffirmed her belief in the importance of precedent.[54] This last point concerning the importance of precedent may be especially important for the future of nonremedial affirmative action in higher education under *Bakke*'s diversity rationale:

> *Adarand* teaches us a valuable lesson about Justices O'Connor and Kennedy. . . . Joined . . . only by Justice Kennedy, [Justice O'Connor] carefully crafted one section of *Adarand* in light of her 1992 [*Planned Parenthood v.*] *Casey* opinion (coauthored with Justices Kennedy and Souter), which cautioned against overruling hugely important cases around which major social expectations have crystallized. . . . Thus a big "plus" for *Bakke* [and its interest in improving student learning] is its social importance. An entire generation of Americans has been schooled under *Bakke*-style affirmative action. . . . Only a handful of modern Supreme Court cases are now household words in America. But *Bakke*—like *Brown* and *Roe*—is surely one of them.[55]

Given this analysis, there is likely a strong case to be made for affirmative action in higher education based on the interest in improving student learning, though more needs to be done to fully develop that case.

2. Enhancing Students' Civic Values

Another educational goal that may be furthered by promoting racial diversity in a university's student body is the goal of enhancing students' civic values. Education has long been viewed in our democratic society as "the very foundation of good citizenship."[56] "[M]uch of the point of education is to teach students how others think and to help them understand different points of view—to teach students how to be sovereign, responsible, and informed citizens in a heterogeneous democracy."[57] The theory here is that by bringing together and promoting constructive interactions among students from diverse racial and ethnic backgrounds, universities can help break down racial fears and stereotypes and cultivate the values of tolerance, justice, and respect for others that make all students better citizens:

> If a far-flung democratic republic as diverse—and at times divided—as late twentieth-century America is to survive and flourish, it must cultivate some common spaces where citizens from every corner of society can come together to learn how others live, how others think, how others feel. If not in . . . universities, where? If not in young adulthood, when?"[58]

Evidence linking racial diversity in the student body to the goal of enhancing civic values would likely include research demonstrating that students who study in racially diverse environments can be more likely to develop positive racial attitudes and to more fully embrace our multicultural democracy. "National studies dealing with changes during the college years in attitudes and values related to civil rights, civil liberties, racism, anti-Semitism, or general tolerance for nonconformity uniformly report shifts toward social, racial, ethnic, and political tolerance and greater support for the rights of individuals in a wide variety of areas."[59] Less evidence, however, has focused directly on the question of whether racial diversity itself can promote such outcomes. Nonetheless, some important research does exist, and additional evidence is being developed.

This evidence includes longitudinal studies linking racial diversity to several civic outcomes. For example, Patricia Gurin found:

> Students who experienced diversity in classroom settings and in informal interactions showed the most engagement during college in various forms of citizenship, and the most engagement with people from different races and cultures. They were also the most likely to acknowledge that group differences are compatible with the interests of the broader community. These effects continued after the students left the university setting. Diversity experiences during college had impressive effects on the extent to which graduates in the national study were living racially and ethnically integrated lives in the post-college world.[60]

Furthermore, Alexander Astin found that increased student diversity experiences, as well as increased faculty and institutional commitment to diversity, were positively associated with such civic outcomes as increased cultural awareness among students and/or increased student commitment to promoting racial understanding.[61] Moreover, a recent study by Sylvia Hurtado, which is included in this volume, found that students who studied with someone from a different racial or ethnic background reported positive growth in such civic outcomes as "the acceptance of people of different races/cultures, cultural awareness, tolerance of people with different beliefs, and leadership abilities."[62]

These longitudinal findings are supported by additional survey evidence. For example, in a recent study by William Bowen and Derek Bok, the vast majority of black and white graduates surveyed said that attending a racially diverse college helped improve their ability "to work effectively and get along well with people from different races."[63]

Some important studies also have looked specifically at the long-term effects of diversity on civic outcomes. For example, in a recent report summarizing lessons from school desegregation research, which is published in this volume, Janet Ward Schofield indicates that students who attend desegregated schools are more likely to live and work in integrated environments as adults.[64]

In addition, the link between racial diversity in the student body and the goal of inculcating civic values can perhaps be established through existing research demonstrating that interactions among different types of people can, in certain circumstances, promote tolerance and understanding. This theory is widely known as the "contact hypothesis," which states that "contact with members of a negatively stereotyped group might ameliorate attitudes both toward the specific group member or members with whom contact occurred, and toward the group as a whole."[65] Numerous studies have provided support for the contact hypothesis if certain conditions are met. These conditions include that 1) the interaction occur between persons of equal status, 2) the interaction afford persons the chance to get to know each other, and 3) the interaction be cooperative and in pursuit of mutual goals.[66] Therefore, the contact hypothesis likely lends support for the role of racial diversity in promoting such civic values as racial tolerance and understanding, provided that universities make the commitment to foster cross-racial, cooperative learning opportunities.

Finally, there is the question of whether this civic interest is likely to be found compelling. The goal of enhancing civic values is at the heart of *Bakke*'s diversity rationale and is often analyzed as part of the interest in improving student learning described above. Therefore, the prior analysis of the likely views of each justice concerning whether the interest in student learning is "compelling" likely applies here as well. However, these interests are properly disaggregated to point out an important difference: Unlike the student learning interest, the civic interest does not necessarily depend on judgments about individuals' viewpoints. In other words, even if the lesson that students of different races learn from interacting with each other in a university setting is that there is no viewpoint correlated with race (i.e., that students from different racial backgrounds do not in fact see any issues differently in any consistent way), that would likely be an extremely valuable lesson toward instilling students of all races with the tolerance and understanding necessary for them to function as good citizens in our multicultural, democratic society. As Justice Stevens explained in *Wygant v. Jackson Board of Education*, referring to the value of racial diversity in school faculty:

> In the context of public education, it is quite obvious that a school board may reasonably conclude that an integrated faculty will be able to provide benefits to the student body that could not be provided by an all-white, or nearly all-white, faculty. For one of the most important lessons that the American public schools teach is that the diverse ethnic, cultural, and national backgrounds that have been brought together in our famous "melting pot" do not identify essential differences among the human beings that inhabit our land. It is one thing for a white child to be taught by a white teacher that color, like beauty, is only "skin deep"; it is far more convincing to experience that truth on a day-to-day basis during the routine, ongoing learning process.[67]

This distinction could make a difference to Justice O'Connor, who in her *Metro* dissent indicated her opposition to affirmative action programs that are based on the assumption that a person's race determines how he or she thinks.[68] As explained above, I believe that this criticism concerning race and viewpoint misunderstands the relevance of racial diversity in the higher education context. Nonetheless, to the extent that the criticism can be avoided, the case for the goal of enhancing civic values as a compelling interest may be even stronger than that for improving student learning.

3. Promoting Students' Preparation for Employment

A third educational goal that may be served by promoting racial diversity in a university's student body is the interest in preparing students for future employment. The theory behind this economic interest is that racial diversity in higher education is a vital tool for promoting students' professional development by teaching them the value of diverse perspectives and how to work and communicate effectively with persons from different backgrounds.[69] This interest likely grows more important as business environments become more diverse, the domestic marketplace becomes more diverse, and the global marketplace expands. "As the population of the country becomes ever more diverse, . . . the need to work effectively with individuals of other races will become an increasingly inescapable reality to members of every racial group."[70] In short, racial diversity in higher education can make all students more qualified for future employment by preparing them for success in an increasingly diverse business world.

Evidence linking racial diversity in the student body to the goal of improving students' professional development would likely include studies showing that employers value employees who have "cross-cultural competencies" and that graduates of diverse universities are more comfortable, effective, and successful working in diverse business environments.

There is growing evidence from the business arena that employers value diversity and persons able to function effectively in diverse environments.[71] This is based, in part, on evidence that diverse work groups, including racially diverse groups, can promote greater problem solving (i.e., generate ideas that are more creative, effective, and feasible) than homogenous groups, but only when those heterogeneous groups are able to be managed effectively.[72] Furthermore, evidence from several studies shows that students who learn in diverse environments are more likely to choose to work in diverse business settings.[73] Finally, a recent study by Kermit Daniel, Dan Black, and Jeffrey Smith, which is published in this volume, presents preliminary evidence that attending a college with a more diverse student body may have a positive effect on the future wages of both black and non-black men, though diversity seems to have a lesser effect or no effect on the future wages of women.[74] This suggest that there may be a market value to learning in diverse environments.[75]

In many ways, the value of diversity in promoting students' preparation for employment is an extension of the benefits of improved student learning and enhanced civic values discussed above, for it relies on the belief that students will take the lessons learned from educational diversity on campus into the workplace. Therefore, evidence related to the value of diversity in promoting teaching and learning and enhancing civic values should be relevant here as well. This relationship among the educational benefits of diversity extends to the question of whether the goal of promoting student's preparation for employment is likely to be found compelling by the Supreme Court. Given the strong case that can be made for both the teaching and learning and civic values rationales, there is likely a strong case to be made for the goal of enhancing students' professional development as a compelling interest that can justify affirmative action, but more needs to be done by both the higher education and business communities to develop that case.

4. Other Potentially Compelling Goals

On a different level than the three educational goals described above, which emanate from Justice Powell's opinion in *Bakke*, promoting the inclusion of racial minorities at selective universities may serve other potentially compelling, nonremedial interests, two of which I will discuss briefly.

First, racial diversity may promote the potentially compelling goal of producing well-educated professionals to practice in underserved areas. Significantly, the achievement of this goal is not based on the interaction among students of different races. In fact, this interest is not really concerned with the race of students at all. Rather, the theory here is that promoting minority enrollment will remedy the lack of essential-service providers, such as medical professionals, in underserved communities because such communities tend to be largely minority communities and minority graduates are more likely to practice in those communities.

Evidence linking the objective of racial diversity to the goal of remedying the lack of essential-service providers in society would likely include evidence that there is a lack of certain types of professionals practicing in certain communities and that minority professionals are more likely to practice in those areas. Such evidence does exist for some fields.

The most apparent example is the medical profession, which was at issue in *Bakke*. There is substantial evidence of disparities regarding access to physicians in certain segments of society.[76] While there are such shortages in poor communities regardless of race, studies indicate that "[t]he supply of physicians was much more strongly associated with the proportion of black and Hispanic residents in the community areas than with the areas' income level."[77] Furthermore, studies show that black and Hispanic medical school graduates are significantly more likely to practice in these underserved areas.[78] A recent study by Timothy Ready, included in this volume, provides an overview of several studies showing that minority physicians are more likely than white physicians to work in disadvantaged and/or predominantly minority communities.[79] Therefore, affirmative action in medical school admissions would likely further the goal of facilitating health care to all citizens.

This interest may be compelling in some circumstances where the need for certain service providers is itself compelling. For example, in *Bakke*, Justice Powell suggested that the state's interest in "facilitating the health care of its citizens" by expanding health services in underserved communities was arguably compelling enough to justify the use of race-based affirmative action at Davis Medical School, but Justice Powell rejected the interest in large part because there was no evidence that minority graduates were more likely to practice in such underserved communities.[80] Such evidence now exists. However, affirmative action programs designed to promote this interest may be unlikely to withstand strict scrutiny for a different reason—there may be race-neutral means available to further this goal (i.e., the program would not be necessary or narrowly tailored). For example, a university could reserve admissions slots for students who pledge to practice in underserved communities after graduation. Therefore, the question of whether this goal is compelling may be moot. On the other hand, evidence that such efforts are not likely to produce lasting solutions could be important. To the extent that race-neutral means are not likely to be effective, race-based means could be justified.

Second, promoting the inclusion of racial minorities at selective universities may serve the goal of remedying racial stratification by producing well-educated minorities to serve at advanced levels in society. This interest rests in part on the notion that universities are prime forces of social mobility and can, therefore, help overcome racial stratification in society. However, this interest may also have an instrumental component: The theory here is that it may be appropriate to use affirmative action to admit minority students to study in certain fields because there is a compelling interest in having a sufficient number of minority graduates in certain positions in society.

In part, evidence linking racial diversity to the goal of remedying racial stratification would include evidence that increasing minority representation in higher education can help overcome gaps in society. There is ample evidence that higher education is a major force for overcoming racial disparities. For example, there is substantial evidence that obtaining a college degree promotes greater earnings, and that this effect is even greater for persons of color than for whites.[81] A recent study by Kermit Daniel, Dan Black, and Jeffrey Smith, included in this volume, found that attending a high-quality college has a positive effect on the future wages of blacks that is approximately three time greater than the effect on wages of non-blacks.[82] Yet despite this evidence, it may be unlikely that the present Supreme Court would find that universities are the appropriate actors to decide to use affirmative action to pursue this goal of remedying racial stratification, which seems akin to the goal of remedying societal discrimination.

However, as stated above, there may be specific cases where evidence shows that increasing the number of minorities serving in select positions in society has an instrumental value that is itself compelling, and where universities are so closely connected to producing individuals to serve in those positions that affirmative action would be justified. Consider, once again, the medical profession. It is clear that there is an underrepresentation of minority physicians in society.[83] Furthermore, there may be an instrumental value to having a sufficient number of minority physicians in society (not to be confused with the interest discussed above in providing underserved communities with physicians of any race) to ensure the highest quality care for persons of color.[84] Thus, it is possible that affirmative action in medical school admissions could be necessary to promote this goal.[85]

But how would the Supreme Court view this interest? It is highly unlikely that the Court would permit universities to use affirmative action solely to promote the social mobility of persons of color. That interest is largely akin to the interest in overcoming "societal discrimination," which the Supreme Court has clearly indicated is not sufficiently compelling to justify affirmative action by any entity except perhaps the federal government.[86] Even where there is an instrumental value to the promotion of minorities in a given field, the use of affirmative action may raise concerns for the Court. This justification promotes a largely pluralistic view of society in which persons of different races are best served by persons of their same race. This runs contrary to American principles of individualism and to much of the Supreme Court's jurisprudence on race. Nonetheless, this interest may be worth pursuing in defense of a university's affirmative action program in specific circumstances where there is a particularly compelling need for minority professionals and a close connection between the education an institution provides and the availability of such professionals in society.[87]

Objective of Promoting Racial Diversity

In the case of nonremedial affirmative action in university admissions, the objective is promoting racial diversity in the student body, which most often means increasing minority representation at predominantly white universities. However, vague objectives, such as "promoting racial diversity," are sometimes detrimental because they lead to confused, imperfect policy choices.[88] What makes an objective "operational" is that it is defined precisely enough so that it is easy to understand what is expected and to determine whether the objective has been achieved. In the case of affirmative action in university admissions, this need to clearly articulate a policy's objective raises additional questions — most importantly, exactly what level of racial diversity is appropriate?[89]

The proper level of diversity a university should pursue necessarily depends on what goal(s) of higher education the university is trying to promote. For example, if the goal is remedying racial stratification in society, then the appropriate level of diversity is likely tied to existing gaps in society. This conclusion illustrates why it is unlikely that the goal of remedying racial stratification will be found to be compelling in most cases. Promoting this interest would permit a discrete university to use affirmative action to admit any number of minority applicants it believed appropriate until societal discrimination was remedied, a situation the Court has rejected.[90]

However, if the goals that a university is seeking to serve are the educational goals of improving teaching and learning, enhancing civic values, or improving professional development among its students, then the appropriate levels of diversity are tied to the levels necessary to achieve those goals by promoting discussions and interactions among students of different races. In other words, some "critical mass" of minority representation is likely necessary to create sufficient opportunities for communication and interactions across racial lines. Furthermore, there is some evidence that minority student participation and interactions across racial lines are dependent, in part, upon the level of comfort minority students feel on campus.[91] A critical mass of students from a given minority group may increase the level of comfort that students from that group feel on campus by providing a community base.[92] Finally, studies show that increasing campus diversity leads to increased cross-racial interactions. For example, a study by Chang, which appears in this volume, shows that increased diversity on campus is positively correlated with the establishment of interracial friendships, even when controlling for student and campus characteristics.[93]

Given the limited, though growing, number of studies concerning the educational value of diversity and the fact that institutional missions and circumstances will vary, we cannot know what level of minority enrollment is optimal to benefit all students. However, there seems to be some agreement between proponents and opponents of affirmative action that tokenism is likely insufficient to realize the educational benefits of diversity and that proportionality in racial representation is not necessarily required to further those educational goals.[94] Between those extremes is a range within which educators are likely due some deference concerning the level of diversity that is optimal to fulfill their educational goals.

Strategy of Affirmative Action

The strategy at issue here is race-based affirmative action in student admissions. It is the use of this race-based strategy that implicates strict scrutiny and requires universities to show that the strategy is narrowly tailored to serve a compelling interest.[95] The compelling interest prong was addressed above. The narrowly tailored prong requires, in part, that the race-based strategy of affirmative action be necessary in the sense that there are no race-neutral means available to achieve the program's compelling interest(s). To the extent that race-neutral means are available, race-based means likely cannot be utilized.

For example, as mentioned above, it may be possible to implement race-neutral means to promote the goal of remedying the lack of essential-service providers in society. A university could, for example, reserve admissions slots for students who pledge to practice in underserved communities after graduation.[96] To the extent that such race-neutral means are effective, race-based affirmative action programs designed to achieve that goal are unlikely to pass strict scrutiny even if the goal is found to be compelling.

However, it is more difficult to see how race-neutral means could effectively achieve the educational goals of improving teaching and learning, enhancing civic values, and improving professional development among all students (assuming these goals are found to be compelling). With regard to each of these goals, the very point is to expose students to persons from different racial backgrounds and/or perspectives. It is unlikely that these goals could be fully achieved without promoting at least some level of racial diversity on campus.[97] Furthermore, evidence indicates that absent intentional efforts to promote the admission of underrepresented minorities to certain selective universities, racial diversity at those institutions would decrease significantly.[98] Therefore, assuming that any of these goals are found to be compelling, affirmative action in student admissions, properly designed, may be a necessary means of achieving that goal.

Design of Race as "Plus Factor"

In the case of nonremedial affirmative action in university admissions, the legally required design is dictated by Justice Powell's decision in *Bakke*. In order for a university's affirmative action program to pass constitutional muster, it must avoid racial quotas and seek to promote a broad-based, individualistic notion of diversity in which race is "but a single though important element."[99] In other words, race may only constitute a single plus factor in a particular candidate's file along with other factors designed to promote diversity in other important dimensions. Admissions programs that do not follow this design will not likely pass strict scrutiny.

It is perhaps appropriate to inquire whether this design of affirmative action, where race is just one element of diversity among many, can truly result in a racially diverse student body, or whether this individualistic notion of diversity is disingenuous because race is really the predominant factor in student admissions. The evidence indicates that while race is only one factor in admissions at selective universities, it is a substantial factor in some cases. According to one study, at those selective universities with average SAT scores in the top 20 percent of all four-year institutions, black and Hispanic applicants were found to be 8–10 percent more likely to be admitted than white students with similar qualifications.[100] "This differential was as large as that associated with having an "A–" average in high school rather than a "B" or having an SAT score of 1400 rather than 1000."[101]

However, for several reasons, this does not necessarily undercut *Bakke*'s plus-factor design. First, the primary factor in admissions at highly selective universities is always academic ability (i.e., all students admitted, through affirmative action or otherwise, come from the pool of qualified candidates).[102] Second, it is clear that universities seek to promote diversity in student admissions based on multiple factors in addition to race (e.g., geographic diversity),[103] but many of these factors are likely well represented at all levels of qualified students. Therefore, a university may not have to take as substantial affirmative action to achieve diversity with regard to most of these characteristics. Third, universities do give substantial weight to other particularistic factors beyond race in student admissions. The most obvious example is alumni preferences, which evidence indicates are often more substantial than race-based preferences at selective universities.[104] Finally, race is likely given substantial weight in admissions at selective universities when choosing among qualified applicants because racial diversity is viewed by educators as an important resource for achieving the goals of higher education.

Conclusion

The above policy framework and analysis indicate that there is likely a strong case to be made for affirmative action in university admissions designed to promote the objective of increasing racial diversity in the student body to further several core goals of higher education, specifically the educational goals of improving student learning, enhancing students' civic values, and/or promoting students' preparation for employment. However, making the case for affirmative action in higher education will require a substantial commitment from the higher education community. For more than 20 years, the higher education community relied heavily on Justice Powell's decision in *Regents of the University of California v. Bakke* to justify affirmative action in higher education. The Fifth Circuit's decision in *Hopwood v. Texas*, and more recent challenges to affirmative action, can be either a clarion call or a death knell.

Based on the above analysis, I conclude that the higher education community must take several steps to build its case for nonremedial affirmative action in higher education.

First, the higher education community must increase efforts to use racial diversity more effectively to further the goals of improving student learning, enhancing civic values, and improving professional development. Racial diversity in the student body is merely a tool or resource. Evidence shows that, like any resource, if such diversity is not used properly and effectively, it is likely to be wasted or even counterproductive. For too long, universities simply provided this complex tool for their students to use without providing guidance on how to use it or creating significant opportunities to do so. This is rapidly changing,[105] but more changes are likely merited. A recent study by Jeffrey Milem, which appears in this volume, indicates that institutions with the greatest diversity are often the least likely to have adopted practices to maximize the benefits of diversity.[106] Further efforts should be taken to formalize the use and benefits of diversity. These efforts could likely include pedagogical changes (such as the enhancement of cooperative learning situations), curricular changes (such as the inclusion of multicultural issues in new and existing courses), and/or extracurricular changes (such as the promotion of community service projects that provide neutral contexts for positive cross-racial interactions).[107] Such efforts would illustrate the institution's commitment to diversity as a means to one or more of the potentially compelling educational goals identified above. Furthermore, such formal programs would create additional opportunities to evaluate the role of diversity in achieving these potentially compelling goals, which leads directly to the next point.

Second, the higher education community must evaluate more rigorously the value of racial diversity in the student body to its educational goals. Universities must have a sufficient basis in evidence to support nonremedial affirmative action. While some significant evidence is available, further social science and other evidence should be developed per the evidentiary links identified above. Such evidence can likely help establish that racial diversity is necessary to promote the educational benefits of diversity and that the use of affirmative action to promote such benefits is not pretextual.[108]

Third, the higher education community must implement affirmative action appropriately and only to the extent necessary to further its articulated nonremedial goals (except where remedial goals are independently justified). This means that universities must make the investment necessary to follow *Bakke*'s "plus factor" design in admissions and must set numerical targets at appropriate levels to achieve its goals, which may mean levels less than proportional representation. If the goals related to promoting the educational benefits of diversity are truly compelling, then universities should be willing to make the commitments and sacrifices necessary to pursue those and only those goals.

Fourth, the higher education community must clearly explain and promote, both on campus and to the public at large, its vision concerning the value of racial diversity in higher education and the role and function of affirmative action in fostering that diversity. Affirmative action faces not only legal challenges, but also political challenges. Building the case for affirmative action means educating and affecting public discourse as well the courts. The primary justification for affirmative action today rests on the educational benefits that accrue to all students from learning in diverse environments, and education leaders can play an important role in ensuring that persons from all racial and ethnic backgrounds fully understand and appreciate those benefits.

Notes

1. See, for example, *Adarand v. Pena,* 515 U.S. 200, 227 (1995); *Richmond v. J. A. Croson Co.,* 488 U.S. 469, 500 (1989).
2. *Regents of the University of California v. Bakke,* 438 U.S. 265 (1978).
3. Studies show that race is most often a factor in student admissions only at highly selective universities, specifically "those [universities] with average SAT scores in the top quintile of four-year institutions." Thomas Kane, Racial and Ethnic Preference in College Admissions 2 (1997) (conference paper) "[A]t the less exclusive institutions that eighty percent of 4-year college students attend, race plays little if any role in admissions decisions." Id.

4. The distinction between "nonremedial" and "remedial" affirmative action is not absolute. However, remedial affirmative action is based directly on the need to *remedy* past or present discrimination, while nonremedial affirmative action is based on the interest in promoting more forward-looking benefits, including the educational benefits that may accrue to all students from attending diverse institutions of higher education.

5. See Phillip Zelikow, *Foreign Policy Engineering: From Theory to Practice and Back Again*, 18 International Security 143 (Spring 1994) (dividing policy engineering into seven interrelated parts, including the four discussed here).

6. This policy analysis provides a different approach for understanding the application of the strict scrutiny standard to affirmative action in higher education, including the compelling interest and narrow tailoring requirements. It is not, however, meant to cover all aspects of the strict scrutiny standard. For a more complete overview of the law, see Scott R. Palmer, *Diversity and Affirmative Action: Evolving Principles and Continuing Legal Battles*, in this volume.

7. *Bakke*, 438 U.S. 265 (1978).

8. See id. at 312-15 (opinion of Powell, J.). "The atmosphere of 'speculation, experiment and creation'—so essential to the quality of higher education—is," Justice Powell wrote, "widely believed to be promoted by a diverse student body." Id. at 312.

9. *Hopwood v. Texas*, 78 F.3d 932 (5th Cir. 1996), *cert. denied*, 518 U.S. 1033 (1996).

10. Id. at 945–46 (emphasis added).

11. See *Bakke*, 438 U.S. at 307 (opinion of Powell, J.).

12. See, for example, Patricia Gurin, *Expert Report, in* The Compelling Need for Diversity in Higher Education, *Gratz v. Bollinger*, 97-75321, and *Grutter v. Bollinger*, 97-75928 (E.D. Mich. 1997) (identifying three categories of goals supported by racial diversity in the student body—1) learning outcomes, 2) democracy outcomes, and 3) outcomes related to living and working in a diverse society); One America in the 21st Century: Forging a New Future, The Report of the President's Advisory Board on Race 66 (1998) ("Diversity improves teaching and learning by providing a range of perspectives that enrich the learning environment; strengthens students' critical-thinking skills by challenging their existing perspectives; teaches students how to interact comfortably with people different than themselves and thereby how to function as good citizens and neighbors; improves students' preparation for employment by teaching them the value of different perspectives, how to function in diverse business settings, and how to communicate effectively in our increasingly diverse domestic marketplace and the expanding global marketplace; and fosters the advancement of knowledge by spurring study in new areas of concern.").

  The concept of "educational benefits of diversity" is used here as an umbrella encompassing several educational goals that may, individually or in sum, be "compelling." The three goals listed above are interrelated and can be divided in several different ways. In addition, other educational goals may also be relevant to certain forms of diversity in higher education, such as the goal of *promoting the advancement of knowledge*—providing diverse perspectives to stimulate research and writing in new areas of concern.

13. See, for example, Goodwin Liu, *Affirmative Action in Higher Education: The Diversity Rationale and the Compelling Interest Test*, 33 Harvard Civil Rights-Civil Liberties Law Review 381, 407 (1998) ("The main function of strict scrutiny's evidentiary requirements, I argue, is to ensure that racial classifications purportedly adopted for legitimate governmental purposes do not actually stem from invidious, unconstitutional motives.").

14. *Bakke,* 438 U.S. at 312 (opinion of Powell, J.) (quoting *Sweezy v. New Hampshire,* 354 U.S. 234, 263 (1957) (Frankfurter, J., concurring in the result)).

15. See, for example, *Wygant v. Jackson Board of Education,* 476 U.S. 267, 277–78 (plurality opinion); id. at 292 (O'Connor, J., concurring).

16. See *Wittmer v. Peters,* 87 F.3d 916, 920–21 (7th Cir. 1996), *cert. denied,* 519 U.S. 1111 (1997).

17. See, for example, Neil Rudenstine, Report to the Harvard University Board of Overseers, 1993–1995, 33 (January 1996) ("Th[e] conception of a diverse student body as an 'educational resource'—comparable in importance to the faculty, library, or science laboratories—is the most direct expression of an idea that we have seen emerging over the course of more than a century.").

18. For a review of the research literature concerning the value of diversity in higher education, See, for example, Gurin, *supra* note 12, at 151 (Appendix B); Jeffrey Milem, *The Educational Benefits of Diversity: Evidence from Multiple Sectors, in* Compelling Interest: Examining the Evidence on Racial Dynamics in Colleges and Universities (prepublication draft) (1998).

19. See, for example, Stephen E. Gottlieb, *Compelling Governmental Interests: An Essential But Unanalyzed Term in Constitutional Adjudication,* 68 Boston University Law Review 917, 937 (1988) ("[W]ith few exceptions, the Court has failed to explain the basis for finding and deferring to compelling governmental interests.") Some legal commentators have suggested that the Court has adopted a "know it when I see it approach" to identifying compelling interests, id. (quoting *Jacobellis v. Ohio,* 378 U.S. 184, 197 (1964) (Stewart, J., concurring), and that "compelling, even more than beauty, [may be] in the eyes of the beholder," David Schimmel, *Is Bakke Still Good Law? The Fifth Circuit Says No and Outlaws Affirmative Action,* 113 Education Law Reporter 1052 (1996) (quoting Lino Graglia, Texas Lawyer, Sept. 25, 1995, at 25).

20. *Bakke,* 438 U.S. at 313 (quoting William Bowen, *Admissions and the Relevance of Race,* Princeton Alumni Weekly 7, 9 (Sept. 26, 1977)).

21. See, for example, Akhil Reed Amar & Neal Kumar Katyal, *Bakke's Fate,* 43 UCLA Law Review 1745, 1749 (1996) ("Integrated education . . . does not just benefit minorities—it advantages all students in a distinctive way, by bringing rich and poor, black and white, urban and rural, together to teach and learn from each other as democratic equals.")

22. *Hopwood,* 78 F.3d at 946.

23. See, for example, The Four Americas: Government and Social Policy Through the Eyes of America's Multi-Racial and Multi-Ethnic Society, Harvard Survey Project 25–37 (Dec. 1995) (illustrating differences in viewpoints by race with regard to several issues). Also see Gary Orfield, *Introduction,* in this volume.

24. Tanya Y. Murphy, *An Argument for Diversity Based Affirmative Action in Higher Education,* 95 Annual Survey of American Law 515 (1996).

25. Note, *An Evidentiary Framework for Diversity as a Compelling Interest in Higher Education,* 109 Harvard Law Review 1357, 1370 (1996) (quoting John D. Wilson, Student Learning in Higher Education 29 (1981)). Racially diverse perspectives may, of course, be more relevant to some issues than others. See, for example, Amar & Katyal, *supra* note 21, at 1778 ("Of course, diversity cannot function in the same way, or be as important, in every academic context. There may be settings where diversity may not have much educational importance at all (graduate school in math, perhaps) and other settings where it will matter a great deal (college, for example).")). But at a university, racially diverse perspectives are likely to be relevant to a significant number of subjects and experiences.

26. See *Hopwood*, 78 F.3d at 945.

27. See, for example, Affirmative Action Review: Report to the President 20–25 (July 1995) (presenting evidence of continued racial stratification and discrimination in American society).

28. Adolphous Levi Williams, Jr., *A Critical Analysis of the Bakke Case*, 16 Stanford University Law Review 129, 225 (1989). "However unpleasant it may be, the issue of race is still very much an unresolved issue in the United States. As desirable as it might be to set this issue to one side, pretend it does not exist, or acknowledge its existence and accord it only minimal importance, the historical evidence and realities (for example to small percentage of Afro-American[s] in the professions) lead us in the opposite direction and to another conclusion; specifically, that race must be considered now and in the foreseeable future." Id. at 229.

29. See *Hopwood*, 78 F.3d at 940 (suggesting that the goal of equal protection is to make race irrelevant).

30. This criticism, of course, suggests an important argument in support of non-remedial affirmative action in faculty recruitment to support the educational benefits of diversity. See *University and Community College System of Nevada v. Farmer*, 930 P.2d 730 (Nov., 1997), *cert. denied*, 118 S. Ct. 1186 (1998) (upholding under a Title VII challenge a university's affirmative action plan to promote faculty diversity where there was also a manifest racial imbalance in the work force). But see *Taxman v. Board of Education of the Township of Piscataway*, 91 F.3d 1547 (3d Cir. 1995) (holding unlawful under Title VII a school board's decision to layoff a white high school teacher rather than an equally qualified black teacher to maintain faculty diversity because only remedial affirmative action programs whose purposes mirror Title VII were deemed lawful).

31. See, for example, Ernest T. Pascarella & Patrick T. Terenzini, How College Affects Students 620 (1991) ("Consistent with evidence on the impact of student-faculty interaction, students' interactions with their peers also have a strong influence on many aspects of change during college. Included are such areas as intellectual development and orientation; political, social, and religious values; academic and social self-concept; intellectual orientation; interpersonal skills; moral development; general maturity and personal development; and educational aspirations and educational attainment.")

32. Nannerl O. Keohane, *The Mission of the Research University, in* The Research University in a Time of Discontent 157 (Jonathan R. Cole, Elinor G. Barber, & Stephen R. Graubard eds., 1994).

33. *Bakke,* 438 U.S. at 313 n.48 (quoting Bowen, *supra* note 20, at 9).

34. Note, *supra* note 25, at 1370.

35. See, for example, Gurin, *supra* note 12, at 100.

36. Mitchell J. Chang, *The Positive Educational Effects of Racial Diversity on Campus,* in this volume.

37. See, for example, Alexander Astin, *How Are Students Affected?* 25 Change 44 (1993); Octavio Villalpando, Comparing the Effects of Multiculturalism and Diversity on Minority and White Students' Satisfaction with College (ASHE Annual Meeting Paper) 16 (Nov. 9, 1994).

38. See, for example, Gabriel J. Chin, *Bakke to the Wall: The Crisis of Bakkean Diversity,* 4 William and Mary Bill of Rights Journal 881, 888–89 (1996).

39. Neil L. Rudenstine, *Student Diversity and Higher Learning,* in this volume.

40. See, for example, Richard A. White, *Law School Faculty Views on Diversity in the Classroom and the Law School Community* (Preliminary Report for the American Association of Law Schools) (2000); Geoffrey Maruyama & Jose F. Moreno, *University*

Faculty Views About the Value of Diversity on Campus and in the Classroom (Report for the American Council on Education and the American Association of University Professors) (2000).

41. Roxane Harvey Gudeman, *Faculty Experience with Diversity: A Case Study of Macalester College,* in this volume.

42. Gary Orfield & Dean Whitla, *Diversity and Legal Education: Student Experiences in Leading Law Schools,* in this volume.

43. Id.

44. Maurianne Adams & Yu-hui Zhou-McGovern, The Sociomoral Development of Undergraduates in a "Social Diversity" Course 31 (Paper presented at the Annual Meeting of the American Educational Research Association) (Apr. 1994).

45. Susan Sturm & Lani Guinier, *The Future of Affirmative Action: Reclaiming the Innovative Ideal,* 84 California Law Review 953, 1024 (1996) (citing L. Richard Hoffman & Norman R.F. Maier, *Quality and Acceptance of Problem Solutions by Members of Heterogeneous Groups,* 62 Journal of Abnormal & Social Psychology 401 (1961)). Of course, not all of the effects of diversity, especially cultural diversity, on problem-solving are positive. "Although culturally diverse groups have the potential to generate a greater variety of ideas and other resources than culturally homogeneous groups, they need to overcome some of the group interaction problems that make group functioning more difficult." Warren E. Watson & Kamalesh Kumar, *Differences in Decision Making Regarding Risk Taking: A Comparison of Culturally Diverse and Culturally Homogeneous Task Groups,* 16 International Journal of Intercultural Relations 53, 61 (1992).

46. See *Adarand,* 115 S. Ct. at 2119 (Scalia, J., concurring in part) ("To pursue the concept of racial entitlement—even for the most admirable and benign purpose—is to reinforce and preserve for future mischief the way of thinking that produced race slavery, race privilege and race hatred. In the eyes of government, we are just one race here. It is American."); id. (Thomas, J., concurring in the judgment) ("In my mind, government-sponsored racial discrimination based on benign prejudice is just as noxious as discrimination inspired by malicious prejudice. In each instance, it is racial discrimination, plain and simple.").

47. See, for example, Amar & Katyal, *supra* note 21, at 1768 ("William Rehnquist voted for Allan Bakke once, and his writings and opinions reveal no faith in Lewis Powell's diversity theory.").

48. See, for example, *Metro Broadcasting, Inc. v. FCC,* 497 U.S. 547, 601–02 (Stevens, J., concurring) ("The public interest in broadcast diversity—like the interest in an integrated police force, diversity in the composition of a public school faculty, or diversity in the student body of a professional school—is in my view unquestionably legitimate.").

49. See *Adarand,* 115 S. Ct. at 2120 (Stevens, J., dissenting, joined by Ginsburg, J.), id. at 2131 (Souter, J., dissenting, joined by Ginsburg and Breyer, J.); id. at 2134 (Ginsburg, J., dissenting, joined by Breyer, J.). Justice Ginsburg's explanation, joined by Justice Souter, concerning the Court's denial of *certiorari* in *Hopwood* is perhaps also evidence of their support for affirmative action in the higher education context. See *Texas v. Hopwood,* 116 S. Ct. 2581 (1996) (indicating that the issue of whether universities can use race as one factor in admissions is "an issue of great national importance" that will be decided another day).

50. See Amar & Katyal, *supra* note 21, at 1757–58, 1769.

51. *Metro,* 497 U.S. at 3028 (O'Connor, J., dissenting).

52. These differences include the unique role of education in society, the special First Amendment protections of academic freedom that may operate in the higher edu-

cation context, the emphasis placed on individualistic diversity in *Bakke* versus the largely pluralistic diversity at issue in *Metro*, the direct interactions among students in a university environment versus the attenuated interactions between owners of broadcast stations and the public, and the fact that Justice Powell upheld educational diversity under strict scrutiny in *Bakke*. See, for example, Amar & Katyal, at 1747 (1996) (offering several potentially salient distinctions between *Bakke* and *Metro*).

53. See, for example, *Wygant*, 476 U.S. at 286 (O'Connor, J., concurring) ("[A]lthough its precise contours are uncertain, a state interest in the promotion of racial diversity has been found sufficiently 'compelling,' at least in the context of higher education, to support the use of racial classifications in furthering that interest."); id. at 288 n.* ("The goal of providing 'role models' discussed by the courts below [and rejected by the Supreme Court here] should not be confused with the very different goal of promoting racial diversity among the faculty.").

54. *Adarand,* 515 U.S.

55. Amar & Katyal, *supra* note 21, at 1760–70.

56. *Brown v. Board of Education,* 347 U.S. 483, 493 (1954).

57. Amar & Katyal, *supra* note 21, at 1774.

58. Id. at 1749. See also Robert Post, *Introduction: After Bakke, in* Representations 1 (Summer 1996) ("Institutions of higher education are today a primary source of . . . cultural capital. They aspire to cultivate the remarkable and difficult capacity to regard oneself from the perspective of the other, which is the foundation of the critical interaction necessary for active and effective citizenship. . . . In the United States, . . . racial and ethnic identities mark lines of intense political division. If the racial and ethnic rifts that divide us are to be transcended by a democratic state that is legitimate to all sides, there must be articulate participation in public culture that concomitantly spans the lines of these controversies.").

59. Pascarella & Terenzini, *supra* note 31, at 279.

60. Gurin, *supra* note 12, at 101.

61. See Astin, *supra* note 37, at 46–49.

62. Sylvia Hurtado, *Linking Diversity and Educational Purpose: How Diversity Affects the Classroom Environment and Student Development, in* this volume.

63. William G. Bowen & Derek Bok, The Shape of the River 225 (1998).

64. Janet Ward Schofield, *Maximizing the Benefits of Student Diversity: Lessons from School Desegregation Research, in* this volume. See also Marvin P. Dawkins & Jomills Henry Braddock, *The Continuing Significance of Desegregation: School Racial Composition and African American Inclusion in American Society,* 3 Journal of Negro Education 394 (1994).

65. James L Werth & Charles G. Lord, *Previous Conceptions of the Typical Group Member and the Contact Hypothesis,* 13 Basic & Applied Social Psychology 351 (1992). See also Gordon Allport, The Nature of Prejudice (1954) (proposing the contact hypothesis).

66. See Werth & Lord, *supra* note 64, at 352; Donna M. Desforges et al., *Effects of Structured Cooperative Contact on Changing Negative Altitudes Toward Stigmatized Social Groups,* 60 Journal of Personality & Social Psychology 531 (1991); Janet Ward Schofield, *Improving Intergroup Relations Among Students, in* Handbook on Research on Multicultural Education 635, 638–41 (James A. Banks, ed., 1995).

67. *Wygant,* 476 U.S. at 315 (Stevens, J., dissenting) (emphasis added). Some commentators seek to distinguish this *sameness* argument from the *difference* argument for promoting racial diversity. See, for example, Joanne Trautmann Banks, *Foreword, in* Trials, Tribulations, and Celebrations: African-American Perspectives on Health,

Illness, Aging, and Loss xv–xvi (Marian Gray Secundy, ed., 1992). But I see the two as inherently linked. Persons of different races likely have some differences that are real, based on their different cultures and experiences, and others that are based on misperceptions from which our sameness can emerge. But the point is that it does not matter to which theory one subscribes because racial diversity likely promotes civic values among all students in either case. Therefore, this goal for affirmative action cannot be said to turn on the relationship between race and viewpoint.

68. See *Metro,* 497 U.S. at 602 (O'Connor, J., dissenting).

69. See, for example, Milem, *supra* note 18, at 14 ("Colleges must find ways for students to communicate regularly across communities of difference so that they are able to develop fully the crosscultural competencies identified by corporate representatives as being essential to the global competitiveness of their organizations.").

70. Bowen & Bok, *supra* note 63, at 223.

71. See, for example, Secretary's Commission on Achieving Necessary Skills, What Work Requires of Schools: A SCANS Report for America 2000 (1991).

72. See, for example, Poppy Lauretta McLeod et al., *Ethnic Diversity and Creativity in Small Groups,* 27 Small Group Research 248 (May 1996).

73. See, for example, Dawkins & Braddock, *supra* note 64, at 394.

74. Kermit Daniel, Dan A. Black, & Jeffrey Smith, *Racial Differences in the Effects of College Quality and Student Body Diversity on Wages,* in this volume.

75. See id.

76. See, for example, Miriam Komaromy et al., *The Role of Black and Hispanic Physicians in Providing Health Care for Underserved Populations,* 334 New England Journal of Medicine 1305 (May 16, 1996).

77. Id. at 1307.

78. For example, id.; S. N. Keith et al. *Effects of Affirmative Action in Medical Schools: A Study of the Class of 1975,* 313 New England Journal of Medicine 1519–25 (1985).

79. Timothy Ready, *The Impact of Affirmative Action on Medical Education and the Nation's Health,* in this volume.

80. See *Bakke,* 438 U.S. (opinion of Powell, J.).

81. See, for example, *One Statistical Measure of How a College Education Tends to Repair Damage From the Past,* Journal of Blacks in Higher Education 5 (Autumn 1996) (reporting that the median annual income of black high school graduates is approximately 57 percent of white high school graduates, but the income of black *college* graduates is 87 percent of white college graduates). "Whatever the reasons for the continuing economic disparities between the races, it is certain that a college education, more than any other factor, serves to break down racial stereotypes, increase opportunities for African Americans, and decrease the economic gap between blacks and whites." Id.

82. Daniel, Black, & Smith, *supra* note 74. Most important in the context of affirmative action, studies show that minority students who attend selective universities, including those admitted as a result of affirmative action, have higher future earnings than equally qualified minority students who attend less prestigious universities. For example, Kane, *supra* note 3, at 13–14.

83. For example, Sterling M. Lloyd & Russell L. Miller, *Black Student Enrollment in U.S. Medical Schools,* 261 Journal of the American Medical Association 272 (1989) ("Blacks continue to be underrepresented in the medical schools of this country and in the profession of medicine. Blacks represent about 12% of the nation's population, but only 6% of total medical school enrollment, 5% of medical school graduates, 5% of postgraduate trainees, 3% of physicians in practice, and *of* medical school faculties.").

84. See id. For example, there is evidence that black patients are more likely to visit black physicians. This is true even after controlling for the proportion of black residents living in the given community. Komaromy et al., *supra* note 76, at 1301–08. Thus, increasing the number of black physicians could lead to an increase in preventive care and early detection of illness as more black patients would more readily seek medical attention. Furthermore, black physicians may be more likely to understand "the cultural and social context of illness and disability among blacks" and to communicate effectively with black patients regarding those issues. Lloyd & Miller, *supra* note 83. See also Clovis E. Semmes, Racism, Health, and Post-Industrialism: A Theory of African-American Health 1310–34 (1996).

85. See *Bakke*, 438 U.S. at 3 10–11 (opinion of Powell, J.) (indicating that the state's interest in "facilitating the health care of its citizens" is potentially compelling).

86. See, for example, id. at 307–10 (opinion of Powell, J.) (holding that the interest in overcoming societal discrimination is insufficient to justify affirmative action by a university).

87. For example, in *Wittmer v. Peters*, 87 F.3d 916 (7th Cir. 1996), *cert. denied*, 65 USLW 3416 (1997), the Seventh Circuit upheld an affirmative action program for black correctional officers at a juvenile "boot camp" to promote the state's compelling interest in the "pacification and reformation" of youth offenders. Imagine that instead of the boot camp seeking to promote a black officer directly, a local university sought to enroll a black applicant in its correctional-officer training program. In that case, there would perhaps be an argument that, given the state's compelling interest in having some black correctional officers in supervisory positions, the university program would pass strict scrutiny.

88. Zelikow, *supra* note 5, at 162–64.

89. When talking about numbers, it is obviously important to distinguish between targets and quotas. The use of quotas in affirmative action is clearly unconstitutional, See, for example, *Bakke*, 438 U.S. at 314–20, in part because using a quota encourages the requirement of enough minorities to fill the quota regardless of qualifications, See Amar & Katyal, *supra* note 21, at 1751. Numerical targets are intended to be more flexible and aspirational. Numerical targets in affirmative action establish the ideal while recognizing that meeting the targets depends on the availability of qualified minority applicants.

90. See, for example, *Bakke*, 438 U.S. at 307–10 (opinion of Powell, J.) ("[T]he purpose of helping certain groups whom the faculty of the Davis Medical School perceived as victims of 'societal discrimination' does not justify a classification that imposes disadvantages upon persons like respondent, who bear no responsibility for whatever harm the beneficiaries of the special admissions program are thought to have suffered. To hold otherwise would be to convert a remedy heretofore reserved for violations of legal rights into a privilege that all institutions throughout the Nation could grant at their pleasure to whatever groups are perceived as victims of societal discrimination. This is a step we have never approved.").

91. See, for example, Chin, *supra* note 38, at 921 ("Diversity proponents often argue that a 'critical mass' of minority students is necessary to ensure that the students are socially comfortable."). For example, there is evidence that black students attending predominantly white universities experience greater levels of alienation and isolation than their white counterparts at predominantly white universities or their black counterparts at historically black universities. See, for example, Walter R. Allen, *The Color of Success: African-American College Student Outcomes at Predominantly White and Historically Black Public Colleges and Universities*, 62 Harvard Educational Review 26 (Spring 1992); Pascarella & Terenzini, *supra* note 31, at 380. Also,

there is evidence that the social and academic adjustment of black students at pre-dominantly white universities is enhanced by communalism, meaning the tendency for a black student to see him/herself as part of a black community. Chalmer E. Thompson & Bruce R. Fretz, *Predicting the Adjustment of Black Students at Predominantly White Institutions,* 62 Journal of Higher Education 437, 437–38 (July/Aug. 1991) ("The communal student may be more likely to draw from the support of Blacks on campus or in the surrounding community, thereby uniting with community members in the face of adversity rather than withdrawing in isolation.").

92. Importantly, recent studies indicate that a critical mass of minority students will not necessarily result in self-segregation. See, for example, Troy Duster, *The Diversity of California at Berkeley: An Emerging Reformulation of "Competence" in an Increasingly Multicultural World, in* Beyond a Dream Deferred 231, 237 (1993) ("Our research revealed that while the student body is segmented along racial and ethnic lines, there are some important, good social relations and collective problem solving across racial and ethnic lines."); Sylvia Hurtado, Eric L. Dey, & Jesus G. Trevino, *Exclusion or Self-Segregation? Interaction Across Racial/Ethnic Groups on College Campuses* (Paper presented at the Annual Meeting of the American Educational Research Association) (1994) (finding that, in terms of informal interactions, "African Americans are more likely to interact across groups than are whites."). Cross-racial interaction will occur as long as universities seek to promote such cross-racial interaction. In other words, in addition to numbers, "the results of efforts to increase diversity on our campuses may depend very much on what kinds of learning environments are created." Bowen, *supra* note 20, at 21.

93. Chang, *supra* note 36.

94. Compare Amar & Katyal, *supra* note 21, at 1777 (supporting nonremedial affirmative action) ("A critical mass of students of a particular group may be needed so that other students become aware of the group (and of the diversity within the group), but this by no means requires exact proportionality—or anything like it.") and Chin, *supra* note 38, at 894 (opposing nonremedial affirmative action) ("The theory of Bakkean diversity is that it may be beneficial for persons who are not members of a particular group to have contact with others who are. Accordingly, the number of minority students admitted is driven not by the percentage of minorities in the population, but by the number needed to achieve that goal of educational diversity."). See also Gudeman, *supra* note 40 ("When evaluating classroom experiences, faculty reported that diversity enhanced desired educational outcomes more successfully when the representation of diverse groups went beyond that of a solo or token presence.").

95. Some education leaders and researchers are exploring admissions formulas that promote racial diversity using facially race-neutral criteria. See, for example, Linda F. Wightman, *The Threat to Diversity* in *Legal Education: An Empirical Analysis of the Consequences of Abandoning Race as a Factor in Law School Admission Decisions,* 72 New York University Review of Law 48 (1997). Yet existing data indicate that the use of facially race-neutral factors, such as social class, in university admissions is not likely to yield a racially diverse student body at some highly selective universities. For example, Robert Bruce Slater, *Why Socioeconomic Affirmative Action in College Admissions Works Against African Americans,* Journal of Blacks in Higher Education 57–59 (Summer 1995) (showing that using socioeconomic status in admissions at selective universities would result in little more racial diversity than a race-blind system that did not include socioeconomic status); Wightman, *supra* note 95, at 48–59 (finding that neither socioeconomic status, selectivity of undergraduate school, or undergraduate major if used as factors in law school admissions would

result in racial diversity similar to that presently achieved under affirmative action); Kane, *supra* note 3, at 17–19 (finding that because the majority of low-income families are white, a college presently administering a race-based affirmative action admissions plan would have to "grant preferences to six times as many low-income students to 'yield' the same number of black and Hispanic freshmen"). ("No race-blind substitute is likely to cushion the effect of an end to racial preferences. The problem is one of numbers."). Some states have recently adopted "percentage plans" for college admission, but such plans are beyond the scope of this chapter.

96. Even if the effect of such a program was to increase racial diversity, it would not be subject to strict scrutiny because it was not facially or intentionally race-based. See, for example, *Personnel Administrator of Massachusetts v. Feeney*, 442 U.S. 256 (1979) (upholding a Massachusetts veterans' preference policy even though the legislature was fully aware that the policy would have a discriminatory effect on women).

97. Possible race-neutral means for achieving these goals may include incorporating multicultural ideas into the curriculum and/or formalizing efforts to promote racial ethics. Therefore, universities may have to present evidence that such race-neutral efforts are not likely to be effective in racially homogeneous compared to racially diverse environments. To the extent that such race-neutral means are likely to be even partially successful, the Court may look more favorably on the use of affirmative action if those race-neutral means are used in tandem with race-based means. See *Metro Broadcasting, Inc. v. FCC*, 497 U.S. 547, 589–590 n.3 (citing with approval the FCC's prior and continued use of race neutral means to achieve its goals).

98. See, for example, Slater, *supra* note 95, at 57 ("[I]f admissions at [the nation's most prestigious universities] were made on the basis of grade point average and SAT scores, and without regard to race, perhaps 1 percent or 2 percent of all students accepted for admission to these schools would be black."); Wightman, *supra* note 95, at 19–27 (showing that minority admissions to ABA accredited law schools would decrease significantly if only race-neutral criteria were used); Bowen, *supra* note 20, at 19 (finding that the use of exclusively race-blind criteria at selective universities would reduce black enrollment from approximately 8 percent to 2 percent).

99. *Bakke*, 438 U.S. at 315 (opinion of Powell, J.).

100. Kane, *supra* note 3, at 8–9.

101. Id.

102. See, for example, Bowen, *supra* note 20, at 10.

103. See, for example, *Citizens Commission on CAW Rights*, The Resource: An Affirmative Action Guide 9A (1996) (indicating that the University of California at Los Angeles (UCLA) considers not fewer than 17 factors in its admissions process).

104. See, for example, John Larew, *"Who's the Real Affirmative Action Profiteer?" in* Debating Affirmative Action 247, 250 (Nicolaus Mills, ed., 1994) ("At most elite universities during the eighties, the legacy was by far the biggest piece of the preferential pie.").

105. See, for example, Daryl G. Smith, *Organizing for Diversity: Fundamental Issues, in* Handbook of Research on Multicultural Education 532 (James A. Banks, ed., 1995) ("On many campuses across the country, the challenges of creating an organization that embraces diversity so that it can truly begin to educate all students has begun.").

106. Jeffrey F. Milem, *Increasing Diversity Benefits: How Campus Climate and Teaching Methods Affect Student Outcomes,* in this volume.

107. See, for example, Institute for the Study of Social Change, Diversity Project: Final Report, University of California at Berkeley 18–19, 40 (November 1991) ("Data . . . suggest that while *both* African-American and white freshman students want more inter-racial experiences and contacts, *they want them on different terms*. African-Americans want more classes and programs and institutional responses. Whites want more individual, personal contacts developed at their own time and leisure. . . . The task is to provide all students with a range of safe environments and options where they can explore and develop terms which they find comfortable for inter-ethnic/cultural contact.").
108. See Liu, *supra* note 13, at 406–10.

CHAPTER 3

Diversity and Affirmative Action: Evolving Principles and Continuing Legal Battles

SCOTT R. PALMER

Introduction

In the U.S. Supreme Court's 1978 decision in *Regents of the University of California v. Bakke*,[1] Justice Lewis Powell, in an opinion that came to be known as the opinion of the Court, declared that a university's interest in securing the educational benefits that flow from diversity in its student body is a compelling interest that can constitutionally support the use of race as a factor in student admissions.[2] For the last two decades, public and private universities across the country have adopted this diversity rationale as their primary justification for affirmative action programs.[3]

Nearly twenty years after *Bakke*, however, the Fifth Circuit Court of Appeals in *Hopwood v. Texas*[4] rejected the notion that promoting educational diversity is a compelling interest, striking down the affirmative action admissions program at the University of Texas School of Law. A divided panel in *Hopwood* held:

> We agree with the plaintiffs that any consideration of race or ethnicity by the law school for the purpose of achieving a diverse student body is not a compelling interest under the Fourteenth Amendment. Justice Powell's argument in *Bakke* garnered only his own vote and has never represented the view of a majority of the Court in *Bakke* or any other case. Moreover, subsequent Supreme Court decisions regarding education state that nonremedial interests will never justify racial classifications. Finally, the classifications of persons on the basis of race for

the purpose of diversity frustrates, rather than facilitates, the goals of equal protection.[5]

This conflict between *Bakke* and *Hopwood* constitutes the heart of the current legal debate regarding affirmative action in higher education. Several decisions by the Supreme Court establish a trend toward the rigid application of "strict scrutiny" in evaluating all race-based policies and programs.[6] Some legal commentators have argued that this trend may "sound the death knell" for affirmative action in higher education.[7] *Hopwood* is obviously a manifestation of that view.

There is, however, a competing conception of the legal status of affirmative action based on the notion, recently endorsed by a majority of the Court, that strict scrutiny is not "fatal in fact."[8] That view is embodied in the case of *Wittmer v. Peters*,[9] which was decided the same year as *Hopwood*. In *Wittmer*, the Seventh Circuit Court of Appeals upheld an affirmative action employment program for correctional officers at a juvenile "boot camp" in order to further the state's interest in the "pacification and reformation" of youth offenders. *Wittmer*, though occurring outside the higher education context, provides a powerful rebuttal to *Hopwood*. Moreover, while some affirmative action programs in education have recently been held unconstitutional,[10] several courts have also recognized that *Bakke* remains good law and have held or presumed that the nonremedial interest in promoting the educational benefits of diversity, as well as other, related nonremedial interests, can be sufficiently compelling to justify affirmative action.[11]

This chapter provides a brief overview of the legal standards governing affirmative action in higher education, focusing specifically on the diversity rationale, and contrasts the cases of *Hopwood* and *Wittmer*.

The Legal Standard Governing Affirmative Action in Higher Education: Strict Scrutiny

The Supreme Court has established under the Fourteenth Amendment and Title VI of the Civil Rights Act of 1964 that race-based policies or programs will be upheld only where they pass so-called strict scrutiny, which requires that the given affirmative action program serve a compelling interest and be narrowly tailored to achieve that interest.[12] "In short, the compelling interest inquiry centers on 'ends' and asks *why* the government is classifying individuals on the basis of race or ethnicity; the narrow tailoring focuses on 'means' and asks *how* the government is seeking to meet the objective of the racial or ethnic classification."[13] Furthermore, to ensure that legitimate compelling interests for affirmative action are not used as pretexts for discrimination, the Court requires a sufficient "basis in evidence" for the belief that a voluntary affirmative action program is warranted.[14]

In the context of higher education, and more generally, the Supreme Court has to date found only two interests sufficiently compelling to justify voluntary, race-based affirmative action: 1) remedying the present effects of past discrimination[15] and 2), under Justice Powell's opinion in *Bakke*, realizing the educational benefits that flow from a racially diverse student body.[16] The Court has also rejected several interests as insufficient to justify race-based actions. Most significantly, the Rehnquist Court has repeatedly held that the interest in remedying so-called societal discrimination is insufficient to justify affirmative action by any entity except perhaps the federal government: "[A]s the basis for imposing discriminatory legal remedies that work against innocent people, societal discrimination is insufficient and overexpansive." [17]

Assuming that a given affirmative action program is found to serve a compelling interest, the Court has identified several factors to be considered in determining whether the program is narrowly tailored to achieve that interest:

> As it has been applied by the courts, the factors that typically make up the "narrow tailoring" test are as follows: [1] whether the government considered race-neutral alternatives before resorting to race-conscious action; [2] the scope of the affirmative action program and whether there is a waiver mechanism that facilitates the narrowing of the program's scope; [3] the manner in which [it] is used, that is, whether race is a factor in determining eligibility for a program or whether race is just one factor in the decisionmaking process; [4] the comparison of any numerical target to the number of qualified minorities in the relevant sector or industry; [5] the duration of the program and whether it is subject to periodic review; and [6] the degree and type of burden caused by the program.[18]

The Remedial Interest in Overcoming the Present Effects of Past Discrimination

Affirmative action originated more than thirty years ago as a remedial effort to overcome the effects of discrimination. Today, a solid majority of the Supreme Court agrees that this interest remains sufficiently compelling to support race-based affirmative action.[19] The real debate is over the scope of this interest: What "past discrimination" is sufficient to justify affirmative action? What "present effects" are sufficient? What evidentiary link must be established between the past discrimination and the present effects? In examining these questions in the context of higher education, it is useful to distinguish between when a university *must* take affirmative action to overcome the present effects of past discrimination and when it *may* take such action.

The Supreme Court in *United States v. Fordice*[20] defined what remedial actions *must* be taken by states that maintained prior *de jure* segregated systems of higher education. *Fordice* involved a challenge to Mississippi's university system alleging that the state had failed to take sufficient steps to dismantle its prior *de jure* segregated system. Mississippi adopted facially race-neutral university admissions policies in the 1960s, but by the mid-1980s, Mississippi's university system remained racially segregated.[21] The Court in *Fordice* held:

> [A] State does not discharge its constitutional obligations until it eradicates policies and practices traceable to its prior de jure dual system that continue to foster segregation. . . . If policies traceable to the de jure system are still in force and have discriminatory effects, those policies too must be reformed to the extent practicable and consistent with sound educational practices.[22]

Fordice thus requires states to do more to desegregate their universities than simply adopt facially race-neutral admissions policies. Rather, states must at a minimum seek to establish effective neutrality.[23]

The legal standard governing what affirmative actions a university *may* take voluntarily to remedy the present effects of past discrimination is somewhat less clear. The Supreme Court cases most on point are *Wygant v. Jackson Board of Education*,[24] which concerned the use of affirmative action in faculty employment, and *Richmond v. J. A. Croson Co.*,[25] which concerned the use of affirmative action in government contracting.

In *Wygant*, the Court held unconstitutional a collective bargaining agreement that gave special protection to minority teachers against layoffs in order to "remedy societal discrimination by providing 'role models' for minority schoolchildren."[26] In a plurality opinion, the Court rejected this interest, and suggested that only an actor's interest in overcoming its own prior discrimination could constitutionally support such race-based action.[27] The Jackson Board did not have sufficient evidence of such prior discrimination.[28] Furthermore, a plurality held that the affirmative action plan at issue was not narrowly tailored, in any case, because layoffs were too great a price for nonminorities to bear.[29]

Three years later, in *Croson*, the Court held unconstitutional the Richmond City Council's Minority Business Utilization Plan, which required a 30 percent minority set-aside for all city-awarded construction contracts in order to remedy past discrimination in the construction industry.[30] Again, the Court rejected this interest in overcoming societal discrimination.[31] In addition, the Court held that the city's plan was not narrowly tailored because there had been no consideration of available race-neutral means and because the 30 percent set-aside was not tied to any goal "except perhaps outright racial balancing."[32] Finally, speaking for a plurality, Justice O'Connor clarified that the Richmond City Council was not restricted to remedying its own prior discrimination but could, given the proper basis in evidence indicating that such action was necessary, also act to eliminate private discrimination within its jurisdiction.[33]

Though employment and contracting are not the same as higher education admissions, three general principles regarding voluntary remedial affirmative action may be gleaned from the Supreme Court's decisions in *Wygant* and *Croson*. First, a university cannot take affirmative action to remedy the effects of general societal discrimination. Second, a university can take affirmative action to remedy the present effects of its own past discrimination if it has a sufficient basis in evidence for the belief that such action is warranted. Third, a university or other state entity can take affirmative action to remedy prior discrimination by other actors to avoid serving as a "passive participant" in a pattern of discrimination, specifically where affirmative action is taken by a government entity seeking to ameliorate the effects of discrimination within its jurisdiction.

Wygant and *Croson* arguably left some important room for the adoption of voluntary affirmative action programs designed to remedy the present effects of past discrimination, especially by institutions that had previously been *de jure* segregated. However, some lower federal courts applying these holdings in the context of higher education have applied them rigidly, and have thus greatly restricted remedial affirmative action programs at universities in those circuits.

First, in *Podberesky v. Kirwan*,[34] the Fourth Circuit Court of Appeals held unconstitutional the University of Maryland's Banneker scholarship program, a merit scholarship program open only to African American students. The University of Maryland defended the Banneker program as necessary to remedy the present effects of its own past discrimination. The university had previously been *de jure* segregated and offered proof that four present effects of past discrimination existed:

(1) The University has a poor reputation within the African-American community; (2) African-Americans are underrepresented in the student population; (3) African-American students who enroll at the University have low retention and graduation rates; and (4) the atmosphere on campus is perceived as being hostile to African-American students.[35]

However, the Fourth Circuit held that, to sustain affirmative action, the university was required to show not only proof of prior discrimination and present effects, but also proof that the present effects were caused by the prior discrimination, as opposed to general societal discrimination, and that the present effects were sufficient to justify the affirmative action program at issue.[36] The Fourth Circuit held that the University of Maryland was unable to establish these evidentiary links and thus rejected the university's race-based scholarship program.

Second, in *Hopwood v. Texas*,[37] the Fifth Circuit Court of Appeals held unconstitutional the affirmative action admissions program at the University of Texas School of Law. The law school defended its affirmative action admissions program based in part on the need to remedy the present effects of past discrimination—not only its own discrimination but also prior discrimination perpetrated by Texas's primary and secondary school systems and by the University of Texas System as a whole.[38] The Fifth Circuit rejected the law school's arguments, requiring the University of Texas School of Law to justify its affirmative action admissions program based solely on its own prior discrimination.[39] Applying the standard established by the Fourth Circuit in *Podberesky*, the Fifth Circuit held that the "present effects" the law school identified, which were nearly identical to those identified by the University of Maryland in *Podberesky*, were not sufficiently linked to its own past discrimination and could not serve to justify the affirmative action admissions program at issue.[40]

Finally, in the case of *Wessmann v. Gittens*,[41] which involved affirmative action in the primary and secondary school context, the First Circuit Court of Appeals implicitly adopted the *Podberesky* standard over a vigorous dissent and held unconstitutional the Boston Latin School's affirmative action admissions policy. The court accepted that Boston Latin, as part of the Boston public school system, had discriminated in the past and that racial gaps in tests scores were a valid "present effect."[42] However, the majority found that the Boston School Committee had not proven that the present effects were caused by the prior discrimination or that affirmative action was an appropriate remedy to ameliorate those effects.[43]

The legal standard for remedial affirmative action established in *Podberesky* and applied again in *Hopwood* and *Wessmann* expands greatly on the Supreme Court's holdings in *Wygant* and *Croson* and has not yet been endorsed by the Court. If this standard becomes the law of the land, it is unclear how a university can provide sufficient evidence to support affirmative action to overcome the present effects of past discrimination.[44] Perhaps the only clearly established method to prove a link between past discrimination and present effects in the context of higher education admissions is by showing a policy or practice emanating from the *de jure* era that continues to have discriminatory effects, in which case the university is *required* to take remedial action under *United States v. Fordice*.[45] In this sense, *Podberesky, Hopwood*, and *Wessmann* may mean that there are now only two classes of remedial affirmative action programs at universities and/or schools in the Fourth, Fifth, and First Circuits—those that are required under *Fordice* and those that are not allowed under *Podberesky* and its progeny. This possibility puts great pressure on the diversity rationale for affirmative action in higher education in those circuits.

The Nonremedial Interest in Realizing the Educational Benefits of Diversity

Unlike the remedial interest in overcoming the present effects of past discrimination, the nonremedial interest in promoting the educational benefits of diversity seeks to justify affirmative action not as a remedy to make up for past discrimination against a certain group, but as a forward-looking tool that is necessary to promote the educational development of all students. In *Regents of the University of California v. Bakke*,[46] Justice Powell, in his landmark opinion, held that securing the educational benefits that flow from diversity in higher education is a compelling interest that can constitutionally support race-based affirmative action in student admissions.[47] *Bakke* involved a challenge under the Fourteenth Amendment and Title VI to the affirmative action admissions program at the University of California at Davis Medical School. Each year, the Davis admissions program reserved sixteen places in its 100-student entering class for minority students, who were admitted through a special admissions process.

In a fractured opinion, four justices in *Bakke* held that Title VI was coextensive with the Fourteenth Amendment and that the Davis admissions program was constitutional in all respects;[48] four different justices held that the case was governed exclusively by Title VI, that Title VI prohibited all considerations of race in the administration of programs receiving federal funds, and that the Davis admissions program was therefore unlawful.[49] Announcing the judgment of the Court, Justice Powell, as the swing vote, joined the former four justices in holding that the Fourteenth Amendment and Title VI were coextensive and that the medical school was not fully prohibited from considering race in its admissions process. However, Justice Powell joined the latter four justices in declaring the Davis admissions program unconstitutional because it was not narrowly tailored to promote what Justice Powell identified as the medical school's compelling interest, promoting the educational benefits of diversity.[50]

According to Justice Powell, the Davis Medical School's interest in promoting educational diversity was sufficiently compelling to support affirmative action in student admissions.[51] "The atmosphere of 'speculation, experiment and creation'—so essential to the quality of higher education—is," he wrote, "widely believed to be promoted by a diverse student body."[52] Justice Powell found the medical school's interest in educational diversity to be supported by the First Amendment interest in academic freedom, which protects the authority of universities to make their own educational judgments concerning "who may teach, what may be taught, how it shall be taught, and who may be admitted to study."[53]

However, according to Justice Powell, the type of educational diversity that constituted a compelling interest was not pluralistic diversity of certain racial groups, but more individualistic diversity in which race is "but a single though important element":[54] "Ethnic diversity . . . is only one element in a range of factors a university properly may consider in attaining the goal of a heterogeneous student body."[55] Therefore, a narrowly tailored affirmative action program designed to promote educational diversity would not rely on rigid racial quotas or a separate admissions process.[56]

As a result of Justice Powell's opinion in *Bakke*, public and private universities have for the last two decades adopted this diversity rationale as their primary justification for affirmative action programs.[57] However, given the fractured holding of the Court in *Bakke* and the absence of additional guidance from the Court since then, the status of the diversity rationale has remained in some doubt. Furthermore, several decisions by the Court, specifically *Adarand v. Pena*,[58] establish that strict scrutiny applies to all race-based affirmative action programs, whether they are adopted by federal, state, or local government actors, and whether they serve "benign" or "invidious" goals. Finally, dicta from some opinions suggest that only the remedial interest in overcoming the present effects of past discrimination can be sufficiently "compelling" to justify affirmative action.[59] In *Hopwood v. Texas*,[60] the Fifth Circuit Court of Appeals seized on these developments and effectively "overruled" *Bakke* by rejecting educational diversity as a compelling interest.

Hopwood v. Texas and Its Rejection of Educational Diversity

In *Hopwood v. Texas*, as discussed above, the Fifth Circuit Court of Appeals held unconstitutional the affirmative action admissions program at the University of Texas School of Law. The law school's admissions system evaluated African American and Mexican American applicants separately from other applicants based on reduced admissions standards.[61] The law school defended its affirmative action admissions program based in part on *Bakke's* diversity rationale. It was relatively clear that the law school's admissions program did not meet the narrow tailoring requirements laid out in *Bakke*. Nonetheless, a majority of the panel eschewed this more narrow ground for holding the law school's admissions program unconstitutional. "[T]enuously stringing together pieces and shards of recent Supreme Court opinions,"[62] a divided panel in *Hopwood* rejected educational diversity as a compelling interest that can justify affirmative action in higher education.

The Fifth Circuit's rejection in *Hopwood* of the diversity rationale proceeded in three stages. First, the court held that Justice Powell's decision in *Bakke* garnered only his vote and, therefore, was not binding precedent.[63] Second, the court held that recent Supreme Court precedent indicated that the *only* potentially compelling interest was overcoming the present effects of past discrimination, and that educational diversity was, therefore, not compelling.[64] Third, the court held, without evidentiary support, that race is as irrelevant to university admissions as blood type, that the use of race in university admissions improperly stereotypes minority applicants, and that the use of race fuels racial hostility.[65] The court concluded, "In sum, the use of race to achieve a diverse student body, whether as a proxy for permissible characteristics, simply cannot be a state interest compelling enough to meet the steep standard of strict scrutiny."[66]

The *Hopwood* decision can be criticized on numerous grounds, but the most important point to note here is that *Hopwood* is not the end of the story. In *Wittmer v. Peters*,[67] Chief Judge Richard Posner and the Seventh Circuit offer a vastly different and largely persuasive view of the present state of nonremedial affirmative action programs under the Supreme Court's jurisprudence.

Wittmer v. Peters and Support for Nonremedial
Affirmative Action

In *Wittmer v. Peters*, the Seventh Circuit upheld an affirmative action employment program for correctional officers at a "boot camp" for youth offenders. The affirmative action program was intended to promote qualified black correctional officers to vacant lieutenant positions in order to facilitate the penological goals of the boot camp.[68] The defendant state official, warden of the youth detention center, presented expert evidence that the boot camp program was not likely to be successful without some black officers in supervisory positions.

Chief Judge Posner, writing for a unanimous court, upheld the affirmative action employment program, finding it narrowly tailored to serve a compelling interest.[69] First, the court rejected the plaintiffs' contention, embraced by the Fifth Circuit in *Hopwood*, that recent Supreme Court precedent indicated that only the remedial interest in overcoming the present effects of past discrimination could ever justify race-based affirmative action:

> The plaintiffs argue that the only form of racial discrimination that can survive strict scrutiny is discrimination designed to cure the ill effects of past discrimination by the public institution that is asking to be allowed to try this dangerous cure. There is dicta to this effect. And certainly it is the most frequently mentioned example of a case in which discrimination is permissible. But there is a reason that dicta are dicta and not holdings, that is, are not authoritative. A judge would be unreasonable to conclude that no other consideration except a history of discrimination could ever warrant a discriminatory measure unless every other consideration had been presented to and rejected by him. The dicta on which the plaintiffs rely were uttered in cases that did not involve, by judges who had never had cases that involved, the racial composition of a prison staff. Such cases were not, at least insofar as one can glean from the opinions, present to the minds of the judges when they considered and rejected other grounds for discrimination and expressed that rejection in sweeping dicta that we have mentioned. The weight of judicial language depends on context, by these plaintiffs ignored. . . . [T]he rectification of past discrimination is not the only setting in which government officials can lawfully take race into account.[70]

Second, the court implicitly held that the state's interest in the "pacification and reformation" of youth offenders was sufficiently compelling to justify affirmative action.[71] In so holding, the court noted that a majority of the Supreme Court had recently endorsed the idea that strict scrutiny is not inevitably "fatal in fact."[72] Furthermore, the court placed great weight on the fact that the defense presented sufficient expert evidence of the penological necessity of the affirmative action program. On this latter point, the court said:

> It is not enough to say that of course there should be some correspondence between the racial composition of a prison's population and the racial composition of the staff; common sense is not enough; common sense undergirded the pernicious discrimination against blacks now universally regretted. . . . In any event that is not the justification advanced. The black lieutenant is needed because the black inmates are believed unlikely to play the correctional game of brutal drill sergeant and brutalized recruit unless there are some blacks in authority in the camp. This is not just speculation, but is backed up by expert evidence that the plaintiffs did not rebut. The defendants' experts—recognized experts in the field of prison administration—did not rely on generalities about racial balance or diversity; did not for that matter, defend a global racial balance. They opined that the boot camp in Greene County would not succeed in its mission of pacification and reformation with as white a staff as it would have had if a black male had not been appointed to one of the lieutenant slots.[73]

Wittmer and *Hopwood* obviously evaluate different nonremedial interests and different programs designed to achieve those interests. Nonetheless, *Wittmer* establishes, at least in the Seventh Circuit, that nonremedial interests can be sufficiently compelling to justify affirmative action. *Wittmer* also confirms that a sufficient basis in evidence can be established to justify nonremedial affirmative action. Furthermore, while *Wittmer* does not speak directly to whether educational diversity constitutes a compelling interest in the higher education context, it would be somewhat puzzling if the interest in rehabilitating youth offenders was sufficiently compelling to justify affirmative action, but the interest in promoting the educational and socio-moral development of university students was not so compelling. Correctional facilities may be unique institutions, but so are universities.

Finally, several recent cases follow on *Wittmer* and further rebut *Hopwood*. Most directly on point is *Smith v. University of Washington Law School.*[74] In *Smith,* the U.S. Court of Appeals for the Ninth Circuit held that Justice Powell's opinion in *Bakke* constitutes binding precedent establishing that a university's nonremedial interest in promoting the educational benefits of diversity can be sufficiently compelling to justify affirmative action. According to the Ninth Circuit:

> The district court correctly decided that Justice Powell's opinion in *Bakke* described the law and would require a determination that a properly designed and operated race-conscious admissions program at the law school of the University of Washington would not be in violation of Title VI or the Fourteenth Amendment. It was also correct when it determined that *Bakke* has not been overruled by the Supreme Court. Thus, at our level of the judicial system Justice Powell's opinion remains the law.[75]

Furthermore, in *Gratz v. Bollinger*,[76] the U.S. District Court for the Eastern District of Michigan recently upheld the University of Michigan's current affirmative action admissions policy because the university presented "solid evidence" that it has a compelling interest in promoting the educational benefits of diversity. The court said, "This Court is persuaded, based upon the record before it, that a racially and ethnically diverse student body produces significant educational benefits such that diversity, in the context of higher education, constitutes a compelling governmental interest under strict scrutiny."[77] In *Johnson v. Board of Regents of the University System of Georgia*, however, the U.S. District Court for the Southern District of Georgia rejected Justice Powell's diversity rationale for affirmative action at the University of Georgia.[78]

Conclusion

This brief legal overview indicates that the law governing affirmative action in higher education is at a crucial point in its development. Several key cases are pending,[79] and there is a strong chance that the Supreme Court will address the issue in the near future. The higher education community must, therefore, use this time to build upon Justice Powell's opinion in *Regents of the University of California v. Bakke* and develop its case for the educational value of diversity.

Notes

1. *Regents of the University of California v. Bakke*, 438 U.S. 265 (1978).
2. See id. at 312–15 (opinion of Powell, J.).
3. See, for example, Tanya Y. Murphy, *An Argument for Diversity Based Affirmative Action in Higher Education*, 95 Annual Survey of American Law 515, 536 (1996) ("Although affirmative action was created specifically for remedial purposes, today the

primary, and perhaps only, justification for the retention of affirmative action programs is educational diversity.").

4. *Hopwood v. Texas,* 78 F.3d 932 (5th Cir. 1996), *cert. denied,* 518 U.S. 1033 (1996).
5. Id. at 944.
6. See, for example, *Adarand v. Pena,* 515 U.S. 200 (1995).
7. For example, Leland Ware, *Tales from the Crypt: Does Strict Scrutiny Sound the Death Knell for Affirmative Action in Higher Education?,* 23 Journal of College and University Law 43, 44 (1996); Donald L. Beschle, *"You've Got to Be Carefully Taught": Justifying Affirmative Action after Croson and Adarand,* 74 North Carolina Law Review 1141, 1180 (1996).
8. For example, *Adarand,* 515 U.S. at 237 ("[W]e wish to dispel the notion that strict scrutiny is 'strict in theory, but fatal in fact.'" (quoting *Fullilove v. Klutznick,* 448 U.S. 448, 519 (1980) (Marshall, J., concurring in the judgment))); id. at 275 (Ginsburg, J., dissenting, joined by Breyer, J.).
9. *Wittmer v. Peters,* 87 F.3d 916 (7th Cir. 1996), *cert. denied,* 519 U.S. 1111 (1997).
10. For example, *Wessmann v. Gittens,* 160 F.3d 790 (1st Cir. 1998) (holding unconstitutional the Boston Latin School's affirmative action admissions policy because it was not narrowly tailored); *Tuttle v. Arlington County School Board,* 189 F.3d 431 (4th Cir. 1999) (holding unconstitutional the Arlington Traditional School's affirmative action admissions policy because it was not narrowly tailored); *Eisenberg v. Montgomery County Public Schools,* 1999 WL 795652 (4th Cir. 1999) (holding unconstitutional the Montgomery County, Maryland, student assignment policy because it was not narrowly tailored); *Johnson v. Board of Regents of the University of Georgia System,* 106 F.Supp.2d 1362 (S.D. Ga. 2000) (holding that the University of Georgia's affirmative action admissions policy violated Title VI of the Civil Rights Act of 1964).
11. See, for example, *Smith v. University of Washington Law School,* 233 F.3d 1188, 1201 (9th Cir. 2000) (holding that Justice Powell's decision in *Bakke* is binding precedent and denying, in part, plaintiff's motion for summary judgement in a suit challenging the University of Washington Law School's prior affirmative action admissions policy) ("[T]he Fourteenth Amendment permits University admissions programs which consider race for other than remedial purposes, and educational diversity is a compelling governmental interest that meets the demands of strict scrutiny of race-conscious measures."); *Wessmann,* 160 F.3d at 796 ("It may be that the *Hopwood* panel is correct and that, were the [Supreme] Court to address the question today, it would hold that diversity is not a sufficiently compelling interest to justify a race-based classification. It has not done so yet, however, and we are not prepared to make such a declaration in the absence of a clear signal that we should. . . . Instead, we assume arguendo—but we do not decide—that *Bakke* remains good law and that some iterations of 'diversity' might be sufficiently compelling, in specific circumstances, to justify race-conscious actions."); *Tuttle,* 189 F.3d at 439 ("We have interpreted *Bakke* as holding that the state 'is not absolutely barred from giving any consideration to race' in a non-remedial context. Although no other Justice joined the diversity portion of Powell's concurrence, nothing in *Bakke* or subsequent Supreme Court decisions clearly forecloses the possibility that diversity may be a compelling interest. Until the Supreme Court provides decisive guidance, we will assume, without so holding, that diversity may be a compelling governmental interest . . ."); *University and Community College System of Nevada v. Farmer,* 930 P.2d 730, 734-35 (Nev. 1997)), *cert. denied,* 118 S. Ct. 1186 (1998) (upholding against a Title VII challenge the University's affirmative action faculty employment policy) ("[T]he *Bakke* plurality held that in the limited setting of a graduate

school, an attempt to attain a diverse student body through a preferential treatment admissions policy is not per se unconstitutional as long as race is one of several factors used in evaluating applicants. . . . We also view the desirability of a racially diverse faculty as sufficiently analogous to the constitutionally permissible attainment of a racially diverse student body countenanced by the *Bakke* Court."); *Brewer v. West Irondequoit Central School District*, 2000 U.S. App. LEXIS 9866 (2d Cir. 2000) (holding that the State's interest in reducing *de facto* segregation is a compelling interest that can justify the use of race in student assignment policies) ("[T]he Fifth Circuit is the only circuit since *Bakke* to hold that a non-remedial state interest, such as diversity, may never justify race-based programs in the educational context. . . . More importantly, this Circuit has not previously taken the position that diversity, or other non-remedial state interests, can never be compelling in the educational setting. In fact, binding precedent in this Circuit . . . explicitly establishes that reducing *de facto* segregation . . . serves a compelling government interest."); *Hunter v. Regents of the University of California*, 190 F.3d 1061, n.6 (9th Cir. 1999) (upholding the use of race in student assignment to an elementary school operated by UCLA to support the state's compelling interest in promoting and disseminating research to improve urban education) ("The appellant argues that only an interest in remedying past discrimination can justify [the school's] use of race/ethnicity as one of a number of factors in its admissions process. We disagree. The Supreme Court has never held that only a state's interest in remedial action can meet strict scrutiny."); *Gratz v. Bollinger*, 122 F.Supp.2d 811, 824 (E.D. Mich. 2000) (holding that the University of Michigan had established that its interest in educational diversity is sufficiently compelling to justify its current affirmative action admissions policy) ("The Court is persuaded, based on the record before it, that a racially and ethnically diverse student body produces significant educational benefits such that diversity, in the context of higher education, constitutes a compelling governmental interest under strict scrutiny."). But see, for example, *Johnson*, 106 F.Supp.2d at 1371 (holding that the University of Georgia's affirmative action admissions policy violates Title VI because the university's diversity rationale is "amorphous at best" and, therefore, not compelling).

12. For example, *Adarand,* 515 U.S. at 235.
13. Memorandum from Walter Dellinger, Assistant Attorney General, U.S. Department of Justice, to General Counsels 10 (June 28, 1995).
14. See, for example, *Wygant v. Jackson Board of Education*, 476 U.S. 267, 277–78 (1986); *Richmond v. J. A. Croson Co.*, 488 U.S. 469, 500 (1989). See also, for example, Goodwin Liu, *Affirmative Action in Higher Education: The Diversity Rationale and the Compelling Interest Test*, 33 Harvard Civil Rights-Civil Liberties Law Review 381, 409 (1998) ("[T]he function of the evidentiary hurdles within the 'compelling interest' test is to smoke out unconstitutional motivations that take the form of 'simple racial politics,' 'illegitimate racial prejudice,' or 'unthinking racial stereotypes.'").
15. See, for example, *Wygant*, 476 U.S. at 286 (O'Connor, J., concurring) ("The Court is in agreement that, whatever the formulation employed, remedying past or present racial discrimination by a state actor is a sufficiently weighty interest to warrant the remedial use of a carefully constructed affirmative action program.").
16. *Bakke*, 438 U.S. at 311-15 (opinion of Powell, J.). See also *Wygant*, 476 U.S. at 286 (O'Connor, J., concurring) ("Additionally, although its precise contours are uncertain, a state interest in the promotion of racial diversity has been found sufficiently 'compelling,' at least in the context of higher education, to support the use of racial considerations in furthering that interest; *Smith*, 233 F.3d at 1201 (holding that Justice Powell's opinion in Bakke is binding precedent). But see, for example, *Hop-*

wood v. Texas, 78 F.3d 932 (5th Cir. 1996), *cert. denied*, 518 U.S. 1033 (1996) (rejecting the idea that Justice Powell's statement concerning educational diversity constituted a holding of the Court).

17. *Wygant*, 476 U.S. at 276. The Court has also held that a school's interest in providing "role models" for minority students is insufficient to justify affirmative action
in faculty hiring. *Wygant*, 476 U.S. at 274–76 (plurality opinion). The Court seemed
to equate this goal with the goal of alleviating general societal discrimination, and
the interest in promoting educational diversity was expressly distinguished. Id. at
289 n.*(O'Connor, J., concurring). In *Bakke*, Justice Powell declared that the interest in increasing the number of minorities in a given profession is insufficient to
justify affirmative action by a university. Justice Powell's analysis of this interest,
however, was cursory; he seemed to view this goal as equivalent to valuing race for
race's sake. Justice Powell also presumed in *Bakke* that the interest in increasing the
number of medical professionals practicing in underserved areas *could* be sufficiently compelling to justify affirmative action by a university, but Justice Powell
found no evidence that the program at issue in *Bakke* was necessary or designed to
achieve that goal. *Bakke*, 438 U.S. at 310–11.

18. Memorandum from Walter Dellinger, *supra* note 13, at 19–20. See also *U.S. v. Para-
dise*, 480 U.S. 149, 171 (1987) (plurality opinion); id. at 187 (Powell, J., concurring).
Not every factor will likely be relevant in every case. Memorandum from Walter
Dellinger, *supra* note 13, at 19–20.

19. For example, *Wygant*, 476 U.S. at 286 (O'Connor, J., concurring). All of the justices
would likely agree that where present, intentional discrimination has been established, some form of prospective race-based remedy can be appropriate. But they
differ in the extent to which they approve of group-based remedies to correct for
past injustices against other members of a group. Nonetheless, only Justice Scalia
and perhaps Justice Thomas have "adopted anything that approaches a blanket
prohibition on race-conscious remedies." Memorandum from Walter Dellinger,
supra note 13, at 6.

20. *United States v. Fordice*, 505 U.S. 717 (1992).

21. Id. at 724–25.

22. Id. at 728–29 (holding several policies of Mississippi's university system "constitutionally suspect" under this standard).

23. The Court's holding in *Fordice* can best be understood in the context of earlier Supreme Court decisions concerning the obligation of prior *de jure* segregated institutions to desegregate. In *Brown v. Board of Education*, 347 U.S. 483 (1954), the Court
held with regard to primary and secondary schools that "separate educational facilities are *inherently* unequal." Id. at 495 (emphasis added). States that had been operating *de jure* segregated systems of education at the time of *Brown* had an affirmative obligation to cure the effects of that prior segregation. See, for example, *Green
v. New Kent County School Board*, 391 U.S. 430, 437–38 (1968) ("School boards . . .
operating state-compelled dual systems [at the time of *Brown*] were . . . clearly
charged with the affirmative duty to take whatever steps might be necessary to
convert to a unitary system in which racial discrimination would be eliminated
root and branch"). However, in *Bazemore v. Friday*, 478 U.S. 385 (1986), the Court
held with regard to state-funded and -operated clubs that had been *de jure* segregated that states had an obligation only to adopt facially race-neutral membership
policies. Thus, the question in *Fordice* was, in effect, whether colleges and universities were more like primary and secondary schools or like voluntary clubs. One
way to understand the decision in *Fordice* is that the Court adopted a middle
ground. *Fordice* in effect creates a presumption that any university practice emanat-

ing from the *de jure* segregated era and continuing to have discriminatory effects is viewed as intentional discrimination and is thus subject to strict scrutiny. This reading of *Fordice* is perhaps modest because it is not that different from other cases that have held that the intent to discriminate is judged from the time at which the law or policy at issue was originally adopted. See, for example, *Hunter v. Underwood*, 471 U.S. 222 (1985) (holding unconstitutional a provision of the Alabama Constitution of 1901, which disenfranchised persons convicted of crimes of moral turpitude, based on general evidence that the provision was originally enacted for a discriminatory purpose).

24. *Wygant v. Jackson Board of Education*, 476 U.S. 267 (1986).

25. *Richmond v. J. A. Croson*, 488 U.S. 469 (1989).

26. *Wygant*, 476 U.S. at 269–84 (plurality opinion).

27. Id. at 274 ("This Court never has held that societal discrimination alone is sufficient to justify a racial classification, rather, the Court has insisted upon some showing of prior discrimination by the governmental unit involved before allowing limited use of racial classifications in order to remedy such discrimination.").

28. Id. at 272.

29. Id. at 283.

30. *Croson*, 488 U.S. at 476–511.

31. See id. at 500–02.

32. Id. at 507–08.

33. Id. at 491–92 (plurality opinion) ("[A] state or local subdivision (if delegated the authority from the State) has the authority to eradicate the effects of private discrimination within its own legislative jurisdiction. . . . Thus, if the city could show that it had essentially become a 'passive participant' in a system of racial exclusion practiced by elements of the local construction industry, we think it clear that the city could take affirmative steps to dismantle such a system.").

34. *Podberesky v. Kirwan*, 38 F.3d 147 (4th Cir. 1994), *cert. denied*, 514 U.S. 1128 (1995).

35. Id. at 152.

36. Id. at 153–54.

37. *Hopwood v. Texas*, 78 F.3d 932 (5th Cir. 1996), *cert. denied*, 518 U.S. 1033 (1996).

38. Id. at 948. The law school's reasoning was likely that it is merely a part of the overall system of education administered by the State of Texas, and by permitting affirmative action at the law school, the state was merely acting to remedy discrimination in one part of its education system that had discriminatory effects in another. See id. at 953–54.

39. Id. at 948–52. According to the court, "Even if, arguendo, the state is the proper government unit to scrutinize, the law school's admissions program would not withstand our review. For the admissions scheme to pass constitutional muster, the State of Texas, through its legislature, would have to find that past segregation has present effects; it would have to determine the magnitude of those present effects; and it would need to limit carefully the 'plus' given to applicants to remedy that harm." Id. at 951.

40. Id. at 952–55. The "present effects" identified by the University of Texas School of Law included "[1] the law school's lingering reputation in the minority community, particularly with prospective students, as a 'white' school; [2] an underrepresentation of minorities in the student body; and [3] some perception that the law school is a hostile environment for minorities." Id. at 951 (quoting *Hopwood v. Texas*, 881 F. Supp. 551, 572 (W.D. Tex. 1994)).

41. *Wessmann v. Gittens*, 160 F.3d 790 (1st Cir. 1998).

42. Id. at 800–01.

43. Id. at 802–08. In dissent, Judge Lipez argued that the Boston Latin program was justified by the school's remedial interest in overcoming the present effects of past discrimination, and that the majority had adopted the wrong standard in requiring the defendant School Committee, rather than the plaintiff, to prove the link between prior discrimination and present effects:

   > In my view, the majority judges the Committee's proof of causation unsatisfactory because the majority misperceives the Committee's evidentiary burden in defending its affirmative action program. . . . A government entity need not admit conclusive guilt for past discrimination's current effects before going forward with a remedial plan. Instead, it must satisfy the court that the evidence before it established a prima facie case of a causal link between past discrimination and the current outcomes addressed by the remedial program. If this prima facie case is not effectively rebutted by a reverse discrimination plaintiff, who always retains the burden of proving illegality of the affirmative action program, the government has met its burden of establishing a compelling interest under strict scrutiny analysis.

44. See, for example, Murphy, *supra* note 3, at 515 ("This strict standard of review and the seemingly impossible factual basis necessary to satisfy this heightened scrutiny imply that remedial action in higher education is no longer a valid justification for affirmative action.").
45. See *supra* text accompanying notes 20–23.
46. *Regents of the University of California v. Bakke*, 438 U.S. 265 (1978).
47. Id. at 312–15 (opinion of Powell, J.).
48. See id. at 324–79 (Brennan, J., concurring in part and dissenting in part, joined by White, Marshall, & Blackmun, J. J.).
49. See id. at 408-21 (Stevens, J., concurring in part and dissenting in part, joined by Burger, C. J., and Rehnquist & Stewart, J. J.).
50. See id. at 271–72 (opinion of Powell, J.).
51. Id. at 311–12.
52. Id. at 312.
53. Id. at 312–13 (quoting *Sweezy v. New Hampshire*, 354 U.S. 234, 263 (1957) (Frankfurter, J., concurring in the result)).
54. Id. at 315.
55. Id. at 314.
56. See id. at 316–18.
57. See, for example, Murphy, *supra* note 3, at 536.
58. *Aderand v. Pena*, 515 U.S. 200 (1995).
59. See, for example, *Metro Broadcasting, Inc. v. FCC*, 497 U.S. 547, 612 (1990) (overruled in part by *Adarand*, 515 U.S. 200 (1995)) (O'Connor, J., dissenting) ("Modern equal protection doctrine has recognized only one [compelling] interest: remedying the effects of racial discrimination.").
60. *Hopwood v. Texas*, 78 F.3d 932 (5th Cir. 1996), *cert. denied*, 518 U.S. 1033 (1996).
61. See id. at 934–38 (explaining the University of Texas School of Law's admissions process).
62. *Hopwood v. Texas* ("Hopwood II"), 84 F.3d 720, 722 (5th Cir. 1996) (Politz, J., dissenting from denial of rehearing en banc) ("The majority of the panel [in *Hopwood*] overruled *Bakke*, wrote far too broadly, and spoke a plethora of unfortunate dicta.").
63. *Hopwood*, 78 F.3d at 944.
64. Id. at 944–45.

65. Id. at 945–46.
66. Id. at 948.
67. *Wittmer v. Peters*, 87 F.3d 916 (7th Cir. 1996), *cert. denied*, 519 U.S. 1111 (1997).
68. See id. at 917. ("The idea [of the boot camp] is to give inmates an experience similar to that of old-fashioned military basic training, in which harsh regimentation, including drill-sergeant abuse by correctional officers, is used to break down and remold the character of the trainee.")
69. See id. at 918–19.
70. Id. at 919 (criticizing *Hopwood v. Texas*, 78 F.3d 932, 944 (5th Cir. 1996)) (other citations omitted).
71. See id. at 920.
72. Id. at 918. See also *Adarand*, 515 U.S. at 237; id. at 275 (Ginsburg, J., dissenting, joined by Breyer, J.).
73. Id. at 919–20. Of potentially great relevance to making the case for educational diversity as a compelling interest, the court, in deciding how much and what type of evidence was necessary to justify the affirmative action program at issue, expressly recognized that the amount and type of evidence required was dependent upon the amount and type of evidence available. Id. at 920. The court did suggest that "after correctional boot camps have been around long enough to enable thorough academic (or academic-quality) study of the racial problems involved in their administration, prison officials can[not] continue to coast on expert evidence that extrapolates to boot camps from the experts' research on conventional prisons." Id. at 920–21. However, the court also recognized that boot camps have been in existence since 1983, and it still upheld the affirmative action program at issue based on limited direct evidence. Id. at 921.
74. *Smith*, 233 F.3d at 1188 (denying, in part, plaintiff's motion for summary judgment in a suit challenging the University of Washington Law School's prior affirmative action admissions policy).
75. Id. at 1201. See also, for example, *Hunter v. Regents of the University of California*, 190 F.3d 1061 (9th Cir. 1999) (upholding the use of race in student assignment to an elementary school operated by UCLA to support the state's nonremedial compelling interest in promoting and disseminating research to improve urban education); *Brewer v. West Irondequit Central* 2000 U.S. App. LEXIS 9866 (2d Cir. 2000) (holding that the state's nonremedial interest in reducing *de facto* segregation is a compelling interest that can justify the use of race in student assignment policies).
76. *Gratz*, 122 F.Supp.2d at 811.
77. Id. at 824.
78. *Johnson*, 106 F.Supp.2d at 1375 (holding that Justice Powell's opinion was not binding precedent and that the university's interest in educational diversity was too "amorphous" to be compelling).
79. See, for example, *Smith*, 233 F.3d at 1188 (University of Washington Law School); *Gratz*, 122 F.Supp.2d at 811 (University of Michigan); *Johnson*, 106 F.Supp.2d at 1362 (University of Georgia); *Grutter v. Bollinger*, 97-72598 (E.D. Mich.) (challenging the University of Michigan Law School's affirmative action admissions policy).

CHAPTER 4

Maximizing the Benefits of Student Diversity: Lessons from School Desegregation Research

JANET WARD SCHOFIELD

Introduction

The goal of this paper is to consider the implications for higher education of the large body of existing research on the effects of desegregation at the elementary and secondary school level. I recognize that there are significant differences between precollegiate and collegiate education, as well as important differences among the many kinds of institutions that make up the U.S. higher education system. I do not assume that the outcomes of having a diverse student population at the K–12 level will necessarily be the same as those resulting from diversity at the college level; nor do I assume that the specific approaches that work in the former environment will necessarily be appropriate for the latter. But as someone who has spent much of the past twenty-five years studying the impact of racially mixed primary and secondary schooling on students, I will try to present here some basic ideas and general lessons that appear likely to be useful in thinking about how to maximize the potential benefits of diversity for college students.

The Outcomes of K–12 School Desegregation

A large and rich set of studies exists on the outcomes of school desegregation at the K–12 level, especially with regard to its effects on African American students.[1] These studies, when combined with relevant theory and research in social psychology, give some insight into the processes through which these outcomes can be achieved. Moreover, this research has been systematically assessed and synthesized by several scholars in the past two or three decades, and there is reasonable consensus about what is known (Cook, 1984; Krol, 1978; Mahard & Crain, 1989; Schofield, 1995a; Stephan & Stephan, 1996; St. John, 1975).

First, we know that desegregated primary and secondary schools enhance the academic progress of African American students, although not necessarily to the same extent in every area or at every grade level. There are also some indications of achievement benefits for Hispanic students. Second, although there is some evidence that desegregation may increase the suspension rate for minority students, there is also reason to believe that it cuts the dropout rate—a more important factor, in the end, given the substantial negative economic consequences of failing to complete high school.

Third, and perhaps most important, desegregation appears to have modest positive long-term occupational consequences for African Americans, including (a) fostering higher occupational aspirations and more consistent career planning linked to these aspirations, (b) increasing earnings modestly, and (c) increasing the likelihood that they will work in professions in which blacks have traditionally been underrepresented.

Although the reasons for these outcomes are undoubtedly complex, the research suggests certain specific mechanisms that appear to play a role, including (a) the positive impact of desegregation on the years of college completed by African American males, (b) the positive effect of the use of desegregated social networks in job searches on the salary ultimately obtained, and (c) the unfortunate but apparently undeniable fact that some employers harbor negative attitudes about hiring minority graduates of urban high schools with large minority student enrollments, but hold more positive attitudes about minority graduates of suburban schools.

Research has also demonstrated a variety of ways in which school desegregation at the precollegiate level appears to help break the cycle of racial isolation, in which individuals from different racial or ethnic groups avoid each other in spite of the fact that this limits their occupational, social, and residential opportunities. So, for example, African Americans who attended desegregated schools are more likely as adults to live and work in racially mixed environments than their peers who attended segregated schools.

Although there is much less research on the effects of desegregation on whites, there are some parallel findings. For example, one study (National Opinion Research Center survey, cited in Aspira of America, 1979) found that desegregated white students were more likely to report both having had a close African American friend and having had African American friends visit their homes than were their counterparts in predominately white schools.

Outcomes Depend on Educational Process

There is one additional, very important finding about precollegiate school desegregation. Although some benefits appear to be common outcomes of attending a racially or ethnically mixed school, the mere fact of having a diverse student body does not automatically lead to them. Rather, the specific nature of the situation in which students find themselves has a crucial effect on a wide range of outcomes.

This has led researchers to the conclusion that attaining a diverse student body is just the first step in a long process, and that attention to the many specifics of that process is absolutely vital if one wants to maximize the potential benefits of diversity and minimize the potential problems (Braddock & McPartland, 1988; Schofield, 1995b). The fact that minority students in predominantly white institutions routinely report higher levels of stress and alienation than their white peers (Allen & Haniff, 1991; Loo & Rolison, 1986) and that, consistent with this, their college attrition rates are markedly higher (Bennett, 1995; Keller, 1988–1989) suggests that this lesson should be heeded at the college level as well.

Although it may seem obvious that the college environment is crucial to maximizing the positive effects of diversity, policymakers and social scientists learned a similar lesson at the precollegiate level the hard way, over many years. Though this is far from a new thought for many of those concerned with diversity in higher education, much remains to be done in changing colleges and universities so that they maximize the potential presented by diverse student bodies (Allan, 1988; Bennett, 1995; Nettles, 1988; Schoem, Frankel, Zúñiga, & Lewis, 1993).

Institutional Approaches to Desegregation

Research on K–12 desegregation suggests that students' school experiences are influenced greatly by the assumptions of those in power, which are embedded in each institution's everyday policies and practices. An analysis of the ways desegregated schools manage the shift from serving primarily or exclusively white students to enrolling a more diverse student body may be helpful in illuminating the situation in higher education—especially for institutions that have historically served whites but have now begun to enroll increasing numbers of minority students, due either to an active desire to serve a broader constituency or to demographic and economic forces that have made minorities a larger proportion of college-bound youth (Bennett, 1995).

Desegregated schools may be characterized as having one of four distinct orientations, each with important implications for students: 1) business as usual, 2) assimilation, 3) pluralistic coexistence, and 4) integrated pluralism (Sagar & Schofield, 1984).

Institutions taking the first stance, business as usual, try to avoid any particular response to the changing nature of the student body and to carry on in the customary way as far as possible. Those taking the second approach, assimilation, tend to see success as achieving an end point at which minority group members can no longer be differentiated from the white majority in terms of values, orientations, skills, and the like. The changes necessary to produce this end state, however, are seen as occurring exclusively in minority group members rather than as occurring in majority group members as well. The pluralistic coexistence approach recognizes and accepts groups' different historical experiences and values, but makes no effort to foster increased understanding, acceptance, or interaction between them.

The fourth approach, integrated pluralism, starts with the recognition and acceptance of differences, but adds an emphasis on fostering respect and interaction. It differs from the other approaches in that it explicitly affirms the educational value inherent in exposing all students to a diversity of perspectives and behavioral repertoires, and in that it is structured to achieve mutual information exchange, influence, and acceptance.

The first three approaches to educating a diverse student body at the precollegiate level all have significant drawbacks, as will be discussed below. The last one, integrated pluralism, is most likely to produce the positive outcomes of desegregation discussed earlier. Little research has been done on the basic modes of institutional response at the college level.

The Negative Consequences of Resegregation

The research on K–12 desegregation underlines the importance of anticipating the possibility—even the probability—of resegregation, and of implementing active policies to prevent it. The first three institutional approaches to desegregation described above share a major drawback: through quite different mechanisms, each one appears to be associated with resegregation that is likely to undermine many of the positive outcomes summarized earlier (Pettigrew, 1969; Sagar & Schofield, 1984).

The research does not suggest that there is anything necessarily wrong with students who have common interests, values, or backgrounds associating with each other to achieve valued ends. In fact, this can serve useful functions at both the collegiate and precollegiate levels (Tatum, 1995, 1997). The problems arise when schools are set up in a way that segregates and ghettoizes minority students; when the apparently voluntary clustering by race or ethnicity stems from fear, hostility, or discomfort; or when such clustering is not part of a varied set of experiences that includes the kind of significant participation in the life of the larger community that promotes meaningful contact and ties with those outside one's own group. Unfortunately, such situations are not uncommon. For example, a large survey of black undergraduates at predominately white institutions found that almost two-thirds reported little or no integration into general student activities, and over 40 percent reported that white students often or always avoided interaction with them outside the classroom (Allen, 1988).

In such cases, research and theory suggest, resegregation undercuts the development of cross-group ties that appear to account for a number of the positive outcomes mentioned above. If resegregation is normative and pervasive, for example, students are unlikely to form relationships across racial and ethnic boundaries that will later be useful in job searches.

Resegregation also undercuts the school's potential to offer an environment in which students from diverse backgrounds can learn about others through classroom and social experiences. Institutions of higher education recognize the importance of experience with certain kinds of diversity in many ways, from admissions policies that value geographic diversity to study-abroad programs. If it is useful for American students to learn about other countries through living in them and meeting their people, should it not also be useful for them to learn more about their own country through extended, meaningful experiences with their peers from different racial or ethnic backgrounds? This seems especially true, given that many students come from backgrounds that make such experiences prior to college unlikely.

Factors Conducive to Achieving Integrated Pluralism

Support of Relevant Authorities

The school desegregation literature and related social psychological theory and research suggest some general principles that should be useful in promoting integrated pluralism in college. Consistent support from those in authority is crucial (Allport, 1954; Hawley et al., 1983). Specifically, principals in desegregated schools have been found to play at least four important roles in promoting desirable outcomes (Schofield, 1995b). First, they have an enabling function—that is, they make choices that facilitate or impede practices that promote positive outcomes, including choices about the allocation of funds. Second, they can serve as models. Although there is no guarantee that others will follow, this appears to be helpful. Third, they can sensitize others, because they are well placed to argue effectively for the importance of attention to issues salient to them. Finally, they have the power to sanction others, to actively reward positive practices and discourage negative ones.

It seems reasonable to expect that those in positions of leadership in higher education can contribute to positive relations on campus in these same ways. Indeed, Pettigrew (1998) outlines a number of specific ways this can be done. Furthermore, it should be recognized that leadership can exist at a variety of levels. Leadership by faculty may be important in affecting students' academic and social experiences, just as leadership at the policy level is important in shaping institutional practices and policies. For example, dissatisfaction with racial disparities in academic outcomes can lead to the development of teaching strategies that improve performance for all, but most especially for black and Latino students (Kleinsmith, 1993). Further, concern about fostering positive intergroup relations can lead to innovative approaches to breaking down barriers and increasing students' knowledge about themselves and others (Tatum, 1995; Zúñiga & Nagda, 1993).

Cooperation toward Mutually Valued Goals

Probably the most unequivocal finding in the research on school desegregation is that cooperation between members of different groups can play an important role in fostering academic achievement and building positive relationships and strong ties among students (Slavin, 1985, 1992, 1995). Cooperation must be carefully structured, however. Positive outcomes are most likely when students from different backgrounds work together toward shared goals that would not be attainable otherwise, and when all can make a valuable contribution. The clarity of this finding, combined with its impact on both academic and social outcomes, has led thousands of elementary and secondary schools around the country to adopt cooperative learning models for at least some of their students' work.

Generally speaking, changes of this sort may be hard to achieve in higher education. Collegiate work is, if anything, even more individualistic than precollegiate work, and older students have and expect more autonomy than younger students. Further, college professors are unlikely to have experience in methods of cooperative teaching and learning. Finally, differences in academic preparation can pose serious barriers to productive cooperation (Schofield, 1980). Nevertheless, it is worth noting that a report prepared by the Department of Labor during the Bush administration listed interpersonal skills, including the ability to work on teams with others and to work well with people from culturally diverse backgrounds, among the five basic competencies needed to function effectively in the workplace (Secretary's Commission on Achieving Necessary Skills, 1991).

Indeed, the U.S. population is becoming increasingly diverse and many people work in relatively large institutional settings. Most workers would therefore profit from educational experiences that prepare them to work cooperatively with people of varied racial and ethnic backgrounds. Focusing attention on how to give students experience working productively on teams may yield benefits of the kind discussed earlier, and also prepare them better for work and for citizenship in a heterogeneous nation.

The desegregation literature also suggests that the classroom is not the only, or even the best, arena for fostering cooperation between students of different backgrounds. Extracurricular activities affect both student development and school climate (Braddock, Dawkins, & Wilson, 1995). Cooperation across racial and ethnic boundaries in the context of sports, arts organizations, clubs, and other such activities is especially effective in building mutual respect, friendship, and shared social identity (Schofield, 1995b).

Stephan and Stephan (1985) suggest that people often feel considerable anxiety at the prospect of interacting with those of different backgrounds and that this can get in the way of forming constructive relationships built on cooperation. Furthermore, research suggests that both majority and minority group members may bring expectations and behavior patterns to mixed situations that impede full and equal participation by all (Cohen, 1980, 1984). Thus, one cannot assume that students will automatically seek opportunities of this sort, or that any and all cooperative experiences will improve intergroup relations. Careful thought must be given to ways of making them attractive and effective.

Equal Status for Members of All Groups
Equal status for members of all groups is another condition that helps produce positive outcomes, whereas unequal status can cause problems (Schofield, 1995b). Previous work on equal status in desegregated settings has distinguished between equal status within the contact situation and that outside it. Because race and ethnicity are so strongly associated with

social class in the United States, it is frequently true that white students in a given school come from wealthier families than their minority group peers, thus bringing to their interactions a higher social status from outside school. This often creates significant obstacles to attaining equal status within the school, given the strong and persistent correlation between socioeconomic background and academic achievement and the fact that academic achievement itself can create a kind of status hierarchy within a school. Creating positive race relations is more difficult when race and class differences reinforce rather than cut across each other; in such a situation, for example, the effects of poverty may be perceived as innate racial differences. A variety of ways to help promote equal status within schools have been suggested—ranging from ensuring that all groups are well represented in positions of power to adopting policies specifically designed to mitigate the impact of unequal status from outside the school.

Similar issues of status are certainly relevant in higher education. For example, the lower socioeconomic status of minority group students is often reflected in the special intensity of their financial concerns compared to those of their white classmates (Muñoz, 1986; Oliver & Etchevery, 1987). Such differences in background often translate into differences in academic preparation. These differences should be addressed in ways that do not create lower status within the school. They may also result in differential amounts of time students must devote to income-producing activities, with corresponding effects on academic performance and status.

All this suggests that financial aid policies can play a crucial role in giving students equal time to function as students and members of the college community. It further suggests the importance of developing pools of academically talented minority students—not only for the benefit of those students themselves, but also because having them on campus, performing comparably to or even better than their majority group peers, helps create an atmosphere in which the status of different groups outside the institution does not predict the status of individuals inside it.

The equal status finding from K–12 school desegregation research warns us of a serious potential problem with plans to promote racial and ethnic diversity on campus by replacing race-conscious affirmative action in college admissions with a system based on class. Such a system would make it much more difficult for colleges to identify and recruit academically talented minority students from middle-class backgrounds, and would virtually guarantee that a much greater proportion of minorities on campus would come from families of low socioeconomic status (Kane, 1998). It is therefore likely that class-based admissions policies would in fact be counterproductive to the goals of institutions seeking to promote cooperative and positive race relations, as Pettigrew (1998) has argued.

In summary, there is a large body of research that explores the impact of school desegregation at the K–12 level on student outcomes. It suggests that a wide array of positive outcomes do often occur. For example, it appears that school desegregation can contribute to breaking down strong historical social patterns that isolate majority and minority group members from each other in spite of the limitations this imposes on their social, residential, and occupational choices. However, this work also suggests that such outcomes are far from inevitable. Crucial to their attainment are the specific conditions obtaining in the school environment. Although there are many differences between the precollegiate and collegiate education, these findings should be of use to those in higher education who must think through the challenges they are facing as the demographic composition of the pool of college-age students changes and our country struggles to meet its need to prepare all its citizens for productive futures.

Note

1.   Most desegregation research has concerned desegregation's effects on African American students. Thus, my tendency to focus on outcomes for this group is a consequence of the available research base rather than a lack of awareness of the many other diverse groups in this country or the potential importance of the impact of diversity on white students. Readers desiring comprehensive citation information on these studies should refer to Schofield (1995a).

References

Allport, G. W. (1954). *The nature of prejudice.* Cambridge, MA: Addison-Wesley.

Allen, W. R. (1988). The education of black students on white college campuses: What quality the experience? In M. T. Nettles (Ed.), *Toward black undergraduate student equality in American higher education* (pp. 57–85). New York: Greenwood Press.

Allen, W. R., & Haniff, N. Z. (1991). Race, gender, and academic performance in U.S. higher education. In W. R. Allen, E. G. Epps, & N. Z. Haniff (Eds.), *College in black and white* (pp. 95–109). Albany: State University of New York Press.

Aspira of America, Inc. (1979). *Trends in segregation of Hispanic students in major school districts having large Hispanic enrollment: Ethnographic case studies* (Final Report, Vol. 2). New York: Author. (ERIC Document Reproduction Service. No. ED 190 271)

Bennett, C. I. (1995). Research on racial issues in American higher education. In J. A. Banks & C. A. McGee Banks (Eds.), *Handbook of research on multicultural education* (pp. 663–682). New York: Simon & Schuster Macmillan.

Braddock, J. H., Dawkins, M. P., & Wilson, G. (1995). Intercultural contact and race relations among American youth. In W. D. Hawley & A. W. Jackson (Eds.), *Toward a common destiny* (pp. 237–256). San Francisco: Jossey-Bass.

Braddock, J. H., & McPartland, J. M. (1988). Some cost and benefit considerations for black college students attending predominantly white versus predominantly black universities. In M. T. Nettles (Ed.), *Toward black undergraduate student equality in American higher education* (pp. 87–104). New York: Greenwood Press.

Cohen, E. (1980). Design and redesign of the desegregated school: Problems of status, power, and conflict. In W. G. Stephan & J. R. Feagin (Eds.), *School desegregation: Past, present, and future* (pp. 251–278). New York: Plenum Press.

Cohen, E. (1984). The desegregated school: Problems in status, power, and inter-ethnic climate. In N. Miller & M. B. Brewer (Eds.), *Groups in contact: The psychology of desegregation* (pp. 77–96). Orlando, FL: Academic Press.

Cook, T. D. (1984). What have black children gained academically from school integration? Examination of the meta-analytic evidence. In T. Cook, D. Armor, R. Crain, N. Miller, W. Stephan, H. Walberg, & P. Wortman (Eds.), *School desegregation and black achievement* (pp. 6–42). Washington, DC: National Institute of Education.

Hawley, W., Crain, R. L., Rossell, C. H., Schofield, J. W., Fernandez, R., & Trent, W. P. (1983). *Strategies for effective desegregation: Lessons from research.* Lexington, MA: Lexington Books, D. C. Heath.

Kane, T. J. (1998). Misconceptions in the debate over affirmative action in college admissions. In G. Orfield and E. Miller (Eds.), *Chilling admissions: The affirmative action crisis and the search for alternatives* (pp. 17–31). Cambridge, MA: Harvard Education Publishing Group.

Keller, G. (1988–1989). Review essay: Black students in higher education: Why so few? *Planning for Higher Education, 17,* 43–57.

Kleinsmith, L. J. (1993). Racial bias in science education. In D. Schoem, L. Frankel, X. Zúñiga, & E. Lewis (Eds.), *Multicultural teaching in the university* (pp. 180–190). Westport, CT: Praeger.

Krol, R. A. (1978). *A meta-analysis of comparative research on the effects of desegregation on academic achievement.* Unpublished doctoral dissertation, Western Michigan University, Kalamazoo. (University Microfilms No. 79-07962)

Loo, C. M., & Rolison, G. (1986). Alienation of ethnic minority students at a predominantly white university. *Journal of Higher Education, 57,* 58–113.

Mahard, R. E., & Crain, R. L. (1989). *The influence of high school racial composition on the academic achievement and college attendance of Hispanics.* Paper presented at the annual meeting of the American Sociological Association, New York.

Muñoz, D. G. (1986). Identifying areas of stress for Chicano undergraduates. In M. A. Olivas (Ed.), *Latino college students* (pp. 131–192). New York: Teachers College Press.

Nettles, M. T. (Ed.). (1988). *Toward black undergraduate student equality in American higher education.* New York: Greenwood Press.

Oliver, J., & Etchevery, R. (1987). Factors influencing the decisions of academically talented black students who attend college. *Journal of Negro Education, 56,* 152–161.

Pettigrew, T. F. (1969). The Negro and education: Problems and proposals. In I. Katz & P. Gurin (Eds.), *Race and the social sciences* (pp. 49–112). New York: Basic Books.

Pettigrew, T. F. (1998). Prejudice and discrimination on the college campus. In J. L. Eberhardt & S. T. Fiske (Eds.), *Confronting racism: The problem and the response* (pp. 263–279). Thousand Oaks, CA: Sage.

Sagar, H. A., & Schofield, J. W. (1984). Integrating the desegregated school: Problems and possibilities. In M. Maehr & D. Bartz (Eds.), *Advances in motivation and achievement: A research annual* (pp.203–241). Greenwich, CT: JAI Press.

Schoem, D., Frankel, L., Zúñiga, X., & Lewis, E. A. (Eds.). (1993). *Multicultural teaching in the university.* Westport, CT: Praeger.

Schofield, J. W. (1980). Cooperation as social exchange: Resource gaps and reciprocity in academic work. In S. Sharon, P. Hare, C. Webb, & R. Hertz-Lazarowitz (Eds.), *Cooperation in education* (pp. 160–181). Provo, UT: Brigham Young University Press.

Schofield, J. W. (1995a). Review of research on school desegregation's impact on elementary and secondary school students. In J. A. Banks & C. A. McGee Banks (Eds.), *Handbook of research on multicultural education* (pp. 597–616). New York: Simon & Schuster Macmillan.

Schofield, J. W. (1995b). Improving intergroup relations among students. In J. A. Banks & C. A. McGee Banks (Eds.), *Handbook of research on multicultural education* (pp. 635–646). New York: Simon & Schuster Macmillan.

Secretary's Commission on Achieving Necessary Skills. (1991). *What work requires of schools: A SCANS Report for America 2000.* Washington, DC: Government Printing Office.

Slavin, R. E. (1985). Cooperative learning: Applying contact theory in desegregated schools. *Journal of Social Issues, 41,* 45–62.

Slavin, R. E. (1992). When and why does cooperative learning increase achievement? Theoretical and empirical perspectives. In R. Hertz-Lazarowitz & N. Miller (Eds.), *Interaction in cooperative groups* (pp. 145–173). Cambridge, Eng.: Cambridge University Press.

Slavin, R. E. (1995). Cooperative learning and intergroup relations. In J. A. Banks & C. A. McGee Banks (Eds.), *Handbook of research on multicultural education* (pp. 628–634). New York: Simon & Schuster Macmillan.

Stephan, W. G., & Stephan, C. W. (1985). Intergroup anxiety. *Journal of Social Issues, 41,* 157–175.

Stephan, W. G., & Stephan, C. W. (1996). *Intergroup relations.* Boulder, CO: Westview Press.

St. John, N. H. (1975). *School desegregation: Outcomes for children.* New York: John Wiley & Sons.

Tatum, B. D. (1995). Talking about race, learning about racism: The application of racial identity development theory in the classroom. *Harvard Educational Review, 62,* 1–24.

Tatum, B. D. (1997). Identity development in adolescence: "Why are all the black kids sitting together in the cafeteria?" In B. D. Tatum (Ed.), *"Why are all the black kids sitting together in the cafeteria?" And other conversations about race* (pp. 52–74). New York: Basic Books.

Zúñiga, X., & Nagda, B. A. (1993). Dialogue groups: An innovative approach to multicultural learning. In D. Schoem, L. Frankel, X. Zúñiga, & E. A. Lewis (Eds.), *Multicultural teaching in the university* (pp. 233–248). Westport, CT: Praeger.

CHAPTER 5

Is Diversity a Compelling Educational Interest? Evidence from Louisville

MICHAL KURLAENDER
JOHN T. YUN

Desegregated schools are under serious attack. During the past decade, some lower federal courts have moved to dismantle existing desegregation orders and to prohibit districts not under court-ordered desegregation from using race as a factor in school assignment plans. School districts interested in continuing their desegregation efforts may now be required to prove to the courts that racial and ethnic diversity serves a compelling, educational purpose.

There currently exists surprisingly little documentation on the impact of racial and ethnic diversity on the educational experience of all students. To date, most research has focused on its impact on black students and consists largely of analyzing test scores. There has been very little effort to evaluate how diversity affects the learning of white, Latino, and Asian students. Yet this information is critical not only to proving compelling educational value legally, but also to achieving a richer understanding of the overall impact of racially and ethnically diverse schools on the moral, intellectual, and social development of students. As judges and school boards make policy decisions that dramatically alter the learning environment, we need a better understanding of whether diversity enhances educational outcomes in measurable ways. Through this study, we extend the research available on this critical question and assess whether or not there is a compelling educational interest to diversity in the Jefferson County, Kentucky, schools for both white and minority students.

The data used in this chapter are from a survey about student experiences with diversity in their schools and classrooms. We surveyed a group of high school students—primarily in the 11th grade—from the Jefferson County School District in Louisville, Kentucky. We identified several important educational outcomes—critical thinking skills, future educational goals, and citizenship—and disaggregated the data by racial groups. We also created composite variables from these questions that represent the students' aspirations for higher education and their comfort levels living and working in multiracial environments. These composites were used as outcomes in several linear regression models designed to complement the disaggregated individual survey question results.

We selected high school juniors, since most have experienced many years of desegregated education but are not yet preoccupied with the distractions common to seniors. To this end we constructed a survey instrument for the express purpose of evaluating how diversity impacts certain educational outcomes. The major research question we are trying to answer is whether diversity enhances educational outcomes in measurable ways. We frame several specific research questions that address and inform this larger issue, specifically:

1) Are the classes and lessons in the Louisville classrooms diverse?
2) Are the perceived opportunities for learning similar across races?
3) Can school-level diversity change student attitudes about living and working in diverse settings?

Data on research question one establish that the school system we are examining is indeed diverse. This is a precondition for determining whether or not diversity can affect educational outcomes. If a relatively desegregated district like Jefferson County does not show high levels of diversity in its curriculum or student body, clearly the other questions are moot. Research question two provides a criterion for determining whether or not desegregated schooling provides an equal opportunity of success for all students. If more diverse environments do equalize opportunity for success, then aspirations—as an indicator of perceived opportunity—should also become more equal between racial/ethnic groups in desegregated environments. Thus, this question asks, in this school system, are the perceived opportunities equal among races? Research question three looks to shed light on whether diversity in school-level variables—like curriculum—are actually associated with better educational outcomes.

Clearly, as these research questions show, gauging the impact of segregation and diversity on educational outcomes represents a difficult challenge. The challenge is further complicated by the legal, social, political, and educational contexts in which these issues are being debated. To understand the scope and significance of this research we need to look at several factors beyond the research questions and examine their relationships to one another. First, we detail the current state of segregation in the United States, including the trends toward resegregation observed in recent years. We then examine the legal framework that circumscribes use of plans to desegregate public schools. From there we proceed to a summary of existing research describing the benefits of desegregated schools. We end by describing the methods and results of our current study, where we establish the level of diversity in the Louisville classrooms and examine how that diversity affects the educational outcomes outlined.

As the following pages detail, both black and white students attending high school in the Jefferson County School District in Louisville, Kentucky, report benefiting greatly from the diversity of their schools. They report strong educational benefits in all three categories: critical thinking skills, future educational goals, and principles of citizenship. The uniformity in responses by racial and ethnic groups affirms the finding of Justice Lewis Powell in *Regents of the University of California v. Bakke* (1978) that diverse educational settings foster stronger learning experiences for all students and help to prepare them to live and work in a multiracial society.

Segregation

A 1999 report released by The Civil Rights Project at Harvard University, *Resegregation in American Schools*, outlines the trends of resegregation in our nation's schools, as well as the rapid demographic changes that our schools are facing.[1] As the nation becomes more racially and ethnically diverse, separation by race is becoming more pronounced in our schools. Today, the country's largest school systems are only serving a small minority of white students, and the dramatic increase in the minority school-age population demands new ways of thinking about segregation and the success of multiracial schools. The greatest progress toward desegregation in the South after the U.S. Supreme Court's *Brown v. Board of Education* decision came between the mid-1960s and the early 1970s. The 1964 Civil Rights Act led to increased enforcement of *Brown*, and authorized busing.[2] By the mid-1970s the South was the most integrated region of the country for both blacks and whites.[3] According to the *Resegregation* report, this degree of progress began to turn around in the late 1980s. The more recent increase in segregation is occurring in regions that have historically been the most integrated within the United States, with the largest percentage of black enrollment.

Kentucky, along with Delaware, showed the largest declines in segregation during the busing era of the 1970s, partly because both states implemented a city-suburban desegregation plan in the large metropolitan areas where the majority of minority students lived.[4] The changing patterns of black segregation in Kentucky over the last 30 years is illustrated by the exposure index which shows the percentage of white students in schools attended by the typical black student.[5] In 1970, the typical black student in Kentucky attended a school that was 49 percent white. By 1996, this figure had increased to 69.1 percent.[6] From 1970 to 1980 there was an increase of nearly 25 percent in the number of white students attending schools that black students were attending; from 1980 to 1996 that percentage fell by 5.2 percent.[7] More than a million U.S. students have been desegregated in countywide districts, including both city and suburban neighborhoods, for more than a quarter century. Aside from Louisville and Wilmington, which were merged by the courts, these are districts that had countywide systems before desegregation. Such systems lead the nation in the depth and stability of their integration.

Legal Framework

Recent court decisions have moved districts from mandatory integration under *Brown* to voluntary policies. Districts once required by the court to desegregate are now filing for unitary status, claiming that the district has eliminated all of the effects of past discrimination.[8] The dominant theme in these decisions is that the courts should withdraw their oversight after a few years and return control to local officials.[9] By the late 1990s some lower federal courts took more dramatic action, prohibiting school districts not under court-ordered desegregation from taking any explicit steps to preserve integration, such as maintaining racial balance in magnet schools. This has often led to serious intensification of segregation and created minority schools with very high concentrations of poverty. If a school district is not under a federal desegregation order, it would have to prove a "compelling interest" to justify considering race in any way to maintain desegregated schools. In *Bakke,*[10] the Supreme Court's key decision on this issue in higher education, the Court held that the most important such "compelling interest" would be the educational value gained for all students in college from exposure to diversity. In the 1999 *Wessmann v. Gittens*[11] case, which prohibited the continuation of desegregation goals at the magnet school, Boston Latin, the federal court held that

Boston Public Schools had not adequately demonstrated a compelling interest that supported a race-sensitive admissions policy. In more recent decisions in Rochester, New York, and Louisville, the fact that diversity can be a compelling interest was clearly recognized.[12] This survey represents an effort to assess whether or not there is such a benefit in the Jefferson County schools for both white and minority students.

In his decisive opinion in the *Bakke* case, Justice Powell outlined the ways in which diversity serves to enhance education. This opinion has served as the cornerstone of affirmative action policies that consider race as a factor in university admissions. In *Bakke*, Powell relied on earlier Supreme Court decisions related to the importance of interracial preparation for the professions and on Harvard College reports describing how a diversity of experiences can contribute to the overall learning environment. These emphasize that the university community should reflect the diversity in our society in order to produce richer educational possibilities for students to gain understanding. The Harvard report cited in *Bakke* states, "The effectiveness of our students' educational experiences has seemed to the Committee to be affected as importantly by a wide variety of interests, talents, backgrounds, and career goals as it is by a fine faculty and our libraries, laboratories and housing arrangements."[13] At the time of *Bakke*, the Court simply accepted the judgment of the educational authorities about what they saw as an obvious relationship. Now the lower courts are raising the standard of proof.

As the only Supreme Court opinion that speaks to the rationale behind the use of race-conscious policies with the goal of diversity, *Bakke* is also important in the K–12 educational context. The benefits of diversity derived from learning among students of different backgrounds accrue just as readily at the elementary and secondary levels as at the postsecondary level. Increasing exposure and interaction among students of different races increases opportunities for learning and enhances civic values. In fact, as the nation becomes increasingly diverse, exposure to people of different ethnic and racial backgrounds earlier in the education process can only help to reduce stereotypes and promote democracy for all people. Yet most of the earlier research on K–12 desegregation is limited to benefits for black students.

Research on the Benefits of School Desegregation

There are many studies from the K–12 desegregation literature that provide evidence on the benefits of studying in a diverse environment. There are three primary categories of student outcomes—enhanced learning, higher educational and occupational aspirations, and social interaction among members of different racial and ethnic backgrounds—that may be enhanced in the integrated (diverse) classroom.[14] Minority students who attend more integrated schools have increased academic achievement and higher test scores.[15] The increase in achievement for minority children has often been attributed to access to the better educational resources, competition, and networks present in desegregated or predominantly white schools.[16] Desegregated schooling is also associated with higher educational and occupational aspirations. Segregated schools that are predominantly non-white often transmit lower expectations for students and offer a narrower range of occupational and educational options.[17] In addition, perpetuation theory[18] teaches us that only when students are exposed to sustained desegregated experiences will they lead more integrated lives as adults. Thus, desegregated experiences lead to increased interaction with members of other racial groups in later years.[19]

In addition to the above research, recent studies in higher education suggest that more diverse educational environments increase all students' level of critical thinking skills.[20] Gurin's 1999 study finds that students from all racial and ethnic groups educated in diverse settings more readily participate in a pluralistic society. Gurin's work in the higher education context suggests that much can be learned about the impact of diversity in high school on student experiences with, and attitudes toward, people of a race or ethnicity different from their own.

Overall, there is substantial evidence that desegregated schooling is associated with positive educational outcomes for minority students.[21] Yet, as stated earlier, little has been done to examine the impact of racial diversity and desegregation on minority students' white peers. Further, current court decisions around the country that aim to remove race from school assignment plans suggest that some courts assume that desegregation is no longer a compelling educational need. This study attempts to address this research void and provide empirical evidence to inform future decisions about the value of desegregation.

Survey Site

Louisville offers an important place for study because it has achieved unusually low levels of racial segregation since its city and suburban schools were merged in 1975. At that time, a federal court ordered the Jefferson County schools to desegregate. Community resistance was extremely intense, and this transition was one of the most difficult experienced by any city at the height of the desegregation era. The Jefferson County schools have operated independently of the court order since 1980, but Louisville has retained city-suburban desegregation and is attempting to preserve desegregation in spite of a federal court decision forcing a change in magnet school policies.

In recent years, Kentucky's public schools have been among the nation's least segregated as a result of the merger between city and suburban schools. Both blacks and whites in the greater Louisville area have been educated in much more diverse schools than children living in most American communities. Since Jefferson County is a large urban area with very diverse white and black populations and a political tradition that is middle of the road on most issues, it offers a valuable setting in which to assess the experiences of students enrolled in schools that have been substantially desegregated.

The desegregation plan in Louisville was initially a purely mandatory student assignment plan between city and suburban schools, but in recent years the plan has come to rely on choice and magnet schools combined with desegregation standards. A survey of the citizens of Jefferson County in 1996 showed that a large majority of citizens preferred to continue school desegregation efforts and to rely strongly on choice and desegregation standards. The survey also revealed a strong desire to avoid segregated black schools, particularly among black citizens, of whom only 15 percent wanted one-race schools.[22] In addition, a 1996 survey of Jefferson County Public School graduates reveals students' attitudes about the importance of desegregated schooling. Graduates were asked whether they agree or disagree with the statement, "I think it is important for my long-term success in life that schools have students from different races and backgrounds in the same schools."[23] Over 83 percent of black graduates said they very strongly agreed, as did 77 percent of whites, and only about 3 percent of black and white graduates said they disagreed with this statement.[24] Overall enrollment in the district has been much more stable in the last decade than that of other large central city systems, all of which had experienced an initial loss of white students after desegregation orders were implemented. In the current school year, all of the Jefferson County high schools have substantial integration, ranging between one-fifth to one-half black students (see Table 1).

Methods and Instrumentation

The principal instrument used in this research, the Diversity Assessment Questionnaire (DAQ), consists of a 70-item student questionnaire. The instrument was developed by researchers brought together by The Civil Rights

Project at Harvard University (CRP), in collaboration with the National School Boards Association's Council of Urban Boards of Education.[25] It is designed to be a classroom-administered questionnaire that asks students about their experiences in their school and classrooms. The survey also includes questions about students' future goals, educational aspirations, attitudes, and interests. The instrument was pretested by researchers at the CRP through focus groups at two different high schools and five different classrooms—each with a very different racial composition. The results reported in this paper are part of a larger study currently undertaken by the CRP using the DAQ that is under way at several other school districts around the country.[26]

The Jefferson County School District administered the survey in early 2000. The district drew a representative sample of juniors, from which they obtained the excellent response rate of over 90 percent resulting in 1,164 returned surveys.[27] All of the high schools in the district participated in the study, and the sample drawn from the district is proportional to the total enrollment of each school. All of the results were computed in simple frequency tables and then calculated in percentages by racial group. We chose to include all people who responded to each question since we wanted to include the maximum number of opinions in each table. As a result, the number of people responding to each question varies by few respondents. The number of nonresponses on any given question is no higher than 5 percent, resulting in a total sample size for each question ranging from 1,287 to 1,158.

To measure the impact of diversity on three broad educational outcomes, we used several composite variables created from indicators in the DAQ questionnaire as both outcomes and predictors. Using Cronbach's alpha reliability and confirmatory principal component analysis, we determined the utility and reliability of these constructs and created them for use in the regression analysis (see Appendix for further discussion).[28] We analyze two different outcomes: higher education aspirations (HIEDASP) and comfort levels for living and working with members of other races (LIVE_WORK). The HIEDASP variable summarizes student responses to three questions about their future educational aspirations. The LIVE_WORK variable measures student responses to seven questions about their attitudes and interest toward living and working in a multiracial setting. To examine our specific research questions relative to both these outcomes, we also needed to create two composite predictor variables, institutional student support (SUPPORT) and the perceived curricular diversity of the school (CURDIV). The first predictor, SUPPORT, is a composite based on students' perceptions of the level of support they re-

TABLE 1 *1999–2000 High Schools in Jefferson County by % African American*

High School	Total Enrollment	% African American
Atherton	1087	20.1%
Ballard	1655	19.4%
Brown	188	39.9%
Butler	1560	20.8%
Central	985	48.8%
Doss	1014	32.0%
DuPont Manual	1754	23.7%
Eastern	1593	26.7%
Fairdale	909	25.7%
Fern Creek	1276	26.6%
Iroquois	1029	44.2%
Jeffersontown	1008	29.3%
Louisville Male Traditional	1621	25.4%
Moore	588	40.5%
Pleasure Ridge Park	1777	18.9%
Seneca	1643	20.6%
Shawnee	581	48.0%
Southern	1425	20.9%
Valley	952	27.4%
Waggener	897	32.4%
Western	582	42.6%
TOTAL	24,124	27.4%

ceive from teachers and school staff in terms of their higher education aspirations. The second predictor, CURDIV, is a composite based on students' reported level of diversity in the curricula of their social studies and English courses. All of the variable descriptions and corresponding DAQ survey questions can be found in the Appendix (Tables A and B).

To analyze the general benefits of a diverse student body, we presented direct student responses to the DAQ questionnaire. To further investigate the impact of perceived curricular diversity (CURDIV) and teacher support (SUPPORT), we conducted an ordinary least squares (OLS) regression analysis estimating the relationship between these constructs to two outcomes, HIEDASP and LIVE_WORK—controlling for race, father's education, mother's education, and gender.[29]

The Student Population

The survey is targeted toward high school juniors. However, due to the presence of mixed-grade classrooms, only about 81 percent of our sample is in the 11th grade; 8 percent of the respondents are in 12th grade; and 11 percent are in the 10th grade. Due to the small number of students from Asian, Hispanic/Latino, and Native American racial or ethnic backgrounds, for the purposes of this study we have broken down student respondents into the following three racial groups: white, African American, and other. All of the results from the survey are presented by these three categories (see Tables 2 and 3).

TABLE 2 *Race/Ethnicity Breakdown of the Sample*

African American	Asian American	Hispanic/ Latino	Native American	White	Other	Total
26.1%	2.1%	2.0%	1.8%	62.4%	5.67%	100%

TABLE 3 *Race/Ethnicity Breakdown of the Sample as Presented in This Study*

African American	White	Other	Total
26.13%	62.36%	11.51%	100%

Students come from families with widely varied levels of education—about one-sixth have graduate degrees, one-eighth are high school dropouts, and a there is a wide spread in between (see Table 4).

TABLE 4 *Parental Levels of Education*

Highest Level of Education Completed	Mother	Father
Grade School	2.3%	2.1%
Some High School	9.2%	10.4%
High School Graduate	26.6%	26.9%
Some College	17.2%	12.5%
College Graduate of Two-Year School	9.9%	6.3%
College Graduate of Four-Year School	11.7%	13.1%
Masters Degree	10.0%	9.2%
Graduate Degree	5.1%	6.1%
Not Sure	8.0%	13.5%
TOTAL	100%	100%

Results

*Students' Perception of the Level of Diversity in Their School and
Classrooms*

We asked students in the Jefferson County School District to describe the
level of diversity in their school and classes. Table 5 illustrates the extent
to which students report that their school environment is diverse. Among
the white students in the survey, close to 85 percent report that "quite a
few" or "about half" of the students in their schools are from other racial
or ethnic groups. Over 60 percent of African American students report
that "quite a few" or "about half" of the students are from other racial or
ethnic groups. Not surprisingly, a large percentage of students from other
racial or ethnic groups, including Asians, Hispanic/Latinos, and Native
Americans, report that "quite a few," "about half," and "most" of the students are from racial or ethnic groups that are different from their own.

TABLE 5 *Student Reports of School Racial Composition*

In My School:	White	Black	Other
A FEW students are from racial or ethnic groups that are different from my own.	10.1%	19.5%	17.8%
QUITE A FEW, BUT LESS THAN HALF the students are from racial or ethnic groups that are different from my own.	39.1%	27.4%	22.5%
ABOUT HALF the students are from racial or ethnic groups that are different from my own.	45.6%	35.3%	30.2%
MOST of the students are from racial or ethnic groups that are different from my own.	5.1%	17.8%	29.5%

In the classroom, perceptions of the level of diversity were quite different from perceptions of school-level diversity. In fact, all students report a higher percentage of segregation by race in all four subject areas
(social studies, English, math, and science). Overall, students in the district report higher levels of segregation within classrooms than by school.
This could be a result of academic tracking, but our study did not explore
the reasons for this pattern.

Very few students, however, report that their classes lack a substantial
presence of other racial groups. Therefore, while classes may be less diverse than the school as a whole, we are nonetheless exploring the experience of students attending diverse schools with fairly diverse classes.

I. Critical Thinking Skills: Classroom Experiences, Peer Interaction, and Student Learning—Are These Classes Diverse?

In *Bakke*, Justice Powell argued that the value of diversity is grounded in the experiences students from diverse racial and ethnic backgrounds bring to the learning environment and their interactions. Patricia Gurin, a professor of psychology at the University of Michigan, conducted an extensive longitudinal study at the University of Michigan, the results of which indicate that interaction with peers from diverse racial backgrounds—both in the classroom and informally—is positively associated with a host of learning outcomes.[30] Gurin argues that diverse universities offer a climate that produces active engagement, requiring students to think in deeper, more complex ways. By exposing students to multiple, even contradictory and unfamiliar perspectives about issues, they learn to think more critically.[31] Her results have important implications for the high school setting by suggesting that educational environments producing a source of multiple and different perspectives can increase students' level of critical thinking skills and establish more complex forms of learning.

All of these theories about how diversity functions in an educational environment rely on one factor—the actual presence of diversity in the classroom and curriculum. Therefore, to address the question of how diversity has affected the educational experiences of high school students in Louisville, the DAQ survey asked about the presence of diversity in the curriculum and about learning experiences that would promote the type of rich discussion and educational opportunities that lead to better educational outcomes. In other words, as research question one asks, "Are these classes and lessons diverse?"

Table 6 includes the results from a series of survey questions that address the level of diversity in the English and social studies curriculum and whether students perceive the curriculum as contributing to their overall understanding of different points of view. Several important observations can be made from these student responses. Students reported a greater level of diversity in the social studies/history curriculum than in the English curriculum, with 45 percent of the social studies students reporting that they frequently read about the experiences of many different cultures and racial and ethnic groups, but only 19 percent of the English students reporting in the "frequently" category. In general, students from all racial groups report about the same level of diversity in the curriculum, which is apparent in looking across the rows in Table 6, suggesting that different racial groups perceive the level and impact of curricular diversity in roughly the same way.

TABLE 6 *Curricular Diversity*

Q13. *In your social studies class, how often do you read about the experiences of many different cultures and racial and ethnic groups?*

	White (%)	African American (%)	Other (%)
Frequently	46.5	45.0	43.3
Sometimes	39.8	41.2	42.5
Rarely	10.5	11.4	11.0
Never	3.2	2.4	3.1

Q15. *Do you think these different viewpoints have helped you to better understand points of view different from your own?*

	White (%)	African American (%)	Other (%)
Helped a Lot	33.2	28.6	25.2
Helped Somewhat	54.2	60.1	57.7
Had No Effect	12.3	9.8	13.8
Had Negative Effect	0.3	1.4	3.3

Q17. *In your English class, how often do you read about the experiences of many different cultures and racial and ethnic groups?*

	White (%)	African American (%)	Other (%)
Frequently	19.5	19.2	17.2
Sometimes	47.2	36.1	43.8
Rarely	27.6	32.6	31.3
Never	5.7	12.0	7.8

Q18. *During classroom discussions in your English class, are racial issues discussed and explored?*

	White (%)	African American (%)	Other (%)
Frequently	9.7	11.3	17.2
Sometimes	35.7	33.8	30.5
Rarely	41.6	32.4	38.3
Never	13.1	22.5	14.1

About 90 percent of students from all racial and ethnic groups report that exposure in the curriculum to diverse cultures and experiences has helped them to better understand points of view different from their own. This skill is critical to understanding and living in the world both socially and economically, particularly as many future economic opportunities will involve contact with people who are from different cultures and may hold divergent worldviews. Later in this chapter, we explore students' reports of diversity in the curriculum and predict other educational outcomes, such as citizenship and attitudes toward living and working in multiracial settings.

We also studied the level of positive interaction among students from different racial and ethnic backgrounds. We asked students to describe their comfort level with various degrees of peer interaction in the classroom around issues of race. Table 7 outlines the results from this series of questions by racial group. A large majority of students (about 90%) from all racial groups report being comfortable or very comfortable discussing controversial issues related to race. Similarly, 95 percent of African American and 92 percent of white students report being comfortable or very comfortable working with students from different racial and ethnic backgrounds on group projects.

Ninety percent of all races felt comfortable or very comfortable learning about the differences among people from other racial and ethnic groups, and these results extend to working with students from other language backgrounds. These results suggest that the students in the Jefferson County school system are quite comfortable with peer interactions across races.

Clearly the level of diversity in these classes is quite high, as is the level of comfort discussing race-related issues. Thus the prerequisite of diversity exists. We explore in the following sections whether that diversity can influence student educational outcomes.

II. Educational Goals for the Future and College Access—
Are the perceived opportunities for learning similar across races?

A second educational outcome or goal measured by this survey is whether learning in a diverse educational setting affects students' educational goals and aspirations. In order to gauge the educational aspirations of high school students, we inquired about students' academic placement in a number of subject areas that lead to college entrance. The interpretation of our results is limited because we are unable to directly compare the results from Louisville (a racially diverse educational setting) with a less racially diverse educational setting. Thus, answering the question of how these aspirations differ by level of segregation is beyond our reach. However, if success is defined by equalizing opportunity, then aspirations—as an indicator of perceived opportunity—may also become more equal between racial and ethnic groups in desegregated environments. We refer to this as the perceived opportunity hypothesis. We test for this hypothesis in Tables 8 and 9 by comparing the responses to each educational aspiration question across races. If the responses to these questions differ sub-

TABLE 7   *Classroom Peer Interaction (How comfortable are you with the following in your classes?)*

Q19a. *Discussing controversial issues related to race?*

	White (%)	African American (%)	Other (%)
Very Comfortable	45.4	43.9	35.9
Comfortable	44.5	46.3	48.4
Not Very Comfortable	8.4	6.1	10.9
Does Not Apply	1.7	3.7	4.7

Q19b. *Working with students from different racial and ethnic backgrounds on group projects?*

	White (%)	African American (%)	Other (%)
Very Comfortable	61.8	60.0	44.5
Comfortable	30.8	34.9	45.3
Not Very Comfortable	7.1	3.1	6.3
Does Not Apply	0.3	2.0	3.9

Q19c. *Learning about the differences between people from other racial and ethnic groups?*

	White (%)	African American (%)	Other (%)
Very Comfortable	61.2	61.3	52.3
Comfortable	32.4	35.3	39.1
Not Very Comfortable	5.5	1.7	5.5
Does Not Apply	0.9	1.7	3.1

Q19d. *Working with students from other language backgrounds?*

	White (%)	African American (%)	Other (%)
Very Comfortable	45.8	48.5	39.8
Comfortable	40.4	37.6	46.9
Not Very Comfortable	10.7	9.5	8.6
Does Not Apply	3.1	4.4	4.7

stantially across races, this supports an interpretation that perceived opportunities had not been equalized. However, if the answers across racial categories are similar, this supports the interpretation that perceived opportunities are more equal.

The responses to questions about educational aspirations in Tables 8 and 9 reveal close similarities by racial group that imply an equality of perceived opportunity, possibly fostered by the implementation of the desegregation plan. For example, approximately 50 to 60 percent of stu-

TABLE 8 *Educational Aspirations (Please tell us how interested you are in the following:)*

Q22a. *Taking a foreign language after high school.*

	White (%)	African American (%)	Other (%)
Very Interested	13.3	14.7	21.4
Interested	17.6	26.4	24.6
Somewhat Interested	29.2	32.2	27.0
Not Interested	39.9	26.7	27.0

Q22b. *Taking an honors or AP mathematics course.*

	White (%)	African American (%)	Other (%)
Very Interested	31.9	23.6	27.8
Interested	25.0	31.2	27.0
Somewhat Interested	19.9	24.7	21.4
Not Interested	23.1	20.5	23.8

Q22c. *Taking an honors or AP English course.*

	White (%)	African American (%)	Other (%)
Very Interested	31.9	29.9	31.7
Interested	29.6	30.6	26.2
Somewhat Interested	19.5	25.4	23.8
Not Interested	18.9	14.1	18.3

Q22e. *Going to a four-year college.*

	White (%)	African American (%)	Other(%)
Very Interested	63.5	62.0	47.6
Interested	21.2	23.6	31.0
Somewhat Interested	8.7	11.0	10.3
Not Interested	6.7	3.4	11.1

dents from all racial groups indicate that they are "very interested" or "interested" in taking honors or Advanced Placement (AP) mathematics or English courses. Also, roughly even numbers of all students are "interested" or "very interested" in taking a foreign language after high school. A remarkable 80 to 85 percent of students report an interest in attending a four-year college (See Table 8).

The consistency of these numbers across groups is very important and begs the question, "How do these results compare to those in districts with higher levels of segregation?" Unfortunately, we cannot answer this

TABLE 9   *Access to College Information*

Q10. How strongly have teachers, counselors, or other adults in this school encouraged you to attend college?

	White (%)	African American (%)	Other (%)
Strongly encouraged	63.9	58.2	61.4
Somewhat encouraged	28.9	31.7	33.9
Neither encouraged nor discouraged	6.7	9.8	2.4
Discouraged	0.4	0.3	2.4

Q11. How much information about college admissions have your teachers, counselors, or other adults in this school given you? (such as SAT, ACT, financial aid, etc.)

	White (%)	African American (%)	Other (%)
A lot	38.1	39.5	31.8
Some	41.5	39.1	44.2
A Little	15.8	18.0	19.4
None	4.6	3.4	4.7

Q12. How strongly have your teachers, counselors, or other adults in this school encouraged you to take honors and/or AP classes?

	White (%)	African American (%)	Other (%)
Very Strongly	25.8	20.5	18.6
Somewhat strongly	47.1	39.9	49.6
Not at All	26.2	38.2	29.5
Discouraged	1.0	1.4	2.3

until surveys of other districts are complete. However, these results are quite suggestive and show that within this desegregated district the educational aspirations of the different races are quite similar.

Providing access to college is also an important goal for most high schools. Do students in the Jefferson County Schools report adequate support and access to information about college? More important, where there is such racial uniformity in interest to pursue college, is the access to information equally uniform for all racial and ethnic groups? Among white students, 93 percent report having school staff encouragement to attend college; African American students report a similar 90 percent; and among students from other racial and ethnic backgrounds, 95 percent report encouragement. Approximately 80 percent of all students report receiving a lot or some information about college admissions procedures, and less than 5 percent of all students report receiving no information about college admissions.

However, students report different levels of encouragement to enroll in an AP or honors class by racial group. Among white students, 73 percent report that teachers or other school officials encourage them to take AP or honors classes, 68 percent of students from other racial and ethnic groups report this type of encouragement, and only 60 percent of African American students report having teachers or other school staff encourage them to enroll in an AP or honors course. In terms of aspirations, the differences between racial groups are few, whereas in terms of encouragement to enter AP courses, more important differences exist. However, it is important to note that a significant majority of African American, white, and other minority students are being encouraged to attend gateway classes that may ultimately lead to better college or postsecondary education attendance for all racial groups.

Regression Analysis

To complement the findings in Tables 8 and 9, the OLS analysis allows us to see whether there are substantial and statistically significant differences in education aspirations across race, gender, and immigrant status.[32] We are also able to focus on the importance of features such as institutional support (SUPPORT) and curricular diversity (CURDIV) in fostering higher educational aspirations. In addition, by including two separate interaction terms between our school predictors—support for higher educational aspirations and curricular diversity—and the dummy variable (BLACK), we are able to directly test whether these school predictors are statistically different based on race. For instance, a statistically significant and negative coefficient on the interaction between BLACK and SUPPORT would indicate that at higher levels of institutional support black students had lower levels of higher educational aspirations than white students. However, by contrast, a nonsignificant coefficient on this interaction term would suggest that the effect of institutional support worked the same way among black and white students with similar levels of support leading to similar levels of higher educational aspirations, lending support to our perceived opportunity hypothesis.

Results from both the regression analysis and students' straight responses to the survey questions reveal important findings about higher educational aspirations. Table 10 details the models fit to estimate the effect of curricular diversity (CURDIV) and school support (SUPPORT) on students' higher educational aspirations. First notice that in all models (1)–(7) we see that teacher and school staff support does have a positive impact on Louisville students' higher education aspirations. The construct SUPPORT is statistically significant to the $p < .001$ level, controlling for students' background characteristics and curricular diversity. Second, diversity in the curriculum does not have a statistically significant impact on higher education aspirations, when controlling for SUPPORT. Note also that being female in Louisville does not have a statistically significant impact on higher education aspirations.

We also tested the potential differences by race toward higher education aspirations and found that being black in Louisville does not have a significant impact, negative or positive, on higher education aspirations. This confirms what was found in Tables 8 and 9—that black and white students have similar higher educational aspirations—and lends more support to the equally perceived opportunity hypothesis. Finally, we tested the two-way interactions between BLACK and SUPPORT and BLACK and CURDIV to see whether the effect of these two constructs on higher education aspirations (HIEDASP) may differ for black students in the district. Results from the regression models where interactions were tested (models (5), (6), and (7)) do not reveal significant differences by race. This further supports our initial findings from students' responses on the survey. Teacher and school support toward higher education aspirations do have an impact, but this does not differ for black and white students in Louisville.

III. Principles of Citizenship and Democracy—Can school-level diversity change student attitudes about their educational aspirations?

As the nation becomes increasingly multiracial, it is important to understand how the educational environment plays a role in preparing students to live and work among people different from themselves. Do students develop a consciousness of the importance of interacting with people of different backgrounds, and does this have an impact on their future goals? Gurin's work also proposes that students who experience diversity in classroom settings and in informal interactions on campus show the most engagement in various forms of citizenship and the most engagement with people from different races and cultures, both during college and beyond.[33] The first set of questions in Table 11 measures student attitudes toward the importance of working in a multiracial setting. The second set examines how students' high school experiences affected their sense of current events and political/social involvement.

In the first set of questions we examined whether students in Louisville felt prepared to work and live in the diverse settings in which they will increasingly find themselves. We recognize that preparation may come from the home even more than it may from the school. Thus, we attempted to isolate the experience in school from other experiences that may contribute to students' overall attitudes about working in a multiracial setting. The set of questions presented in Table 11 aims to identify students' comfort level with, preparation for, and intention to operate in settings that are racially and ethnically diverse. A basic function of schools is preparing students to work and live among people different from themselves, and this level of preparation and comfort is an educational outcome of diverse school settings.

The results from Louisville students are overwhelmingly positive in this area. Over 85 percent of all students believe that they are prepared to work in a diverse job setting and that they are likely to do so in the future. More than 80 percent of African American and white students report that their school experience has helped them to work more effectively with and get along with members of other races and ethnic groups. Finally, over 90 percent of all students report that they would be comfortable working for a supervisor of a different racial or ethnic background. These results suggest that schools, which are often the place where the changing demographics of the nation are most pronounced, can help to produce young adults who are ready to operate in settings populated by people from a variety of backgrounds.

We wanted to take this hypothesis further to ascertain what types of citizens in a diverse America these schools are producing. We chose to ask students about how their high school experiences may contribute to their interests in a host of democratic principles and actions, all of which are central to the mission of public schooling in a democracy (see Table 12). The responses to these questions were encouraging, with 57 percent of white students, 65 percent of African American students, and 51 percent of other minorities stating that their interest in volunteering in their community has increased. In addition, 47 percent, 60 percent, and 45 percent of whites, African Americans, and other minorities, respectively, responded that their interest in participating in elections had increased. Finally, about 60 percent of African Americans and half of whites and other minority groups said that their interest in taking on leadership roles in their communities had increased.

While it is clear that without a comparison to less diverse districts these student responses cannot be directly attributable to the desegregation plan, it is important to note the results and think about them in the context of questions mentioned earlier, in Table 7. If these students feel "very prepared" to work within diverse environments, work more cooperatively with other racial groups, *and* are more inclined to be involved in

TABLE 10   Results from Regression Models of Higher Education Aspirations (HIEDASP)

	Model (1)	Model (2)	Model (3)	Model (4)	Model (5)	Model (6)	Model (7)
IMMIG	0.682 (0.405)~	0.825 (0.407)*	0.677 (0.408)	0.838 (0.411)*	0.836 (0.412)*	0.838 (0.411)*	0.836 (0.411)*
FEMALE	0.316 (0.180)~	0.167 (0.177)	0.260 (0.182)	0.145 (0.179)	0.151 (0.180)	0.146 (0.179)	0.151 (0.180)
BLACK	0.225 (0.203)	0.354 (0.200)~	0.300 (0.206)	0.385 (0.203)~	0.054 (0.718)	(0.288) (0.780)	0.043 (0.943)
SUPPORT		0.405 (0.051)***		0.400 (0.053)***	0.400 (0.053)***	0.396 (0.062)***	0.400 (0.062)***
CURDIV			0.076 (0.033)*	0.011 (0.034)	0.001 (0.039)	0.011 (0.034)	0.001 (0.040)
BLKCDIV					0.035 (0.072)		0.034 (0.074)
BLKSUPP						0.015 (0.115)	0.002 (0.119)
#of Obs.	1094	1071	1069	1049	1049	1049	1049
F-stat.	2.34~	17.81***	3.01*	13.85***	11.57***	11.54***	9.91***
R-squared	0.01	0.06	0.01	0.06	0.06	0.06	0.06

Standard errors in parentheses.   Significance levels: ~$p < .10$; *$p < .05$; **$p < .01$; ***$p < .001$

TABLE 11 *Attitudes about Working in a Multiracial Work Setting*

Q23. After high school, how prepared do you feel to work in a job setting where people are of a different racial or ethnic background than you are?

	White (%)	African American (%)	Other (%)
Very Prepared	55.1	54.9	55.6
Somewhat Prepared	40.0	39.9	35.7
Not Prepared	3.3	4.1	5.6
Reluctant to Do So	1.6	1.0	3.2

Q24. Do you believe your school experiences have helped you, or will help you in the future, to work more effectively and to get along better with members of other races and ethnic groups?

	White (%)	African American (%)	Other (%)
Helped a Lot	35.2	36.1	30.2
Helped Somewhat	45.6	46.7	35.7
Had No Effect	15.9	14.8	30.2
Hurt My Ability	3.3	2.4	4.0

Q26. How likely do you think it is that you will work with people of different racial and ethnic backgrounds?

	White (%)	African American (%)	Other (%)
Very Likely	43.4	49.5	44.1
Likely	42.2	39.2	39.4
Not Likely	6.0	8.9	11.8
Do Not Know	8.4	2.4	4.7

Q27. How comfortable would you be with a work supervisor who was of a different racial or ethnic background than you are?

	White (%)	African American (%)	Other (%)
Very Comfortable	58.6	50.9	53.6
Somewhat Comfortable	35.3	46.2	35.2
Not Comfortable	4.0	1.8	7.2
Reluctant	2.2	1.1	4.0

their community in positions of leadership, this has profound implications for the level and direction of political and economic discourse in our country. But can schools effect these types of changes on students? We can answer this question and assess whether the actual classroom environment has had an impact on these students' attitudes toward members

TABLE 12   *Attitudes about Civic Participation (Have your high school experiences increased your interest in:)*

Q28a. Current events?

	White (%)	African American (%)	Other (%)
Greatly Increased	20.4	23.5	20.9
Somewhat Increased	55.1	52.2	51.9
No Effect	22.9	22.9	22.5
Decreased	1.6	1.4	4.7

Q28c. Volunteering in your community?

	White (%)	African American (%)	Other (%)
Greatly Increased	20.8	20.3	14.8
Somewhat Increased	36.6	44.7	37.5
No Effect	39.5	31.3	43.0
Decreased	3.1	3.8	4.7

Q28e. Participating in elections?

	White (%)	African American (%)	Other (%)
Greatly Increased	14.6	19.1	16.3
Somewhat Increased	32.4	41.7	29.5
No Effect	49.3	36.1	48.1
Decreased	3.7	3.1	6.2

Q28g. Taking on leadership roles in your school?

	White (%)	African American (%)	Other (%)
Greatly Increased	28.9	39.5	20.9
Somewhat Increased	38.0	39.5	44.2
No Effect	29.7	19.6	27.1
Decreased	3.4	1.4	7.8

Q28k. Taking on leadership roles in your community?

	White (%)	African American (%)	Other (%)
Greatly Increased	18.8	27.1	16.3
Somewhat Increased	33.2	36.0	31.0
No Effect	43.6	32.2	46.5
Decreased	4.4	4.8	6.2

Q28l. Voting for a senator or president from a minority racial or ethnic group?

	White (%)	African American (%)	Other (%)
Greatly Increased	12.8	22.6	10.9
Somewhat Increased	25.2	34.9	36.4
No Effect	54.1	36.6	43.4
Decreased	7.8	5.8	9.3

of other racial groups using a simple OLS regression to answer the question: Is the level of curricular diversity related to students' attitudes toward living and working in multiracial settings? As the results in Table 13 seem to indicate, the answer to this question is "yes."

Regression Analysis

Table 13 lists the results of a linear regression model fitted to the outcome LIVE_WORK, which is a composite similar to the HIEDASP variable adddressed in Table 10. LIVE_WORK describes students' attitudes toward living and working in multiracial settings. The regression analysis resulting in Table 13 uses LIVE_WORK as an outcome variable and uses the same predictors as the previous regression model: immigrant status, gender, race, school support for higher educational aspirations, curricular diversity, and the interactions between race and the school variables. Results from Table 13 indicate that there is, in fact, a positive relationship between perceived curricular diversity (CURDIV) and attitudes toward living and working in multiracial settings (LIVE_WORK), since the coefficient on CURDIV in model (7) is positive (b = 0.425) and statistically significant (p < .001). In fact, the effect of perceived curricular diversity is statistically significant in all models (1)–(7) to the p < .001 level, which indicates the robustness of this finding. This finding is very important. It seems to indicate that school variables—as measured by students' perception of a school's curricular diversity—can affect the attitudes of students on this particular outcome. If perceived curricular diversity can affect students' thinking and attitudes, what about student diversity? Again, this study opens up intriguing possibilities that can only be explored by surveying multiple districts with very different levels of segregation.

It is also interesting to note that being an immigrant, a female, and black are all strongly related to attitudes toward living and working in multiracial settings, even controlling for perceived curricular diversity and teacher support. Teacher and school staff support is also positively associated with higher intentions and better attitudes toward living and working in multiracial settings. Finally, in models 5, 6, and 7, we tested for two-way interactions between each of our question predictors and race. This analysis reveals a statistically significant interaction between BLACK and CURDIV, indicating that the impact of perceived curricular diversity on attitudes toward living and working in multiracial settings differs for black and white students. The fact that the coefficient on the CURDIV*BLACK interaction is negative (b = –0.312) and statistically significant (p < 0.01) implies that the relationship between CURDIV and LIVE_WORK is steeper for white students than black students, even

TABLE 13 *Results from Regression Models on Attitudes toward Living and Working in MultiRacial Setting (LIVE_WORK)*

	Model (1)	Model (2)	Model (3)	Model (4)	Model (5)	Model (6)	Model (7)
IMMIG	2.324 (0.659)***	2.379 (0.671)***	2.136 (0.683)**	2.201 (0.668)**	2.192 (0.666)**	2.202 (0.669)**	2.195 (0.667)**
FEMALE	1.621 (0.299)***	1.454 (0.297)***	1.453 (0.295)***	1.354 (0.296)***	1.315 (0.296)***	1.367 (0.297)***	1.320 (0.295)***
BLACK	1.805 (0.333)***	1.995 (0.332)***	1.984 (0.330)***	2.088 (0.331)***	4.905 (1.200)***	1.871 (1.297)	4.171 (1.560)**
SUPPORT		0.607 (0.087)***		0.470 (0.090)***	0.457 (0.089)***	0.450 (0.105)***	0.427 (0.105)***
CURDIV			0.401 (0.054)***	0.331 (0.056)***	0.418 (0.066)***	0.332 (0.056)***	0.425 (0.067)***
BLKCDIV					−0.293 (0.120)*		−0.312 (0.123)**
BLKSUPP						0.033 (0.192)	0.140 (0.196)
#of Obs	1001	981	977	959	959	959	959
F-stat.	23.82***	29.98***	31.28***	29.93***	26.07***	24.92***	22.40***
R-squared	0.07	0.11	0.11	0.14	0.14	0.14	0.14

Standard errors in parentheses. Significance levels: ~p < .10; *p < .05; p < .01; ***p < .001

though, overall, black students in Louisville indicate a stronger intention to live and work in multiracial settings than their white counterparts.

Blacks indicate higher levels of desire to live and work in diverse settings than white students. However, the impact of perceived curricular diversity on intention to live and work in diverse settings is greater for white students. This finding has some important policy implications because it suggests that increasing the diversity of a school can narrow the gap between the attitudes of whites and blacks toward living and working in multicultural environments.

Conclusion

In the past few years, federal district courts have struck down a number of desegregation plans. However, they have been doing so without good information about the potential educational benefits of racially diverse schools. With this survey, we attempt to take the first steps in assessing whether diversity enhances educational outcomes in measurable ways. We relied on survey data from one of the nation's most integrated school districts, the Jefferson County School District in Kentucky. The survey questions Louisville students answered were designed to discern how high school students attending interracial schools believed that the diversity of their schools affected what they have learned, their educational aspirations, and their plans for the future.

In order to explore the concept of diversity benefits, we looked at three specific educational outcomes: 1) peer interaction and critical thinking; 2) educational goals for the future and college access; and 3) principles of citizenship and democracy. By answering three specific research questions involving these outcomes, we've established several key facts about Louisville.

Our findings suggest the important impact of desegregation on this environment. First, in Jefferson County schools there are high levels of diversity in both curricular and social interactions. Second, there is a high level of equality between races in the perceived educational opportunities for students. Finally, we've established that a school's diversity can have an effect on educational outcomes, specifically the outcome of willingness to live and work in diverse environments. In these three results, we see important educational gains that may be attributed to schooling in diverse environments.

In addition, results from the survey and from our analysis of the data indicate that both black and white students attending high school in the Jefferson County schools report benefiting greatly from the diversity of their schools. Students in Louisville report strong educational benefits in all three categories: critical thinking skills, future educational goals, and principles of citizenship. Furthermore, we see a strong uniformity in responses by racial and ethnic groups that provides evidence of a successful integration plan, as defined by greater equalization of opportunity between racial and ethnic groups in desegregated environments. Most important, we see that diversity has a positive impact on learning, on student attitudes, and on important democratic principles. Our results strongly support the findings of the Supreme Court in *Bakke* that diverse educational settings foster stronger learning experiences for all students and help to prepare them to live and work in a multiracial society.

Notes

1. Gary Orfield and John T. Yun, *Resegregation in American Schools* (Cambridge, MA: The Civil Rights Project, Harvard University, June, 1999).
2. Gary Orfield, Susan Eaton, and the Harvard Project on School Desegregation, eds., *Dismantling Desegregation: The Quiet Reversal of Brown v. Board of Education* (New York: New Press, 1996).
3. Orfield et al., *Dismantling Desegregation*.
4. Orfield et al., *Dismantling Desegregation*.
5. Orfield et al., *Dismantling Desegregation*. The exposure index can be interpreted as the percentage of white students in a school attended by the "average" or "typical" black student. See Otis Dudley Duncan and Beverly Duncan, "A Methodological Analysis of Segregation Indexes," *American Sociological Review, 20* (1955), 210–217.
6. Orfield et al., *Dismantling Desegregation*.
7. Orfield et al., *Dismantling Desegregation*.
8. William L. Taylor and Edwin Darden, "Guidance to School Boards on Race and Student Assignment," *Inside School Law, 1,* No. 1 (Winter 1999), pp. 2–5.
9. Orfield et al., *Dismantling Desegregation*.
10. *Regents of the University of California v. Bakke,* 438 U.S. 265 (1978).
11. *Wessmann v. Gittens,* 160 F.3d 790 (1st Cir. 1999).
12. Taylor and Darden, "Guidance to School Boards."
13. Dean of Admissions Fred L. Glimp, "Final Report to the Faculty of Arts and Sciences," *65 Official Register of Harvard University, 25* (1968), 104–105.
14. See Janet Ward Schofield, "Review of Research on School Desegregation's Impact on Elementary and Secondary School Students," in *Handbook of Research on Multicultural Education*, ed. James A. Banks & Cherry A. McGee Banks (New York: Simon & Schuster MacMillan, 1995), pp. 597–616; Janet Ward Schofield, "Maximizing the Benefits of Student Diversity: Lessons from School Desegregation Research," in this volume; Jomills Henry Braddock, "The Perpetuation of Segregation Across Levels of Education: A Behavior Assessment of the Contact-Hypothesis," *Sociology of Education, 53* (1980), 178–186; Amy Stuart Wells and Robert L. Crain, "Perpetuation Theory and the Long-Term Effects of School Desegregation," *Review of Educational Research, 64* (1994), 531–555; James M. McPartland and Jomills Henry Braddock, "Going to College and Getting a Good Job: The Impact of Desegregation," in *Effective School Desegregation: Equality, Quality, and Feasibility,* ed. Willis D. Hawley (London: Sage, 1981); Patricia Gurin, "The Compelling Need for Diversity in Higher Education," expert testimony in *Gratz et al. v. Bollinger et al.* (No 97-75231 E.D. Mich.,

filed 1997) and *Grutter et al. v. Bollinger et al.* (No 97-75928 E.D. Mich., filed 1997), 1999.

15. See Robert L. Crain and Rita E. Mahard, "The Effect of Research Methodology on Desegregation Achievement Studies: A Meta-Analysis," *American Journal of Sociology, 88* (1983), 839–854; Robert L. Crain, "School Integration and the Academic Achievement of Negroes," *Sociology of Education, 44* (1971), 1–26; Schofield, "Review of Research," "Maximizing the Benefits."

16. Wells and Crain, "Perpetuation Theory"; Orfield et al., *Dismantling Desegregation.*

17. Marvin P. Dawkins, "Black Students' Occupational Expectations: A National Study of the Impact of School Desegregation," *Urban Education, 18* (1983), 98–113; Jon W. Hoelter, "Segregation and Rationality in Black Status Aspiration Processes," *Sociology of Education, 55* (1982), 31–39.

18. Braddock, "The Perpetuation of Segregation"; McPartland and Braddock, "Going to College"; Wells and Crain, "Perpetuation Theory."

19. Braddock, "The Perpetuation of Segregation"; McPartland and Braddock, "Going to College"; Wells and Crain, "Perpetuation Theory."

20. Gurin, "The Compelling Need."

21. Schofield, "Review of Research," "Maximizing the Benefits"; William Trent, *Desegregation Analysis Report* (New York: Legal Defense and Education Fund, 1991); Robert L. Crain, "School Integration and Occupational Achievement of Negroes," *American Journal of Sociology, 75* (1970), 593–606; Crain, "School Integration and the Academic Achievement of Negroes."

22. Wilkerson and Associates, "Student Assignment Survey: Summary of July 1996 Findings."

23. Wilkerson and Associates, "Student Assignment Survey."

24. Wilkerson and Associates, "Student Assignment Survey."

25. Researchers from around the country were brought together by The Civil Rights Project, Harvard University, in November 1999 to develop the DAQ instrument.

26. The DAQ instrument will be used in several school districts around the country during the 2000–2001 academic year.

27. There are a total of 6,082 juniors in the Jefferson County School District. The sample drawn was to include one-sixth of the junior population in the district (1,014). The sampling frame included all schools in the district, and the size of the sample within each school was proportional to the school size. The final sample includes 1,128 students, but due to mixed-grade classrooms there are 913 juniors. In this analysis we have chosen to use all of the data, including the 125 tenth graders and 90 twelfth graders in the sample.

28. Abdelmonem A. Afifi and Virginia Clark, *Computer-Aided Multivariate Analysis,* 3rd ed. (London: Chapman & Hall, 1996).

29. We tested for the significance of mother's and father's education, found that they were not significant in any of the models, and thus dropped them from the final analysis.

30. Gurin, "The Compelling Need." Also, a recent study of Harvard and Michigan law school students found powerful effects on learning in various fields of legal studies. See Gary Orfield and Dean Whitla, "Diversity and Legal Education: Student Experiences in Leading Law Schools," in this volume.

31. Ibid.

32. The equations we use for all of these analyses are of the form:

Outcome $= \alpha + \beta_1(\text{IMMIGRANT}) + \beta_2(\text{FEMALE}) + \beta_3(\text{BLACK}) + \beta_4(\text{SUPPORT})$
$+ \beta_5(\text{CURDIV}) + \beta_6(\text{BLACK*CURDIV}) + \beta_7(\text{BLACK*SUPPORT}) + \gamma$

33. Gurin, "The Compelling Need."

Appendix

The composite variables were all constructed the same way. We examined the items in the DAQ and determined which questions represented the appropriate constructs. For each of the constructs we calculated the Cronbach's alpha reliability and performed a principal components analysis. From Cronbach's analysis it was clear that these questions were highly correlated with one another. None of our prospective constructs scored reliabilities below 0.65. Principal components analysis showed that a simple additive construction (each construct equally weighted and summed together) would result in a construct that corresponded to the first eigenvalue for the construct, and would account for over 40 percent of the variance in each of our perspective constructs.

TABLE A   *Description of Outcome Variables in the Analysis of Diversity Effects*

Variable Name	Description	Corresponding Questions (answer choices provided)
HIEDASP	Higher Education Aspirations	How interested are you in the following: *(Very Interested—Interested—Somewhat Interested—Not Interested)* Taking a foreign language after high school? Taking an honors or AP mathematics course? Taking an honors or AP English course? Going to a four-year college?
LIVE_WORK	Interest and intention to live and work in multiracial setting as an adult	How interested are you in the following: *(Very Interested—Interested—Somewhat Interested—Not Interested)* Taking a course focusing on other cultures after high school? Traveling outside of the United States? Attending a racially/ethnically diverse college campus? Living in a racially/ethnically diverse neighborhood when you are an adult? Working in a racially/ethnically diverse setting when you are an adult? How prepared do you feel to work in a job setting where people are of a different racial or ethnic background than you are? *(Very Prepared— Prepared —Somewhat Prepared—Reluctant to do so)* How important is it for you to attend a college that has a racially and ethnically diverse student body? *(Extremely Important—Important—Somewhat Important—Not Important)* How likely do you think it is that you will work with people of racial and ethnic backgrounds different from your own? *(Very Likely—Likely—Not Likely—Do Not Know)*

TABLE B   *Description of Predictor Variables in the Analysis of Diversity Effects*

Variable Name	Description	Corresponding Questions (answer choices provided)
SUPPORT	Sense of school/ teacher support to pursue higher education	How strongly have teachers, counselors, or other adults in this school encouraged you to attend college? *(Strongly Encouraged—Somewhat Encouraged—Neither Encouraged nor Discouraged—Discouraged)*
		How much information about college admissions have your teachers, counselors, or other adults in this school given you? *(A Lot—Some—A Little—None)*
		How strongly have your teachers, counselors, or other adults in this school encouraged you to take honors and/or AP classes? *(Very Strongly—Somewhat Strongly—Not at All—Discouraged)*
CURDIV	Curricular diversity in English and social science classes as measured by course readings/ materials and classroom discussion	In your social studies or history class, how often do you read about the experiences of different cultures and racial and ethnic groups? *(Frequently—Sometimes—Rarely—Never)*
		During classroom discussions in your social studies or history class, how often is a range of viewpoints expressed about the topics you are studying? *(Frequently—Sometimes—Rarely—Never)*
		During classroom discussions in your social studies or history class, how often are racial issues discussed and explored? *(Frequently—Sometimes—Rarely—Never)*
		In your English class, how often do you read about the experiences of different cultures and racial and ethnic groups? *(Frequently—Sometimes—Rarely—Never)*
		During classroom discussions in your English class, how often are racial issues discussed and explored? *(Frequently—Sometimes—Rarely—Never)*

CHAPTER 6

Diversity and Legal Education: Student Experiences in Leading Law Schools

GARY ORFIELD
DEAN WHITLA

Introduction

For more than two decades, the legal foundation for the policies that have permitted the integration of highly selective universities and professional schools has rested on the U.S. Supreme Court's 1978 *Bakke* decision. Justice Lewis Powell's controlling opinion upheld race-conscious admissions policies on the grounds that they support the important goal of producing a diverse student body representing many kinds of experience and points of view, which enriches the discussions and learning experiences on campus.[1] While the value and importance of this goal seemed obvious to many within the university community, the academic world had done little to demonstrate how diversity works on campus and what difference it makes. Recently, there have been sharp challenges from opponents of civil rights, and in 1996 a federal appeals court outlawed affirmative action in Texas in a decision that claimed that student diversity had no educational benefits. There are now a number of lawsuits and referendum campaigns around the country in which the impact of diversity is an important legal or political issue. Direct evidence on the impact of diversity on education is now essential.

This study explores the impact of diversity by asking students how it has influenced their educational experiences. Most discussions about the effects of diversity are simply assertions; people with differing ideologies come up with highly divergent arguments. If a central question is whether or not racial diversity broadens the intellectual life of the university and enriches the educational experience in the student community, there are only two reliable sources—the students and the faculty. This study reports on the experiences of students captured in a high response-rate survey administered by the Gallup Poll at two of the nation's most competitive law schools, Harvard Law School and the University of Michigan Law School, as well as through data collected through an email/Internet survey at five other law schools. The data indicate that the Supreme Court was correct in its conclusions about the impact of diversity in *Bakke* and earlier higher education decisions. It spells out how and in what settings students experience different educational outcomes. The study also explores the differences among students—the experiences of those who believe diversity has a negative influence, as well as the large majority who see important gains.

Trends in Access

There have been vast changes in the level of access to college for minority students since the 1960s, with very encouraging trends over much of that period. Between 1972 and 1996, the percentage of blacks enrolling in college the fall after completing high school rose from 44.6 percent to 56.0 percent, and the percentage of Hispanics enrolling rose from 45.0 percent to 50.8 percent. The percentage of white enrollment rose from 49.7 percent to 67.4 percent. The racial gap between the percentage of black and white high school graduates going on to college was smallest in the mid-1970s. The gap began to widen after *Bakke*, and a variety of policy changes and scholarship cutbacks made college less accessible in the 1980s.

In 1971, among young adults age twenty-five to twenty-nine, 11.5 percent of blacks and 10.5 percent of Latinos had college degrees, compared to 22.0 percent of whites. By 1998, the black rate was up to 17.9 percent and the Latino number was 16.5 percent, but the white rate was 34.5 percent. The gap had been 10.5 percent between blacks and whites in 1971, but grew to 16.6 percent twenty-seven years later. The black enrollment rate actually declined during the 1980s, but then began to grow again.[2] Even before the rollback of college civil rights policies, higher education was far from the ultimate goal of equal access. Professional education also experienced substantial changes. Law school enrollment grew from 1 percent black in 1960 to 7.5 percent in 1995.[3]

Highly selective colleges and professional schools tended to have very small numbers of minority students until the late 1960s and early 1970s. Their normal recruitment and selection systems did not produce significant minority enrollments, and many went through the peak of the civil rights era with few minority students.[4] During the late 1960s, many universities decided to undertake systematic efforts to increase their minority enrollments, often spurred by the social upheaval of urban riots, student protests, federal policy, and the assassination of Martin Luther King Jr. In the Ivy League, the percentage of black students grew between 1967 and 1976 from 1.7 percent to 4.5 percent.[5] There were similar or larger changes in a number of highly selective public universities. These significant changes, at a time when access to leading universities was becoming much more competitive and the country more conservative, led to opposition.

The Legal Issues

Affirmative action in selective universities and professional schools is generally voluntary rather than required by a court order or administrative directive. Courts unquestionably have power to impose race-conscious remedies in cases where a university or school has been found guilty of intentional segregation, but lawsuits and findings of this kind are rare for selective universities outside the South. Aside from southern institutions, where there may be a history of overt discrimination that has never been corrected,[6] there has long been uncertainty and dispute over the degree to which race can or should be taken into account.

The federal courts have raised challenging standards for maintaining racially targeted civil rights remedies. In the past decade, there have been serious battles over such remedies in affirmative action employment, in minority contracting, in voting rights, and in school desegregation. There has been a particularly bitter battle during the past several years over the continuation or abandonment of policies and practices aimed at maintaining integration in the nation's selective colleges and universities. This is a continuation of the intense fight in the 1970s, which led a deeply divided Supreme Court to permit continuation of affirmative action in colleges and universities by a single vote in the 1978 *Bakke* decision.

The Court was so fragmented in *Bakke* between supporters and opponents of race-conscious policies that the case was decided by Justice Lewis Powell, a conservative Virginian appointed by President Richard Nixon. Six of the nine justices wrote opinions in the case, reflecting the divided perspectives. Powell's decisive opinion recognized only one justification for continuing the policy—the pursuit of diversity. Today, only one of the justices who wrote opinions in the *Bakke* case remain on the Court—Justice John Paul Stevens—and the only other continuing member from that time is Chief Justice William Rehnquist, who voted against the University of Cal-

ifornia policy. Since 1989, there have been a string of Supreme Court decisions narrowing—though not forbidding—policies based on race-conscious
remedies in other arenas. However, the Supreme Court has not undertaken
to review any of the major higher education cases. In the lower courts there
have been only two sweeping decisions concluding that *Bakke* is no longer
valid, another strongly attacking the validity of the diversity justification,
and several other recent decisions concluding that *Bakke* is still the law of
the land. Federal courts have outlawed diversity-based, race-conscious admissions: in the 1996 *Hopwood* decision rejecting the University of Texas
Law School's policies and forbidding any consideration of race in admissions, and the August 2000 Georgia case prohibiting the affirmative admissions policies of the University of Georgia.[7] Referenda have ended it in two
others. The California referendum forbidding affirmative action at public
universities has been accepted as valid by a federal court. In Florida the state
government ended affirmative action in 2000.

The basic legal requirements for defending race-conscious policies in
this period of legal development are that the policy responds to a "compelling interest" of the institution that cannot be achieved by another
method and that it is "narrowly tailored" to achieve that interest. In this
setting, lawyers and university officials have looked to Justice Powell's
opinion upholding *Bakke* as providing the best road map to what the
courts might uphold as a compelling interest. In his decision, Powell concluded that "the attainment of a diverse student body . . . clearly is a constitutionally permissible goal for an institution of higher education. Academic freedom, though not a specifically enumerated constitutional
right, long has been viewed as a special concern of the First Amendment.
The freedom of a university to make its own judgments as to education includes the selection of its student body." Powell quoted the Court's 1957
decision in *Sweezy v. New Hampshire:* "It is the business of a university to
provide that atmosphere which is most conducive to speculation, experiment and creation. It is an atmosphere in which there prevail 'the four essential freedoms' of a university—to determine for itself on academic
grounds who may teach, what may be taught, how it shall be taught, and
who may be admitted to study." Powell continued: "The atmosphere . . .
so essential to the quality of higher education is widely believed to be promoted by a diverse student body as the Court . . . noted in *Keyishian,* it is
not too much to say that the 'nation's future depends upon leaders
trained through wide exposure' to the ideas and mores of students as diverse as this Nation of many peoples."

Justice Powell also pointed to another important precedent—the
higher education decisions that had set the stage for *Brown v. Board of Edu-*

cation. The NAACP first won Supreme Court decisions against state-mandated educational segregation at the graduate level, where the Court recognized that associations, contacts, and exchanges with other students were a vital part of the preparation for a profession and could not possibly be equal within segregated institutions. In *Sweatt v. Painter,* the Court made a similar point referring specifically to legal education. The Court's 1950 opinion, by Chief Justice Fred M. Vinson, noted that the University of Texas Law School

> possesses to a far greater degree those qualities which are incapable of objective measurement but which make for greatness in a law school. Such qualities, to name but a few, include reputation of the faculty, experience of the administration, position and influence of the alumni, standing in the community, traditions and prestige.
>
> Moreover, although the law is a highly learned profession, we are well aware that it is an intensely practical one. The law school, the proving ground for legal learning and practice, cannot be effective in isolation from the individuals and institutions with which the law interacts. Few students and no one who has practiced law would choose to study in an academic vacuum, removed from the interplay of ideas and the exchange of views with which the law is concerned.[8]

This decision, made prior to the time of the more liberal Warren Court, seemed to reflect the justices' recognition of what had been significant in their own legal education. Law is an area in which effective analysis and advocacy obviously require as deep an understanding as possible of various points of view on key legal issues and of the social and economic realities in which they arise. In addition, as is true in all professions, personal contacts and relationships, often established during the training period, become vital and invaluable resources in succeeding in the profession and having relationships with other colleagues. When southern states proposed to offer "separate but equal" programs for black law students, thereby denying them these contacts, the Court recognized that they could not possibly offer equivalent opportunities.

Powell's *Bakke* opinion relied heavily on Harvard College's admissions procedures, including an appendix with Harvard's description of the program:

> In recent years Harvard College has expanded the concept of diversity to include students from disadvantaged economic, racial and ethnic groups. When the Committee on Admissions reviews the large middle group of applicants who are deemed capable of doing good work in their courses, the race of an applicant may tip the balance in his favor

just as geographic origin or a life spent on a farm may tip the balance in other candidates' cases. A farm boy from Idaho can bring something to Harvard College that a Bostonian cannot offer. Similarly, a black student can usually bring something that a white person cannot offer.

Harvard's report reasoned: "Faced with the dilemma of choosing among a large number of 'qualified' candidates, the Committee on Admissions could use the single criterion of scholarly excellence. . . . But for the past 30 years the Committee on Admissions has never adopted this approach. The belief has been that . . . Harvard College would lose a great deal of its vitality and intellectual excellence and that the quality of the educational experience offered to all students would suffer."[9] Dean of Admissions Fred Glimp stated further that "the effectiveness of our students' educational experience has seemed to the Committee to be affected as importantly by a wide variety of interests, talents, backgrounds and career goals as it is by a fine faculty and our libraries, laboratories and housing arrangements."[10] Harvard officials had consistently believed that diversity was a fundamental requirement in constructing the best possible educational experience. They were convinced that they knew much more about choosing the best class for a great university than could be discerned from numbers on tests or school transcripts.

Both the *Sweatt* decision in 1950 and the *Bakke* decision almost thirty years later relied on the proposition that a fundamental requirement of both undergraduate education and professional education is that students confront different ideas on campus and learn how to relate to other students who reflect the diversity of society. The best way that universities can make this happen is to consciously select students likely to contribute to diversity.

Rejecting the arguments in support of diversity, the most dramatic negative decision, the 1996 Texas *Hopwood* case, simply denies that diversity has any impact on universities. In this case, the Fifth Circuit Court of Appeals held that race was not associated with any relevant educational diversity. "The use of race, in and of itself, to choose students," the court ruled, "simply achieves a student body that looks different. Such a criterion is no more rational on its own terms than would be choices based upon the physical size or blood type of applicants."[11] In this extraordinary statement the court appeared to embrace the proposition that race and ethnicity are not linked to either different experiences or perspectives that would be relevant to the educational experience. If that were true, of course, any effort to assert a compelling interest in fostering diversity would become an exercise in futility. Colleges would lose the only justification for affirmative action left standing after the *Bakke* decision, and any positive race-conscious efforts would become illegal.

In the July 1999 decision in *Tracy v. Board of Regents of the UGA*, Judge B. Avant Edenfield, of the District Court of the Southern District of Georgia, dismissed a case of a student challenging the university's admissions policies, but then went on to attack the diversity justification for affirmative action. He was skeptical about those who "contend that one's racial or ethnic identity takes precedence over any actual contribution to an atmosphere of speculation, experiment and creation." Advocates of diversity "fail to meaningfully show how it actually fosters educational benefits. At best one can cite to speculative cause and effect 'evidence' that X number of blacks, Hispanics, (etc.) in a given freshman class will somehow translate into a 'better' academic environment."

"Defendants," he wrote, "insist that the preference leads to an increase in ethnic diversity, which, in turn, leads to a more diverse collection of thoughts, ideas and opinions on campus. . . . Hence, an increase in the number of non-Caucasian students will make it possible for all students at UGA to derive the educational benefit that comes from direct exposure to peers from different backgrounds, whose experiences and points of view are different from their own or less different than assumed." The judge concluded that there was no reliable evidence for this argument, implicitly rejecting Justice Powell's conclusion in *Bakke*. This decision, and the conclusion that nothing is actually known about the impact of what Judge Edenfield dismisses as "cosmetic diversity," clearly show the need for evidence regarding the actual impact of racial diversity on students' experiences.

Much of the future of affirmative action depends, in other words, on whether or not diversity really does make a difference to educational experiences. Many of the major defenses by higher education leaders assert that it makes a substantial difference, but they reason primarily from tradition or from philosophic premises without supporting evidence.

Obviously, in a situation in which there are fundamentally differing interpretations of social reality, it is important to establish as many of the relevant facts through research as the subject matter will permit. The best evidence on the impact of diversity will be the actual experiences of students and faculty members comparing diverse classrooms and student bodies to segregated ones. If students and faculty report clear differences in educational experiences, the reasoning of Justice Powell in the *Bakke* case will be strongly supported.

Previous Research

Since minority students began enrolling in substantial numbers at elite universities, there has been considerable research on race relations on campus. Most researchers, however, have not concentrated their attention on the *Bakke* proposition, which many scholars believed to be self-evident, but on the ways in which outcomes could be improved for minority students. The desegregation of colleges, like the desegregation of public schools, raised complex issues of change, of dealing with stereotypes and discrimination, of helping students who were isolated on campus and had to make difficult transitions, and of trying to build successful interracial communities on campuses with very few minority professors and administrators. Changing historically white institutions to successful interracial institutions is a difficult process, and universities often change slowly.[12] This research, while undoubtedly useful for university leaders trying to cope with these challenges, does not address the basic *Bakke* premise. (The fact that there is a great deal of work yet to be done on campus race relations may, on the other hand, help account for the opinion of many law school students that their campuses have not yet done enough.) Extremely little attention was given to documenting the benefits for white and Asian American students, and critics often suggest that blacks, Latinos, and Native Americans gain from affirmative action while white and Asian American students simply lose.

More recently there have been efforts to obtain indirect information about the impact of diversity, often using survey data and other information collected for other purposes to seek out evidence of possible impacts. For example, the large annual surveys of college freshmen and the faculty surveys conducted by UCLA in collaboration with the American Council on Education have data that make it possible to determine whether or not different teaching styles are used by professors working at diverse or homogeneous campuses. Researchers can compare how students feel about their campuses at universities with different racial compositions. A number of researchers have surveyed campus climates and evaluated various programs intended to improve race relations or minority success on campus. There have been a number of efforts to analyze the variety of available data and to summarize what the various studies might possibly show about impacts.[13] Some important work has been done, but it is difficult to reach conclusions on the central questions of the impact of diversity without studying them directly.

Important work has also been done recently on the value of diversity in universities on the lifelong contributions of students. William Bowen and Derek Bok's massive longitudinal study focusing on the long-term success and contributions of black students admitted to highly selective universities, *The Shape of the River: Long-Term Consequences of Considering Race in College and University Admissions,*[14] is the leading example of this kind of work. The *New England Journal of Medicine* has published data showing the influence of minority doctors on providing professional services for minority communities and there has been similar research for law schools.[15] The Bowen and Bok study also shows that there was a great deal of college racial interaction among graduates of twenty-eight selective colleges and that the students believed that campus diversity helped prepare them for living and working with people of different backgrounds. Almost 80 percent of the white students surveyed believed that their college's race-conscious admissions should be continued or even strengthened. The study, however, did not include professional school students and did not explore the impact of diversity on the specific aspects of the education of students.

Studies are under way, and some have been published, on the impact of diversity on the specific educational experiences of faculties. There has also been a national survey of public beliefs about the importance and impact of diversity on higher education. A 1998 national Yankelovich survey found that 94 percent of Americans agreed that "growing diversity makes it more important than ever for all of us to understand people who are different from ourselves," and 75 percent believed that diverse student bodies had positive effects on the education of students (18 percent disagreed).[16]

All of this research had important things to say about diverse campuses. There is still, however, a serious need for explicit information on how interracial campuses produce new patterns of discussion and learning. How this works in specific settings, schools, and courses could greatly help to test the validity of the basic propositions in the *Bakke* decision.

The Need for Student Survey Research

A crucial way to obtain evidence on the way in which diversity changes educational experience is to ask students and faculty members who have had experience in diverse institutions and often had other experiences in nondiverse institutions. The advantages of good surveys are that they seek out a broad range of respondents representing the entire population, use questions that permit a full spectrum of positive and negative answers, and guarantee anonymity. The data is collected by third parties and is collected in a way that permits statistical analysis of the results. There is no other feasible way to get a reliable estimate of changes in beliefs and personal experiences.

Surveys on highly controversial issues may, of course, provide opportunities for people to express their political or ideological views. We realize that constitutional decisions should not depend on polls of political preferences and, for that reason, we have tried to ask questions that call for reporting personal experiences, not whether or not the students approve or disapprove of various laws or court decisions. Students felt free to express a wide variety of views and many offered personal comments and explanations that went beyond the specific questions. Because of our concern that activist students might be much more likely to respond to the survey than other students, we invested heavily in obtaining an exceptionally high response rate for our study of two law schools to make certain that we had the best possible representation of the full range of student views. The findings may not be perfect, but they are far better than any other data available on this subject. Unless we could randomly assign students to segregated and integrated law schools and follow their experiences for years, data of this sort is the best that is likely to be obtainable.

Exploratory Surveys

In response to this vacuum of evidence we began exploratory research on student attitudes in law schools, recognizing that law schools are a particular target in the battle on affirmative action because of the intensely competitive nature of their admissions processes. A short questionnaire was drafted and submitted by email to students at Yale and Harvard law schools in the spring of 1998. The responses were extremely interesting and the approach was tried in more schools the next fall. However, this method was not successful in reaching enough students to produce a reliable response rate. This exploratory research was done through email and Internet at seven law schools—Harvard, Michigan, Virginia, Chicago, Yale, Minnesota, and Iowa[17]—with a response rate varying from 10 percent at Chicago to 23 percent at Yale. A total of 1,937 students responded by Internet, 67 percent whites, 10 percent Asian Americans, 6.5 percent blacks, 4.5 percent Latinos, and 7.4 percent foreign students. The results showed that only 2 percent of students reported no interracial contacts in law school. A majority of all students, and a majority within each racial group, said they had frequent or very frequent interracial contacts. More than half of the whites, Asian Americans, and Hispanics, for example, reported they had at least two close black friends in their school. Seventy-six percent of blacks and 85 percent of Latinos reported at least three close white friends. Obviously there was substantial contact for these students, a dramatic contrast to their experiences prior to law school. Only 12 percent of the white students reported, for example, that they had often had contact with students of other races and ethnicities while growing up. Sixty-four percent of the black students in these selective law schools, in contrast, reported having such frequent contacts. Whites also tended to be far more isolated in high school than law school minority students. Only with college did they experience greater diversity, and law school brought them even more intensive interracial contact and friendships. The data indicate that it is rare for minority students to obtain access to elite law schools without substantial integration experiences in their earlier life, but is quite common for whites. This suggests that whites may receive some of the largest greatest benefits from the policies that desegregate elite colleges and professional schools.

The students responding to the email/Internet survey reported large impacts on their ability to work with and get along with people of other racial and ethnic groups. Fifty-seven percent of black students, 60 percent of Latinos, 46 percent of Asian Americans, and 36 percent of whites reported large impacts on this score. Only 5 percent of students saw little or no benefit in this respect. Less than 2 percent of students believed that diversity lessened the quality of informal discussion at their school, while 70 percent selected the top two categories of positive impact. There were similar results about the quality of classroom discussion.

The email/Internet survey population was primarily white male. In other words, the law school population surveyed was heavily over-represented by white males, the group most likely to oppose affirmative admissions policies in national surveys. These results were fascinating. Almost two thousand students on these seven campuses indicated by large majorities that they believed that there were important intellectual and personal benefits from diverse student bodies, just as Justice Powell had suggested in *Bakke*.

The Yale results were especially interesting, since the school produced the highest response rate and is widely regarded as the nation's most selective law school. Thirty percent of its students responding to the survey had little or no interracial contact while growing up and 22 percent had little or none in high school. While at Yale Law School, only 3 percent said they had little or no contact across racial lines and 55 percent reported a great deal. Forty-three percent reported studying together very often or fairly often and 59 percent checked the two highest categories of impact on their ability to work with others from different backgrounds more effectively in the future. Seventy-four percent said that diversity improved the range of informal discussion at Yale, and 72 percent checked the two highest categories about enrichment of classroom discussion.

Fifty-seven percent said that exchanges with students of other racial and ethnic backgrounds had led them to change their values. In this relatively small school that produces presidents, Supreme Court justices, and other leaders of the bar and politics, a very talented and sophisticated group of students reported major effects of diversity on their understanding and views of important social and legal issues.

We were well aware, however, of the problems with the Internet survey. There was no way for us to reach any scientifically valid conclusion that the views of these students were representative of the overall law school population. Our response rate was far too low to permit statistically valid inferences. The answers might reflect the overall student population, or it could be that only the students most sympathetic to affirmative action were answering our questionnaire.

Interestingly, there were virtually no differences in responses between these small surveys and our later high-response-rate surveys. The responses patterns, whether collected through Internet responses or through the later Gallup interviews, were virtually identical, lending credibility to the entire effort.

The Gallup Poll Surveys

To clear up the uncertainty inherent in low-response surveys, we decided to focus on a limited number of law schools and hire a professional survey research firm of the highest quality to obtain the kind of response rate necessary to determine validly the views of the total student body of some law schools. We contracted with the Gallup Poll to obtain a high response rate to the questionnaire at Harvard Law School and the University of Michigan Law School.[18] Gallup was able, through extensive follow-ups, to reach 79 percent of the students at these two highly selective law schools,[19] a rate that was subsequently raised to 81 percent by follow-up calls from our research team. A total of 1,820 students were surveyed at these two schools. As a result, we have the best available survey data exploring the central propositions set out by the Supreme Court in the *Bakke* decision.

Both of these universities draw large numbers of applicants and place their graduates in excellent positions, but they are different in several respects. Harvard is private, eastern, and faces no legal challenge to its admissions policies; Michigan is public, midwestern, and is facing a lawsuit challenging its admissions practices. In light of these and other differences, one might expect quite different patterns of response, but we found striking similarities in many dimensions. The fact that many of the results parallel those found in the small samples in the seven-campus Internet study also suggests that these findings reflect broadly held opinions.

TABLE 1   *Racial and Ethnic Composition of Gallup Survey Population (in %)*

Black	6.7
Asian	10.3
Foreign	7.6
Hispanic	4.3
White	66.9
Mixed	2.8
Indian	0.6
Refused Question	0.8
Unknown	0.1

TABLE 2   *Frequency of Contact with People of Different Race or Ethnicity while Growing Up (in %)*

	None				Often
	1	2	3	4	5
Harvard Students	10.8	28.7	20.7	15.7	23.7
Michigan Students	12.3	32.4	20.4	15.6	19.3

Among students at these two elite law schools, about one-fourth of Harvard students and one-fifth of Michigan students had frequent contact with students of other racial and ethnic backgrounds when growing up, and two in five had little or no contact. The statistics for high school experience were very similar.

TABLE 3   *Contact with People of Different Race or Ethnicity in Your High School (in %)*

	None				Often
	1	2	3	4	5
Harvard Students	10.8	26.5	19.7	18.9	23.8
Michigan Students	10.4	31.3	22.5	17.7	18.1

Among the U.S. law students in the survey, whites were the least likely to report frequent interracial contact while growing up or in high school, while blacks were most likely to have had such experiences. Thirteen percent of whites reported no interracial contact while growing up and another 37 percent reported very little. The corresponding numbers for African Americans were 4 percent and 2 percent. For Hispanics they were 0 percent and 2 percent. Sixty-three percent of African American students reported they had often had such contact, compared to only 12 percent of whites. The statistics for high school were very similar. In other words, almost no blacks and Latinos who succeeded in enrolling in these elite law schools came from a highly segregated childhood and education, but almost half of the whites did. A national study of school segregation patterns in 1996–1997 showed that whites were by far the most segregated ethnic group in U.S. schools and that they were remaining highly isolated even as the nation's school enrollment reached 36 percent nonwhite.[20] To the extent that interracial experience and understanding is an important educational goal, clearly whites were the group most in need of this experience in law school. Later questions will show that such experiences did, indeed, have a powerful impact.

TABLE 4   *Contact in College with People of Different Race or Ethnicity (in %)*

| | None | | | | Often |
	1	2	3	4	5
Harvard Students	4.8	14.8	27.6	25.5	27.0
Michigan Students	3.2	16.3	28.6	26.1	25.8

Students at these two law schools were much less likely to have a segregated experience in college. Although about two-fifths of students experienced very little interracial contact in high school, less than one-fifth reported this pattern in their colleges and well over half reported high racial contact (categories 4 and 5) in their colleges. A substantial majority of students at both schools reported having a roommate of a different race or ethnicity during college. In law school, about half the Harvard students answering the question and more than two-fifths of the Michigan students reported having such roommates. One student who did not see much value in interracial classes commented, however, that "in the dorms, living with folks of different races has been overwhelmingly positive." One-fifth of the African American law students reported having no close friends of other races, while 37 percent reported three or more and the rest said that they had one or two close friends of another background. Almost no whites reported an absence of friends of other races and ethnicities.

TABLE 5   *Close Friends of Another Racial or Ethnic Background (in %)*

For African American Students

	None	*One*	*Two*	*Three or More*
Harvard	22.6	22.6	18.1	34.5
Michigan	16.8	18.1	20.0	43.7
Combined	20.8	21.2	18.7	37.3

For Asian American Students

	None	*One*	*Two*	*Three or More*
Harvard	11.4	16.8	15.4	54.8
Michigan	13.6	15.2	19.7	50.3
Combined	12.1	16.3	16.7	53.4

For Latino Students

	None	*One*	*Two*	*Three or More*
Harvard	29.3	21.7	17.8	27.8
Michigan	25.8	21.7	20.8	31.5
Combined	28.2	21.7	18.7	29.0

For White Students

	None	*One*	*Two*	*Three or More*
Harvard	1.7	1.7	4.1	91.4
Michigan	0.9	0.92	0.2	94.5
Combined	1.4	1.5	3.5	92.4

In these two law schools, which had made extensive efforts to diversify their classes, almost none of the students reported a total absence of interracial contact—only about one in forty. Another one-seventh of the students had very little contact. But 55 percent of the Harvard students and 60 percent of the Michigan students reported high levels of interracial contact.

TABLE 6   *Contact with People of Different Race or Ethnicity in Law School (in %)*

| | *None* | | | | *Frequent* |
	1	*2*	*3*	*4*	*5*
Harvard Students	2.5	14.0	28.2	29.3	26.0
Michigan Students	2.1	14.0	24.9	29.9	29.2

One-sixth of students in both schools never studied with students of another race and about one-fifth more rarely did. On the other hand, about one-third said that they studied together often or fairly often. This relationship was less common than other relationships. Yet, there were many instances of it, and three-fourths of students had some experiences studying together.

TABLE 7   *Studying with People of Different Race or Ethnicity (in %)*

| | *Never* | | | | *Often* | *Only* |
	1	*2*	*3*	*4*	*5*	*Study Alone*
Harvard Students	17.0	19.6	20.1	14.2	19.1	9.0
Michigan Students	17.0	22.2	17.9	12.9	22.5	7.3

The most important issues on the survey concerned the intellectual impact of diversity on student learning experiences. Students tended to report that their experiences were substantially improved in diverse classes.

TABLE 8   *Racial Diversity Impact on "how you and others think about problems and solutions in classes" (in %)*

	Enhances Experience	*Moderately Enhances*	*No Impact*	*Moderately Detracts*	*Detracts from Experience*
Harvard Students	34.7	33.5	25.1	4.2	1.7
Michigan Students	41.3	31.5	21.5	3.9	1.6

One of the issues the Supreme Court recognized as being very important in the 1950 decision on law school segregation was that "the law school, the proving ground for legal learning and practice, cannot be effective in isolation from the individuals and institutions with which the law interacts."[21] Confirming this view, more than two-thirds of students in each school found diversity to lead to an enhancement of their thinking about problems in their classes. More than one-third saw a very clear benefit. Less than 2 percent found a clearly negative impact, and between one-fifth and one-fourth thought that it made no difference.

When students were asked whether or not diversity had affected their "ability to work more effectively and/or get along better with members of other races," at Harvard 39 percent of the total found that diversity clearly enhanced their ability while another 29 percent found a moderate enhancement, 29 percent saw no impact, and just 4 percent found it to be a moderate or clear detriment. Such clear benefits were seen by 48 percent of the students at Michigan.

TABLE 9   *Racial and Ethnic Diversity's Impact on "your ability to work more effectively or get along better with members of other races" (in %)*

	Enhances Ability	Moderately Enhances	No Impact	Moderately Detracts	Detracts from Ability
Harvard Students	38.6	28.6	28.6	2.4	1.4
Michigan Students	47.8	23.8	24.5	2.2	1.4

College admissions officers and educational leaders often think about enriching the discussion that takes place on campus. Some of that happens in classrooms, and other times it happens in the many informal interactions among students—encounters where students test their ideas and learn from each other. In law schools, which often have large classes, the chance for sustained interaction with faculty members is often limited, but there are many opportunities for intense discussion with fellow students, who are a remarkably gifted group in highly selective law schools.

Two-thirds of Harvard students and nearly three-fourths of Michigan students said that these informal exchanges were enhanced by the diversity of their schools. The vast majority of the remainder said that it made no difference. Only one in sixteen saw any negative impact.

TABLE 10   *Racial Diversity's Impact on "the way topics are discussed informally at meals, over coffee, or at other similar occasions" (in %)*

	Clearly Enhances	Moderately Enhances	No Impact	Moderately Detracts	Clearly Detracts
Harvard Students	35.4	32.7	25.1	4.9	1.6
Michigan Students	42.9	31.0	19.7	4.5	1.6

Obviously, diversity is more relevant to some parts of the law school curriculum than to others. Students typically take a variety of courses such as Contracts, Property, Civil Procedure, and others that may have little direct relationship to race. Students at neither school are required to take any course in civil rights, though these issues arise in courses such as Constitutional Law. However, when asked whether diversity affected "the way topics have been discussed in a majority of your classes," students reported strong influences across their educational experience. Nearly two-thirds of the students reported that most of their classes were better because of diversity. About one-fourth saw no difference, and one in twelve believed that there was some negative impact.

TABLE 11   *Racial Diversity's Impact on "the way topics have been discussed in the majority of your classes" (in %)*

	Clearly Enhances	Moderately Enhances	No Impact	Moderately Detracts	Clearly Detracts
Harvard Students	29.3	33.8	27.3	6.0	2.8
Michigan Students	36.5	29.9	25.0	5.9	2.3

When asked to make an overall assessment of whether diversity was a positive or negative element in their total educational experience, the result was overwhelmingly positive. Eighty-nine percent of Harvard students and 91 percent of Michigan students reported a positive impact, the large majority reporting a strongly positive impact. One student explained: "Being confronted with opinions from different socioeconomic and ethnic realms forces you to develop logical bases for the opinions you have and to discard those not based on such logic. You simply are forced to think more critically about your opinions when you know that people with differing opinions are going to ask you to explain yourself." Less than 1 percent of the students at each school reported a negative impact and less than one-tenth felt that there was no impact. In public opinion research it is very rare to find majorities of this size on any controversial issue.

TABLE 12   *"Do you consider having students of different races and ethnicities to be a positive or negative element of your educational experience?" (in %)*

	Clearly Positive	Moderately Positive	No Impact	Moderately Negative	Clearly Negative
Harvard Students	69.3	19.9	9.7	0.6	0.2
Michigan Students	73.5	17.0	8.6	0.2	0.2

In any interracial setting, in a society highly polarized along racial lines and in which there are active debates about civil rights policy occurring in the community and in politics, there are bound to be experiences of conflict. There were very active political and ideological struggles going on in politics, in the courts, and in many communities at the time these students were surveyed. This is one of the important questions in discussions of the simplest form of the theory of integration, "the contact hypothesis," the idea that simply producing interracial contact solves racial problems. Research shows that the outcome of interracial contact is anything but simple. If adults with fully developed racial concepts and stereotypes are brought together in an unfavorable setting, the result can be reinforcement of their stereotypes, unless the situation is handled well. Neighborhood racial transition often produces this kind of experience. Many white Americans, for example, have stereotypes about black and Latino communities and culture in which elements of class are mixed with elements of different socialization, habits, preferences, etc. Some forms of interracial contact experiences may reinforce their stereotypes rather than change them. Many minority students have stereotypes and fears about contact in their family background—memories, for example, about forms of discrimination. The key to positive interaction has been defined by a number of researchers. Successful contact appears to depend, for example, on "equal status interaction" settings in which people are treated equally and interact as peers. In the survey, we asked students a series of questions about conflicts and their impact to help assess whether or not the law school experience was working positively.

When asked their opinion about whether or not conflicts among students reinforced racial stereotypes, some students said that they did, but only about one in twenty strongly agreed with this idea. Another one-eighth of the students agreed moderately, but a clear majority of students disagreed.

TABLE 13   *Conflicts Because of Racial Differences Simply Reinforce Stereotypical Values (in %)*

	Strongly Agree	Moderately Agree	No Impact	Moderately Disagree	Strongly Disagree
Harvard Students	4.1	12.9	27.8	28.6	25.1
Michigan Students	5.2	12.2	28.1	28.6	25.2

Avoiding conflict, of course, is not a basic goal of higher education. In fact, confronting different opinions and taking ideas very seriously are hallmarks of a good education. This is all the more true for legal education, where students need to understand all sides of conflicts and how to argue difficult issues in contentious, high-stakes settings. When we asked students whether or not conflicts arising from racial differences led them to reexamine their own ideas, many replied affirmatively. One student added a comment noting the impact on his beliefs and values: "I guess I would say that due to my discussions with minorities I've completely changed my viewpoint on affirmative action. And I work closely with a professor who happens to be black and I think that's changed my perception as well."

TABLE 14   *"Do conflicts because of racial differences challenge you to rethink your own values?" (in %)*

	Enhances Rethinking	Moderately Enhances	No Impact	Moderately Detracts	Detracts from Rethinking
Harvard Students	32.6	35.7	17.3	8.5	5.2
Michigan Students	42.4	32.4	14.9	4.8	5.2

Some of the students take the issue further to say that such conflicts eventually lead to "positive learning experiences." Less than one-fifth of the students believe the result is negative, but more than one-fourth see no impact one way or another.

TABLE 15 *Conflicts Because of Racial Differences Ultimately Become Positive Learning Experiences (in %)*

	Enhances Learning	Moderately Enhances	No Impact	Moderately Detracts	Detracts from Learning
Harvard Students	20.3	31.6	29.3	12.5	5.3
Michigan Students	24.3	36.0	26.5	9.1	3.6

Law school students encounter many legal and social issues that tend to be perceived differently among different racial groups in the nation. It is on these issues that the possible impact of racial diversity might be expected to be most apparent. Among various groups of Americans, for example, there are deep differences in the way the criminal justice system is viewed. The strikingly different perceptions of the O. J. Simpson trial were a clear example. The Justice Department's Bureau of Justice Statistics estimates, for example, that blacks males and females are more than six times as likely to be imprisoned as their white counterparts.[22] In diverse settings, students are likely to encounter views very different from their own. A reasonable question to ask would be whether or not they had encountered and thought about different understandings, but we asked a more demanding question: Had the discussions actually changed their view of the issue? Many students reported that the exchanges had altered their viewpoint. A large majority of the students said their views had been affected. Only 9 percent saw no impact and more than one-third reported a "great deal" of change. Obviously, this was a powerful experience for the people who would become the prosecutors, public defenders, lawmakers, and judges of the future.

TABLE 16 *"Have discussions with students of different racial and ethnic backgrounds changed your view of the equity of the criminal justice system?" (in %)*

	A Great Deal	Substantially	Significantly	A Little	Not at All
Harvard Students	32.3	28.4	17.6	12.5	8.6
Michigan Students	38.6	26.7	18.8	6.8	8.8

Criminal justice was one area where the advantages of diversity seemed clear in some of the comments students added to the survey. "You cannot discuss the criminal justice system without having blacks in class," one student concluded. "I cannot see how the law can be properly learned without diverse perspectives and opinions," said another. "This is especially true in constitutional and criminal law. Few white classmates would have paused to think carefully or challenge their thoughts on the law without the contributions of opinions from their minority classmates." Every racial and ethnic group of students reported large changes in their views from interracial discussions of criminal justice issues. Thirty-one percent of whites, 45 percent of Asian Americans, 27 percent of African Americans, and 45 percent of Latinos reported a great deal of change resulting from these exchanges. Among whites, only 8 percent reported that their views had not changed at all.

Much of law and politics in the United States is about the conflict of rights—one person's right to safety v. another person's right to have a gun, one person's right to buy a home v. a suburban community's right to exclude rental and affordable housing, one person's right to a neighborhood school v. others' right to a desegregated school, the right to freedom of the press v. the duty not to libel citizens, the right to build a factory on your land v. the rights of neighbors to be free of pollution. Although rights are often discussed in absolute terms, they are almost always bounded by other rights and duties. We asked students how diversity was related to their understanding of such conflicts. More than three-fourths of the students reported more than a slight impact on their views of such conflicts, with most reporting a fairly strong impact.

TABLE 17   *"Have discussions with students of different racial and ethnic backgrounds changed your view of the issues that need to be considered in resolving serious conflicts over rights?" (in %)*

	A Great Deal	Substantially	Significantly	A Little	Not at All
Harvard Students	24.2	32.3	22.7	12.3	8.5
Michigan Students	31.0	32.6	21.8	7.3	7.0

Understanding the nature of law requires understanding the social and economic conditions in which law is applied. Many laws and court decisions rest on assumptions about such conditions, and in many instances it is necessary to understand such conditions (and the differing views about them) in order to evaluate court decisions, statutes, and legal doctrines. Some law school students come to law school with substantial undergraduate training or practical experience on such issues. Others do not. Often these issues are not addressed substantively in law teaching, which tends to be much more about the principles and precedents or deductive models concerning points of law than about the underlying social realities. Educational experiences in discussions that enable students to understand these issues better may be of great value in understanding legal issues and representing clients.

TABLE 18 *"Have discussions with students of different racial and ethnic backgrounds changed your view of conditions in various social and economic institutions?" (in %)*

	A Great Deal	Substantially	Significantly	A Little	Not at All
Harvard Students	25.1	30.8	22.5	13.7	7.6
Michigan Students	32.0	33.8	19.1	8.9	5.9

One of the vital parts of professional training is to make future lawyers familiar with a broad range of issues that they will be faced with throughout their lives as professionals. Almost nine-tenths of students thought that there would be at least some impact on understanding issues they might confront from their experiences with students of other backgrounds. Forty-four percent of Harvard students and 54 percent of Michigan students expected a "substantial" or a "great deal" of impact. As the Supreme Court noted in its 1950 *Sweatt* decision: "Few students, and no one who has practiced law, would choose to study in an academic vacuum, removed from the interplay of ideas and the exchange of views with which the law is concerned."

TABLE 19 *"Have discussions with students of different racial and ethnic backgrounds changed your view of the kind of legal or community issues that you will encounter as a professional?" (in %)*

	A Great Deal	Substantially	Significantly	A Little	Not at All
Harvard Students	16.1	27.8	27.8	15.2	12.5
Michigan Students	22.9	30.8	24.5	10.7	10.6

The United States is entering a period in which civil rights issues will take on extraordinary importance. There are rapidly changing demographics and deep inequalities and regional differences among racial and ethnic groups. There are, for example, already five states, including the nation's two largest states, in which whites have become a rapidly shrinking statewide minority in the school population. By the time the careers of today's law students end, the Census Bureau projects that the country will have a bare majority of whites in the population and that whites will be only about 40 percent of the school-age population. Blacks, who are already the third largest minority in California and the second largest in three New England states, will, like whites, have to adapt to huge racial changes. In a country whose population growth is being driven by immigration, mostly of non-Europeans who do not speak English, many issues of immigration and language must be resolved.[23] None of these issues is simple, and students tend to have very different understandings of such issues, depending on their own race or ethnicity.

Issues about rights and race have a great deal of saliency in American life and it would not be surprising if law school diversity had only a small impact on the values of a group of highly educated, highly intelligent students who have discussed such issues in their earlier education. Seven out of eight students, however, report that contact with students of diverse backgrounds has led to a change in their values, more than half reporting the highest levels of change. "I think that the level of cultural and ethnic diversity here at Michigan is amazing and wonderful," said one student. "I think that after attending predominantly white schools, being in such a diverse group has strengthened and broadened my personal belief and feelings." Fifty-nine percent of whites, 64 percent of Latinos, 64 percent of Asian Americans, and 46 percent of African Americans report the two highest levels of change in their values concerning civil rights. Clearly, very powerful exchanges are occurring among students in the law school communities on these issues.

TABLE 20   *"Have discussions with students of different racial and ethnic backgrounds changed your values regarding civil rights?" (in %)*

	A Great Deal	Substantially	Significantly	A Little	Not at All
Harvard Students	22.4	28.0	24.9	11.9	12.5
Michigan Students	27.7	27.4	23.4	9.1	12.2

To make the comparisons more explicit, students were asked to compare their classes that were homogeneous with their classes that were diverse in terms of the range of discussion, the level of intellectual challenge, and the seriousness with which alternative views were considered.

Among those who had had both types of classes the number who said that the diverse classes were superior in these respects outnumbered those who found the single-race classes superior by more than ten to one. The majorities reporting better outcomes in diverse classes were even more lopsided on the questions on the range of perspectives and the seriousness with which the alternatives were considered.

Many students commented on these issues. One said, "A more diverse setting enhances education but keys you into viewpoints you may not have considered before." The students remembered "a particular experience; I took a class with 50 students in it—40 were male, none were minorities. Thinking back, the class would've benefited from more diversity." Another noted, "I think that a diverse student body greatly contributes to the learning process, more issues are covered [and] it greatly enhances classroom discussion." A third observed, "Cultural and ethnic diversity is more important in law school than in many other studies." A fourth noted, "Cultural and ethnic diversity is a necessity to have a true understanding of how these issues affect everyone." "I can't imagine," said another, "how serious discussion of the law which affects all Americans can take place without the points of view of all different races."

TABLE 21   *Impacts of One-Race v. Interracial Classes (in %)*

	Homogeneous	Diverse	No Difference	Cannot Answer*
Level of intellectual conflict or challenge greater	3.4	34.4	36.8	25.6
More serious discussions of alternative perspectives	3.2	47.3	24.0	25.6
Discussed greater variety of subjects and examples	2.2	44.3	28.2	25.3

*Basic reason for nonresponse was that the student questioned had had only homogeneous or only diverse classes.

The small minority of students who saw negative results suggested a different impact. One student observed, "In classes with one race, more people are willing to express their views without offending anyone." Another noted, "Invariably, certain minority members will have a chip on their shoulder and destroy the conversation into one of racism and name-calling as opposed to intellectual thought." Another criticized "the politically correct attitude that affects the free expression of the true views of the majority class." These comments might lead one to believe that whites would agree on anti-affirmative action policies if minorities were not present to embarrass them, but this survey shows that white students, by a large majority, support affirmative action in an anonymous questionnaire. Some student critics of affirmative action actually have an incorrect racial stereotype about the real attitudes of their white classmates.

Students were asked, finally, what their opinion on their law school's minority admissions policy should be. The responses showed that the students had widely varying views of the policy priorities. Forty-five percent felt that the existing policies for diversity were insufficient and more should be done. Thirty-six percent believed that the present policies were correct, and 16 percent favored doing less or nothing at all. Only 19 percent of whites and 8 percent of Asian Americans wanted to deemphasize or end affirmative admissions policies.

Obviously legal issues of rights are not decided by opinion polls, but it is interesting that such a large majority of the group of students whose rights are supposedly violated by affirmative action favors doing as much or more than the universities are currently doing. This may well reflect the value of the intellectual benefits white and Asian students believe they gain from diversity. Another interesting finding is that even some of the opponents of affirmative action report intellectual benefits from the policy, since the proportion reporting benefits on some of the questions is significantly higher than the percent favoring the policy.

TABLE 22   *"What should be done about the admissions policy at your law school seeking a student body which includes more underrepresented minorities?" (in %)*

	Strengthen Policy	Maintain Policy	Deemphasize or Discontinue
Harvard Students	47.2	33.4	15.4
Michigan Students	40.1	40.3	16.5

One student commented, "I wouldn't go to a school that didn't have an affirmative action program." Another observed, "A diverse law school classroom is essential to building a democracy of lawmakers, leaders, and [public] servants who will appreciate the broad wealth of personal and group experience throughout the United States." Another student noted, "The lawyers that we make today are going to make the laws we live under tomorrow. If we expect those laws to reflect the vast diversity that is America, our law schools must possess that diversity within their walls today." Another observed, "We learn from other students, [and] to not have affirmative action would seriously detract from the school. Attempts to dismantle such programs are ultimately misguided, short-sighted, and self-destructive."

It is interesting to note that the largest number of students favored not only maintaining but strengthening the affirmative admissions policies. A number explained their views. Some commented on their surprise at how little diversity there was in their school. A substantial number said that the existing programs were not enough and that more should be done, both in admissions and in changing the instructional process. "Most classes are predominantly white," one student noted. "Larger percentages of minority groups will encourage broader participation," another observed. A student who had been at a college with half nonwhite students noted that "discussions about race and diversity were far better and much more informative than in law school, where the population is much less diverse."

Many students pointed to the lack of diversity on their faculties and the ways in which that weakened the potential benefits of diversity: "The faculty is not very diverse, and they need to include more issues in class discussions." Another noted that he "found very little cultural diversity in [the] faculty." Another student complained, "I think it is absolutely unacceptable that Harvard has not made greater efforts to employ [minority] professors." Another noted, "It's not enough just to have a diverse student body, but also faculty and administrative diversity, because it is a matter of having an open feeling about the school which only [having] a diverse student body cannot create." "Student diversity isn't great," said another student, "but it's even worse in the faculty."

Toward Stronger Benefits: Working on Integration

Though students reported major benefits, a number wrote comments indicating that they believed that the experience could be improved, particularly by a more significant effort to deal with social segregation issues. Students thought that there should be more effort by the schools to foster stronger interactions. Another common desire was for more effort to bring students together within the law school. A number of students, particularly at Harvard Law School, pointed to self-segregation as a barrier to stronger interaction. In spite of the reports of a great many interracial friendships and interactions of many sorts, some felt that there were still social barriers and believed that the law school should provide more leadership on that issue. In spite of some "enormously gratifying experiences," one student said that "Harvard Law School has also been the place where I have seen the most racial segregation in comparison to any place that I have been. I find that very odd." A student who thought "diversity is incredibly important" noted that, "as an undergraduate at Stanford . . . relations across racial boundaries were not perfect, but were far better than at Harvard Law School. I think the reason for this was simply that there were more minority students at Stanford." Part of the problem, another student observed, "has to do with the segregation between the racial groups, more so than the numbers." "As a foreign national," another student said, "I'm very disappointed that people are very separated in terms of race." Still another student was "surprised that social culture at Harvard Law School is very segregated." One student said that their law school should take more initiative to bring students together: "We need to do more about it, . . . we're going to live with one another." Still another student observed: "It doesn't help to have diversity when ethnic groups segregate themselves. Priority should be to promote interaction." A Harvard student noted, "I think they need to make a better effort to build student community—in particular, to build interaction between different races."

These students are asking that the law schools move from what most see as a beneficial but sometimes difficult desegregation to a more fully realized integration. This kind of transformation has been a basic issue in the discussion of desegregation in public schools for decades. Both the concern about faculty desegregation and about efforts to produce more positive interactions among students have been goals in school desegregation for more than thirty years. Almost all of the school desegregation plans have faculty desegregation goals and standards, and many schools adopted procedures to assure collaboration across racial lines in classroom assignments and other techniques to build greater success. Law students raising these issues were considering basic elements for a deeper kind of transformation of their schools to genuinely multiracial institutions where equal status interaction was more likely to occur.

Among critics of affirmative action who expressed their personal opinion, most simply favored admissions on traditional academic criteria and some expressed the opinion that racial inequality should be solved somewhere else, usually in schools or undergraduate colleges. One student commented, "It's good to be diverse but you don't want to have unqualified students. I think that it needs to start earlier, at grade school." A few expressed the view that affirmative action harmed minorities. One student, for example, said, "It is damaging to everyone to put people in schools that they would not have been admitted to otherwise."

Some students were conflicted over the policy issues. "It is a really hard question and it is really hard to answer," said one student. "Affirmative action . . . [is] not really a great solution to the problem, but I don't think there is a better one out there to use." Some students mentioned that they would favor more emphasis on poverty in admissions, either as an alternative or as a supplement to the existing policies. "I think that affirmative action should be used on a class-based scale rather than a racially based scale because middle- to upper-class minorities should not receive preferential treatment." Another added, "Race is an inappropriate and unfortunate proxy for socioeconomic class."

Value Change

One of the strongest possible impacts of experiences of diversity would be an actual change in beliefs and values growing out of the interaction. There is clear evidence in other areas of civil rights that new experiences may be related to changed attitudes. For example, there was a massive increase in southern acceptance of sending black and white students to the same schools after desegregation occurred. In 1942, only 2 percent of southern whites favored interracial schools. By 1982 the rate was 82 percent.[24] Although it may be too soon to see such impact in the overall law profession, many of the law students we surveyed reported a large or substantial change in their values growing out of their experiences with diversity at law school. A clear majority, for example, reported a change in their values concerning civil rights.

Foreign Students

It is interesting to note that on a number of questions about the value of diversity, the most negative group was not American whites or Asians but foreign students who have a significant presence at both schools. They accounted for a disproportionate percentage of the opponents on many questions. Since many of these students were products of far less diverse societies and had little need to understand the complexities of U.S. social structures, it is not difficult to understand these attitudes. Even foreign students, however, tended to see advantages of diversity by a substantial margin. On the question of how diversity affected the way that students "think about problems and solutions in class," for example, 4 percent of foreign students believed that it clearly detracted, compared to less than 1 percent of blacks, Asian Americans, or Latinos, and less than 2 percent of whites. The percentage of foreign students who saw some advantage, however, outweighed those who saw some disadvantage by more than 5 to 1. For American whites the ratio was more than 10 to 1.

One foreign student noted, "Coming from a country that has practically no minorities, the whole issue [was] strange in the beginning; after studying here, I recognize the importance of the problem." Another noted that "most of these discussions refer only to Americans and they should be broadened and take into account the races and ethnicities of other countries." Another commented that he or she was "surprised" at "so much emphasis here in the U.S. on ethnic diversity; I think to a certain degree it promises conflict among the races." Another international student had very different views: "I studied in Australia first, and American law studies are much richer because of diversity." Obviously, foreign students returning to their own countries felt much less of an urgent need to understand diversity than did American students.

Conclusion

Law students reflect much of the diversity of the nation and report a wide range of experience and views on issues of race and civil rights. It is clear from this survey, however, that large majorities have experienced powerful educational experiences from interaction with students of other races. Although the plurality of students believe that not enough has been done to realize this potential fully, there are many contacts and friendships that have formed across racial and ethnic lines. White students appear to have a particularly enriching experience, since they are by far the most likely to have grown up with little interracial contact. The values affirmed by Justice Powell and by the Harvard admissions officials cited in the *Bakke* decision appear to be operating in the lives of law students today. It is regrettable that the scholarly world has been so slow in studying these changes. Nevertheless, this data clearly affirms the judgments of the courts and the leaders of legal education thirty-five years ago when they embarked on policies that led to the diversity that most of today's students find so beneficial to their legal education and to understanding critical dimensions of their profession.

Notes

1. There are two other basic arguments for affirmative action. The first, remedying the history of discrimination by universities, has tended to be discounted by the courts in recent years. The courts have assumed that the enactment of civil rights laws and the passage of time have largely eliminated the continuing impact of this history, a conclusion that is strongly disputed by civil rights leaders. The other is the social benefits of affirmative action for the society and the professions. This argument has been central to some of the most important recent research, but was not recognized as a basic justification in *Bakke*.

2. National Center for Education Statistics, *The Condition of Education 1999* (Washington, DC: Government Printing Office, 1999), pp. 116, 126.

3. William G. Bowen and Derek Bok, *The Shape of the River: Long-Term Consequences of Considering Race in College and University Admissions* (Princeton, NJ: Princeton University Press, 1998), p. 10.

4. In the nineteen states that historically had separate black public universities, real integration often did not begin until the 1970s.

5. James E. Blackwell, *Mainstreaming Outsiders: The Production of Black Professionals*, cited in Bowen and Bok, *The Shape of the River*, p. 7.

6. *U.S. v. Fordice*, 112 S. Ct. 2736 (1992).

7. *Tracy v. Board of Regents of the UGA*, 59 F.Supp.2d 1314, 1322 (S.D.Ga 1999).

8. In *Sweatt v. Painter*, 339 U.S., at 633–4.

9. Final Report of W. J. Bender, Chairman of the Admission and Scholarship Committee and Dean of Admissions and Financial Aid, pp. 20 et seq. (Cambridge, MA, 1960).

10. Dean of Admissions Fred L. Glimp, Final Report to the Faculty of Arts and Sciences, 65 *Official Register of Harvard University*, No. 25 (1968), 93, 104–105 .

11. *Hopwood v. State of Texas*, 76 F3d 932 at 945 (5th Cir. 1996).

12. Walter R. Allen, Edgar G. Epps, and Nesha Z. Haniff, eds., *College in Black and White: African American Students in Predominantly White and in Historically Black Public Universities* (Albany: State University of New York Press, 1991); Michael T. Nettles, ed., *Toward Black Undergraduate Student Equality in American Higher Education* (Westport, CT: Greenwood Press, 1988); Patricia Gándara, *Over the Ivy Wall: The Educational Mobility of Low-Income Chicanos* (Albany: State University of New York Press, 1995); Richard C. Richardson, Jr., and Elizabeth Fisk Skinner, *Achieving Quality and Diversity: Universities in a Multicultural Society* (New York: Macmillan, 1991).

13. See, for example, Daryl G. Smith and associates, *Diversity Works: The Emerging Picture of How Students Benefit* (Washington, DC: Association of American Colleges and Universities, 1997).

14. Bowen and Bok, *The Shape of the River*.

15. Miriam Komaromy and associates, "The Role of Black and Hispanic Physicians in Providing Health Care for Underserved Populations," *New England Journal of Medicine, 334*, No. 20 (1996), 1305–1310.

16. Ford Foundation press release, "Americans See Many Benefits to Diversity in Higher Education, Finds First-Ever Poll on Topic," October 6, 1998.

17. Stanford participated briefly, but withdrew.

18. This study was made possible through grants by the Andrew W. Mellon Foundation and an anonymous donor to Harvard University. Derek Bok of Harvard University and Keith Reeves of Swarthmore College participated in discussions on the

design of the survey. Much of the statistical work was done by Jody Clarke, Warren C. Reed, and Elizabeth Yong. Carolyn Howard, Carlin Llorente, and Luke Travis also assisted in data collection and follow-up.

19. Harvard Law School and the University of Michigan Law School are two of the most competitive law schools in the country. Though there are criticisms of the *U.S. News and World Report* rankings, they place Harvard Law School number one in the nation and Michigan Law School number eight. Harvard Law School is ranked number one by reputation among academics, judges, and lawyers, and Michigan Law School is ranked number six, with the reputation scores 4.9 and 4.7, respectively (5.0 the highest). The 1998 undergraduate GPA scores for Michigan Law School are 3.4–3.7, and for Harvard Law School they are 3.7–3.9. Average LSAT scores at both schools are very high.

20. Gary Orfield and John Yun, *Resegregation in American Schools* (Cambridge, MA: The Civil Rights Project, Harvard University, 1999), p. 15, table 11.

21. *Sweatt v. Painter,* 339 U.S. 634.

22. Bureau of Justice Statistics, *Lifetime Likelihood of Going to State or Federal Prison* (Washington, DC: U.S. Department of Justice, 1997).

23. U.S. Bureau of the Census, "Population Projections of the United States by Age, Sex, Race, and Hispanic Origin: 1995–2050," February 1996, pp. 25–1130; Steven A. Holmes, "Census Sees a Profound Ethnic Shift in U.S.," *New York Times,* March 14, 1996.

24. Howard Schuman, Carlotte Steeh, and Lawrence Bobo, *Racial Attitudes in America: Trends and Interpretations* (Cambridge, MA: Harvard University Press, 1985), p. 78.

This survey would not have been possible without the support of the deans of the participating law schools. We are indebted to the high-quality professional work of the Gallup Poll.

CHAPTER 7

The Positive Educational Effects of Racial Diversity on Campus

MITCHELL J. CHANG

Perspective

Does attending a college with a racially diverse population significantly enhance students' educational experiences? Does such diversity on campus create a richer environment for learning? These questions lie at the heart of one of the most contentious issues in higher education today: the use of race-conscious affirmative action in admissions.

Critics of affirmative action argue that diversity by itself has no significant educational benefits and is therefore not a legitimate goal. Moreover, the critics charge, race-conscious policies designed to promote diversity have serious negative effects, including lowering academic standards, "polarizing" campuses, and denying educational opportunities to "more deserving" white students—the "reverse discrimination" argument.

Some recent important judicial and policy decisions on affirmative action have taken note of this controversy. Both the Fifth Circuit Court of Appeals 1996 ruling in *Hopwood v. Texas* and the 1995 decision of the Regents of the University of California to eliminate race-conscious affirmative action were made in part on the grounds that there are no significant educational benefits to having a racially diverse student body.

The arguments on either side of this critically important issue have often been political, ethical, and ideological. Very little empirical research has asked whether there is indeed a direct link between diversity and positive educational outcomes.

This paper represents one attempt to fill that gap. The data analyzed here, though hardly definitive, point unmistakably to the conclusion that campus diversity does indeed have a small but significant positive effect on students' experience of college. Moreover, they offer no support to the arguments of those who say that the results of efforts to promote diversity have been negative.

Research Objectives and Data Sources

Most educators view a diverse student body as an important educational resource, arguing that diversity creates a richer environment for learning (Rudenstine, 1996; Tien, 1996). Students are said to learn most from those who have very different life experiences from theirs (Sleeter & Grant, 1994). Diversity offers the potential, many educators believe, to challenge students and enrich the intellectual dialogue of the college community (Duster, 1993; Moses, 1994). Further, having a racially diverse campus is seen as a powerful way to teach students the realities of the multiracial world they will eventually be living and working in (Astone & Nuñes-Wormack, 1990; Hall, 1981; Tierney, 1993).

Research by Astin (1993b) and Villalpando (1994) found that emphasizing "multiculturalism" through ethnic studies courses, cultural awareness workshops, cross-racial socialization, and discussion of racial issues—to name just a few campus activities—is associated with widespread beneficial effects on a student's academic and personal development, irrespective of the student's race. Their studies, however, did not directly link the level of diversity on campus with these positive effects. The purpose of the study described here was to ask if such a link exists, by measuring the impact of having a racially mixed student population on students' likelihood of socializing with those of different racial or ethnic groups and of discussing issues of race and ethnicity.

This study draws on several major data sources. The primary source of student data is the Cooperative Institutional Research Program (CIRP) database. CIRP is a longitudinal set of very large student and faculty surveys and research, sponsored by the American Council on Education and the Higher Education Research Institute (HERI) at UCLA. The database is designed to assess the impact of college on students, and is generally considered the most comprehensive collection of information on higher education. The CIRP data used in this study included information from two surveys: the 1985 freshman survey and the 1989 follow-up survey of the same college class in their senior year.[1]

The 1985 survey was administered to new college freshmen during orientation programs and in the first few weeks of fall classes. It included information on students' personal and demographic characteristics, high school experiences, and expectations about college, as well as their values, attitudes, life goals, self-confidence, and career aspirations. The survey was completed by 192,453 first-time full-time freshmen at 365 four-year colleges and universities.[2]

Four years later, in the summer and fall of 1989, the follow-up survey was sent to the home addresses of a sample of the 1985 respondents. The 1989 survey repeated the earlier one's questions on values, attitudes, life goals, self-confidence, and career aspirations. It also asked students to reflect on their experiences and perceptions of college. More than 86,000 students were contacted; approximately 30 percent of them responded. The final sample yielded 18,188 students attending 392 four-year colleges and universities. This sample was statistically adjusted for nonresponse and weighted to approximate the national population of students.[3]

Also included in the data set was information on students' SAT and ACT scores, provided by the Educational Testing Service and the American College Testing Program.[4] The 1989 HERI Registrar's Survey provided additional information on which students had earned bachelor's degrees, which were still enrolled in college, and how many years of college each student had completed. These data were linked with the surveys to form a database designed to assess a wide range of student experiences and undergraduate achievements and to provide longitudinal data for studying how different college environments influence student development. Institutional characteristics (size, type, and so on) and undergraduate ethnic enrollments from 1986, both obtained from the data files of the U.S. Department of Education's Integrated Post-Secondary Data System (IPEDS), were merged with student survey data.

The IPEDS enrollment figures for African American, Asian American, Latino, and white undergraduate students were used to create the measure of campus diversity.

Finally, several campus climate measures were developed from responses to the 1989 HERI Faculty Survey and merged with the data sets. The faculty data were collected from full-time teaching personnel at 212 of the same institutions for which longitudinal student data were available. The survey asked faculty members to describe how they spent their time, how they interacted with students, what teaching practices and evaluation methods they used, their perceptions of the institution's climate, and their sources of stress and satisfaction, as well as demographic and biographical questions.[5]

Defining "Racial Diversity"

Although previous research has examined how college students are affected by "racial diversity" (Allen, 1985, 1992; Astin, 1993a; Hsia & Hirano-Nakanishi, 1989; Hurtado, 1992; Pascarella & Terenzini, 1991), there is little consensus on what constitutes a racially diverse student population. Conventional approaches equate color with diversity; that is, the more nonwhites on campus, the more "diverse" the student body. This approach fails to measure heterogeneity, and thus fails to address the educational rationale for maintaining race-conscious admissions practices—namely, that diversity enriches education because students learn most from those who have very different life experiences from their own.

I therefore designed a measure to assess an institution's ability to provide opportunities for all students to interact with others from different racial groups. Percentages of students from different major racial groups were combined to create an overall measure that equates diversity with heterogeneity. The formula, similar to that used for calculating standard deviation, is

$$\sqrt{\frac{(A-m)^2 + (L-m)^2 + (B-m)^2 + (W-m)^2}{4}}$$

where A is the percentage of Asian American students, L is the percentage of Latinos, B is the percentage of blacks, W is the percentage of whites at each particular instituion, and m is the mean, or overall average, of A, L, B, and W across all instituions. This formula yields an inverse measure (the greater the differences from the mean, the less diversity), so the reciprocal of this value was used as the index of diversity.

In effect, this variable measures the variance across all four racial and ethnic groups. For example, if the percentages of the four groups were very similar (e.g., 25%, 25%, 30%, and 20%) at a particular institution, it would have a very low standard deviation, and thus a high index of diversity—in this case, 0.28. If, on the other hand, the percentages were widely disparate (e.g., 80%, 5%, 0%, and 15%) it would have a large standard deviation and a low index of diversity—in this case, 0.03. In this way, I attempted to define racial diversity as an institution's ability to offer opportunities for maximizing cross-racial interaction for all students.

Research Design

This study uses the Input-Environment-Outcome (I-E-O) methodological framework developed by Astin (1991) for assessing the impact of college

TABLE 1 *Input and Outcome Measures*

Freshman Racial Attitudes (From 1985 Freshman Survey)	*Outcome Measures (From 1989 Follow-Up Survey)*
Views[a]	Frequency with which students[b]
"Busing is O.K. to achieve racial balance in the schools."	Socialized with persons from different racial/ ethnic groups
"Realistically, an individual can do little to bring about changes in society."	Discussed racial/ethnic issues

Importance of Goals[c]

Helping to promote racial understanding
Influencing social values

[a] Coded as a four-point scale: 4 = "Agree strongly" to 1= "Disagree strongly."
[b] Coded as a three-point scale: 3 = "Frequently" to 1 = "Not at all."
[c] Coded as a four-point scale: 4 = "Essential" to 1 = "Not important."

environmental variables on student outcomes. According to Astin, the impact of the environment, in this case racial diversity, on specific student outcomes is best observed after controlling for student characteristics measured at college entrance.

Four characteristics of entering freshmen reflecting their views and goals regarding racial or ethnic issues were selected as measures of their racial orientation and were controlled when examining the effects of racial diversity on student behavior as measured four years later (see Table 1). Two outcome measures were selected from the 1989 follow-up survey to examine the effects of racial diversity: the frequency with which students socialized with those of different racial or ethnic backgrounds, and the frequency of their having discussions of racial or ethnic issues. Both of these activities have been shown by earlier research to be associated with students' academic and personal development (Astin, 1993b; Villalpando, 1994).

Researchers have long emphasized the importance of controlling student background characteristics when interpreting the impact of the college environment on outcomes (Astin, 1977; Feldman & Newcomb, 1969; Pascarella & Terenzini, 1991). Because the distribution of students across different college environments is never random, a number of student characteristic, college environment, and student involvement measures were selected as additional controls for this study. Socioeconomic status, race, gender, and measures of student ability have been shown to be consistent predictors of a variety of educational outcomes (Astin, 1982; Featherman & Hauser, 1978; Ortiz, 1986; Pascarella & Terenzini, 1991); this study controls for these differences.

In addition, several college characteristics served as controls to help identify how the effects of racial diversity might vary according to campus environment, following the practice of earlier researchers (Astin, 1977, 1991, 1993a; Pascarella & Terenzini, 1991; Weidman, 1989). These included variables considered important for understanding racial climates on campus: institutional size, location, type, religious affiliation, gender (coed or single-sex), and selectivity. Other measures of peer-group characteristics and faculty environment that have been shown to be important in determining educational outcomes (Astin, 1993a; Astin & Chang, 1995; Hurtado, 1990; Pascarella & Terenzini, 1991) were also included for analysis.

Lastly, a set of variables that measured students' direct involvement and experiences with their institutions was selected from the 1989 follow-up survey. These items were designed to examine variations in students' experiences within individual campuses, and included activities such as enrolling in an ethnic studies course, attending a racial or cultural awareness workshop, being a member of a fraternity or sorority, working full-time while attending college, taking part in intercollegiate or intramural sports, being elected to student government, participating in campus protests or demonstrations, working on a group project for a class, and so on. These particular measures were chosen because they are known to affect some of the outcomes used in this study (Astin, 1977, 1993a; Hurtado, 1990) and are believed to "mediate" the effects of racial diversity (Astin, 1993b).

Analysis and Findings

The various measures of students' initial attitudes and outcomes were combined with all of the control variables in a statistical analysis designed to isolate the effects of racial diversity on the two specified outcomes—the development of interracial friendships and the frequency of discussing racial issues. This analysis was done in relation to 1) student background characteristics, 2) the campus racial diversity measure, 3) other campus characteristics, and 4) intermediate outcomes. Because this model requires a temporal arrangement of variables, college experiences were treated as intermediate outcomes; that is, they occurred after the student's initial exposure to the college environment but while the student was still in college. Variables were entered in the above four-stage se-

TABLE 2   *Student Socialization and Discussion of Racial Issues as a Function of Campus Diversity*

| | Racial Diversity | | | |
Student Outcomes	Simple r	ß1	ß2	ß3
Socialized with someone of a different race	.16***	.11***	.12**	.12**
Discussed racial issues	.08***	.05***	.04**	.02*

ß1 represents the standardized regression coefficient after controlling for student background characteristics.

ß2 represents the standardized regression coefficient after controlling for institutional, peer, and faculty characteristics.

ß3 represents the final standardized regression coefficient.

* $p < .014$, ** $p < .001$, *** $p < .0005$

quence to observe changes in regression coefficients. To determine if the effects of racial diversity made a unique contribution, beyond the effects of other variables, Beta coefficients for the racial diversity measure were observed after controlling for student background and college environment, and again after controlling for intermediate outcomes.

The simple statistical correlations for the racial diversity measure and the two outcomes are .16 and .08 (see Table 2). The last three columns in Table 2 show the corresponding correlations after controlling for student background, college environment, and college experiences. The results show that multiracial diversity is a significant, though not strong, positive predictor of students' likelihood of forming interracial friendships and talking about race and ethnicity, even after students' background and campus environment are taken into account.

One could argue that participating in these two outcome activities is in itself a positive experience. More important, however, is that these experiences have been shown to be associated with beneficial effects on students' academic and personal development, regardless of their race (Astin, 1993b; Villalpando, 1994). To verify these effects, additional analyses were conducted on four educational outcomes: retention, satisfaction with college, intellectual self-confidence, and social self-confidence. These outcomes resemble the measures most often used in "racial diversity" studies (Astin, 1993a, 1993b; Hurtado, 1990). Moreover, these outcome measures have corresponding pretest measures that were selected from the 1985 freshman survey (see Table 3).

TABLE 3 *Educational Outcome Measures*

Outcome Measures (1989 Follow-Up Survey)	Pretests (1985 Freshman Survey)
Self-Concept	
Academic Self-Concept[a] Self-Rating: "intellectual self-confidence"	Academic Self-Concept Identical Self-Rating
Social Self-Concept[a]	Social Self-Concept
Self-Rating: "social self-confidence"	Identical Self-Rating
Retention	
Student Persistence: Earned a bachelor's degree or above Student did not withdraw, transfer, or take a leave of absence	Students' best guess as to the chances they will:[c] Drop out temporarily Earn a BA
College Satisfaction	
Overall college satisfaction rating[b]	Students' best guess as to the chances they will be satisfied with college[c]

[a] Coded as a 5-point scale: 5 = Highest 10% to 1 = Lowest 10%.
[b] Coded as a 4-point scale: 4 = Very Satisfied to 1 = Dissatisfied.
[c] Coded as a 4-point scale: 4 = Very Good Chance to 1 = No Chance.

This further analysis shows that socializing with someone of another racial group is positively related to all four educational outcomes, and that these relationships remained significant even after institutional, peer, and faculty variables were controlled (see Table 4).

But when the effects of other intermediate outcomes were controlled, only the effects on satisfaction with college and social self-confidence remained significant.[6] Thus, socializing with someone of another race appears to have direct effects on two of these educational outcomes, and indirect effects on the other two. Likewise, the experience of talking about racial issues shows significant positive effects on all four outcomes, even after controlling for student background and college environment. When intermediate outcomes were controlled, however, only one of these outcomes, intellectual self-confidence, remained significant.[7]

In sum, these findings strongly suggest that both socializing across racial lines and discussing issues of race are positive educational experi-

TABLE 4   *Educational Outcomes as a Function of Students' Experiences*

Student Outcome	Socialize				Discuss			
	Simple r	ß1	ß2	ß3	Simple r	ß1	ß2	ß3
Retention	.06*	.04*	.04*	.00	.07*	.04*	.03*	.00
Satisfaction with College	.10*	.09*	.08*	.05*	.11*	.07*	.05*	.00
Intellectual Self-Concept	.08*	.03*	.03*	.01	.10*	.06*	.06*	.05*
Social Self-Concept	.10*	.07*	.06*	.04*	.09*	.05*	.04*	.02

ß1 represents the standardized regression coefficient after controlling for student background characteristics.

ß2 represents the standardized regression coefficient after controlling for institutional, peer, and faculty characteristics.

ß3 represents the final standardized regression coefficient.

* $p < .0005$

ences. Because racial diversity on campus increases the likelihood of students' having these experiences, I conclude that diversity has educational benefits in college.

Implications for Policymakers

Attending college with those of other races and ethnicities increases the likelihood that students will socialize across racial lines and talk about racial matters. The more diverse the student body, the more likely that these activities will take place. In turn, these activities have a positive impact on student retention, overall college satisfaction, and intellectual and social self-confidence among all students. Though racial diversity alone does not appear to directly affect every one of these educational outcomes, it very likely affects all of them indirectly.

The statistical correlations found in this study are relatively small, but they are significant—not simply in the mathematical sense but also because they exist at all. Critics of affirmative action in college admissions maintain that diversity has no benefit in itself and that efforts to promote it are counterproductive of positive race relations. This study suggests that these critics are wrong, that campuses where diversity has flourished, largely through the impact of affirmative action, confer significant educational benefits on their students.

Given what we know about the racial climate on U.S. campuses and the corrosive forces in society at large that impede dialogue and understanding, even a small positive impact may be extremely important. The modest benefits we see in this study could perhaps be much larger if policymakers choose to move the clock forward instead of turning it back.

Notes

1. The sample used in this study did not include historically black institutions because the controversy over affirmative action in admissions has ignored these institutions (Hacker, 1992). This is not surprising, as their mission, clientele, and history vastly differ from those of predominantly white institutions (Allen, 1987, 1992; Davis, 1991; Fleming, 1984; Jackson & Swan, 1991; Nettles, 1991; Willie, 1981). Because this study sought to inform the use of affirmative action, it was reasonable to limit the sample in this way. Likewise, this study did not include community colleges because the sample size for that group was too small.
2. See Astin, Green, Korn, and Shalit (1985) for a copy of the survey and a complete description of the sampling procedure.
3. See Higher Education Research Institute (1991) for a copy of the survey and a complete description of the sampling and weighting procedures.
4. ACT scores were converted into equivalent SAT scores by HERI.
5. For detailed information on the Faculty Survey (implementation, sampling, and weighting) see Astin, Korn, and Dey (1990).
6. It is difficult to interpret whether socializing with someone of another racial or ethnic group has a "direct" effect on retention and intellectual self-concept because this particular experience is also an intermediate outcome and a temporal arrangement among intermediate outcomes cannot be established.
7. The same problem described in the preceding footnote applies here.

References

Allen, W. R. (1985). Black student, white campus: Structural, interpersonal, and psychological correlates of success. *Journal of Negro Education, 54,* 134–137.

Allen, W. R. (1987). Black colleges vs. white colleges: The fork in the road for black students. *Change, 19,* 28–34.

Allen, W. R. (1992). The color of success: African American college student outcomes at predominantly white and historically black public colleges and universities. *Harvard Educational Review, 62,* 26–44.

Astin, A. W. (1977). *Four critical years.* San Francisco: Jossey-Bass.

Astin, A. W. (1982). *Minorities in American higher education.* New York: Macmillan.

Astin, A. W. (1991). *Assessment for excellence: The philosophy and practice of assessment and evaluation in higher education.* New York: Macmillan.

Astin, A. W. (1993a). *What matters in college: Four critical years revisited.* San Francisco: Jossey-Bass.

Astin, A. W. (1993b). Diversity and multiculturalism on the campus: How are students affected? *Change, 23,* 44–49.

Astin, A. W., & Chang, M. J. (1995). Colleges that emphasize research and teaching: Can you have your cake and eat it too? *Change, 27(5)*, 44–49.

Astin, A. W., Green, K. C., Korn, W. S., & Schalit, M. (1985). *The American freshman: National norms for 1985*. Los Angeles: UCLA, Higher Education Research Institute.

Astin, A. W., Korn, W. S., & Dey, E. L. (1990). *The American college teacher: National norms for the 1989–90 HERI Faculty Survey*. Los Angeles: UCLA, Higher Education Research Institute.

Astone, B., & Nuñez-Wormack, E. (1990). *Pursuing diversity: Recruiting college minority students*. Washington, DC: George Washington University, School of Education and Human Development.

Chang, M. J. (1999). Does racial diversity matter? The educational impact of a racially diverse undergraduate population. *Journal of College Student Development, 40*, 377–395.

Davis, R. B. (1991). Social support networks and undergraduate student academic-success-related outcomes: A comparison of black students on black and white campuses. In W. R. Allen, E. G. Epps, & N. Z. Haniff (Eds.), *College in black and white* (pp. 143–157). Albany: State University of New York Press.

Duster, T. (1993). The diversity of California at Berkeley: An emerging reformulation of "competence" in an increasingly multicultural world. In B. W. Thompson & S. Tyagi (Eds.), *Beyond a dream deferred: Multicultural education and the politics of excellence*. Minneapolis: University of Minnesota Press.

Featherman, D., & Hauser, R. (1978). *Opportunity and change*. New York: Academic Press.

Feldman, K. A., & Newcomb, T. M. (1969). *The impact of college on students* (vol. 1). San Francisco: Jossey-Bass.

Fleming, J. (1984). *Blacks in college: A comparative study of students' success in black and in white institutions*. San Francisco: Jossey-Bass.

Hacker, A. (1992). *Two nations: Black and white, separate, hostile, unequal*. New York: Ballantine Books.

Hall, S. (1981). Teaching race. In A. James & R. Jeffcoate (Eds.), *The school in the multicultural society* (pp. 58–69). London: Harper.

Higher Education Research Institute. (1991). *The American college student, 1989: National norms for 1985 and 1987 college freshmen*. Los Angeles: Author.

Hsia, J., & Hirano-Nakanishi, M. (1989). The demographics of diversity: Asian Americans and higher education. *Change, 21*, 20–27.

Hurtado, S. (1990). *Campus racial climates and educational outcomes*. Doctoral dissertation, University of California, Los Angeles. Ann Arbor: University Microfilms International, No. 9111328.

Hurtado, S. (1992). Campus racial climates: Contexts of conflict. *Journal of Higher Education, 63*, 539–569.

Jackson, K. W., & Swan, A. L. (1991). Institutional and individual factors affecting black undergraduate student performance: Campus race and student gender. In W. R. Allen, E. G. Epps, & N. Z. Haniff (Eds.), *College in black and white* (pp. 127–141). Albany: State University of New York Press.

Moses, Y. T. (1994). Quality, excellence, and diversity. In D. G. Smith, L. E. Wolf, & T. Levitan (Eds.), *Studying diversity in higher education*. San Francisco: Jossey-Bass.

Nettles, M. T. (1991). Racial similarities and differences in the predictors of college student achievement. In W. R. Allen, E. G. Epps, & N. Z. Haniff (Eds.), *College in black and white* (pp. 175–191). Albany: State University of New York Press.

Ortiz, V. (1986). Generational status, family background, and educational attainment among Hispanic youth and non-Hispanic white youth. In M. A. Olivas (Ed.), *Latino college students*. New York: Teachers College Press.

Pascarella, E. T., & Terenzini, P. T. (1991). *How college affects students.* San Francisco: Jossey-Bass.

Rudenstine, N. L. (1996, March/April). The uses of diversity. *Harvard Magazine,* 48–62.

Sleeter, C. E., & Grant, C. A. (1994). *Making choices for multicultural education: Five approaches to race, class, and gender.* New York: Maxwell Macmillan.

Tien, C. (1996). *Racial preferences? Promoting diversity in higher education: Perspectives on affirmative action and its impact on Asian Pacific Americans.* Los Angeles: LEAP Asian Pacific American Public Policy Institute.

Tierney, W. G. (1993). *Building communities of difference: Higher education in the twenty-first century.* Westport, CT: Bergin & Garvey.

Villalpando, O. (1994). *Comparing the effects of multiculturalism and diversity on minority and white students' satisfaction with college.* Paper presented at the annual meeting of the Association for the Study of Higher Education, Tucson, AZ.

Weidman, J. (1989). Undergraduate socialization: A conceptual approach. In J. Smart (Ed.), *Higher education: Handbook of theory and research.* New York: Agathon Press.

Willie, C. V. (1981). *The ivory and ebony towers.* Lexington, MA: Lexington Books, D. C. Heath.

A draft of this article was first written in December 1996 for The Civil Rights Project, Harvard University. With permission from the editor, a different version of this study was submitted to a research journal for review and has since been published; see Chang (1999).

CHAPTER 8

Linking Diversity and Educational Purpose: How Diversity Affects the Classroom Environment and Student Development

SYLVIA HURTADO

We are facing a U.S. society that is increasingly diverse. In such a society, it is ever more important to provide all college and university students with the skills necessary for success in an increasingly complex world. By the year 2000, most new jobs in the economy will require a postsecondary education, and women and racial/ethnic minorities will compose a majority of the work force (Justiz, 1994). It is projected that by 2010, one out of every three Americans will be Latino, African American, Asian American, or Native American. This projection, however, does not reflect the rapid rate at which racial/ethnic populations are becoming the majority in many states—a change that is already evident in elementary and secondary schools. This demographic shift suggests that the role of higher education will remain essential in training a work force that can both economically sustain communities and forge relationships across the diverse populations that make up American society. Educating a diverse student body remains central to this educational purpose.

Several recent reports issued by the American Association of Colleges and Universities have highlighted the importance of educating students for a diverse democracy. Such an education attends to the representation of various gender and racial/ethnic groups at the institution, the interactions inside and outside of the classroom that affect student learning, and the incorporation of knowledge about diverse groups in society:

> As educators we must address these basic challenges for American pluralism across the curriculum—in the classroom, in the co-curriculum, in the intersections between campus and community. In short, this diversity that is part of American society needs to be reflected in the student body, faculty and staff, approaches to teaching, and in the college curriculum. (AAC&U, 1995, p. 8)

Thus, many campuses today have come to recognize diversity as an educational policy or goal that is consistent with the overall objectives of the institution—to equip graduates with the appropriate technical skills, human relation skills, and ways of thinking that will be useful in a complex and diverse society.

Yet, even while educational policymakers recognize these major demographic changes and the need for higher education to prepare its students accordingly, there exists fierce opposition to policies that promote campus diversity. The most contentious conflicts within the diversity debate have primarily been manifest in challenges to policies that consider race as a factor in college and university admissions. At heart, these challenges have questioned the educational benefits of diversity. For example, the *Hopwood* decision by the Fifth Circuit Court of Appeals in Texas suggested that the benefits of racial or gender diversity within the faculty or student body are no more significant than the benefits of a population diverse in individual characteristics, such as height or blood type. Until recently, higher education policymakers have unfortunately offered relatively little empirical research regarding the impact of diversity on students' educational experiences, aside from assertions based on intuitive notions that student and faculty diversity enhance the education provided by schools. This shortage of documentation has left diversity policies susceptible to legal and political attack. Fortunately, the recent research that has been conducted in this area is beginning to show that institutional progress toward diversity goals can have an impact on students' educational experiences (Hurtado, Milem, Clayton-Pederson, & Allen, 1999; see also Orfield & Whitla, in this volume).

Building on this recent work, this study supplies further evidence of the positive impact of diversity. It gauges diversity's effects on students' self-perceived improvement in the abilities necessary for contributing positively to a pluralistic democracy. The findings, from a nationwide survey of faculty and students at predominantly white four-year colleges and universities, make a strong case for the educational value of student and faculty diversity. A diverse student body provides students with important opportunities to build the skills necessary for bridging cultural differences and may cultivate their capacity for other important learning. The presence of a diverse faculty helps to ensure that students take full advantage of the benefits that diversity offers.

Research on Interaction with Diverse Peers

Much classic and contemporary theory suggests that exposure to diversity plays a key role in student learning and development during the college years. Scholars contend that students' cognitive and social development are intertwined, and as students approach college age they are more likely to apply cognitive abilities and skills to interpersonal situations and social problem-solving (Chickering & Reisser, 1991; Muss, 1988). Both cognitive and social development are also thought to occur through social interaction, spurred by the disequilibrium that results when one tries to reconcile one's own embedded views with those of others (Piaget, 1975). College students who report interactions with diverse peers (in terms of race, interests, and values) have shown a greater openness to diverse perspectives and a willingness to challenge their own beliefs after the first year of college (Pascarella, Edison, Nora, Hagedorn, & Terenzini, 1996). Overall, cognitively complex thinkers rather than dualistic thinkers should be able to develop in-depth and societal perspectives about situations and social problems (Perry, 1970; Selman, 1980). These theories and research support the notion that encountering others who have diverse backgrounds and perspectives can lead to interactions that promote learning and development.

Yet, although diversity is linked with student development in theory, educators must create certain conditions to maximize the potential for learning. Several researchers have supported the notion that learning occurs best when the educational environments support interaction under conditions of equal status (Allport, 1954). In other words, placing students of diverse backgrounds in a classroom is a necessary but insufficient condition for learning. Merely encountering differences can promote feelings of superiority or inferiority among students rather than growth and development. Particular pedagogical techniques promote the type of interaction necessary to create equal status conditions and, thus, learning in diverse environments. For instance, Robert Slavin (1995) and other researchers have consistently shown that students engaged in racially/ethnically diverse cooperative learning groups report cross-racial friendships outside these groups. Overall, cooperative learning has demonstrated value in enhancing the academic achievement of students from all racial/ethnic groups and in reducing prejudice as students improve their interaction skills with students from different backgrounds (Slavin, 1995; Wolfe & Spencer, 1996). Elizabeth Cohen (1994) further reveals that without attention to the structure of peer groups in diverse classrooms and to learning activities that promote interaction on an equal status basis, peer status can actually reproduce inequality and undermine the potential learning that can occur among diverse peers. Furthermore, students exposed to complex instructional activity that takes diversity into account have demonstrated gains in factual knowledge and higher-order thinking skills (Cohen et al., 1997). In sum, active learning pedagogies increase interaction in the classroom because students "learn more than when they are passive recipients of instruction" (Cross, 1987, p. 4). Both research and theory support the notion that students learn a great deal from diverse peers when interaction is facilitated in supportive environments.

Such supportive environments also would conceivably include opportunities for students to encounter unfamiliar and diverse perspectives in the curriculum. For example, research evidence presented in the University of Michigan's affirmative action cases reveals that students' learning and civic participation outcomes are enhanced by exposure to diversity in the college curriculum, and that these effects are enhanced further by facilitated interaction with diverse peers in the classroom (*Gratz et al. v. Bollinger et al.; Grutter et al. v. Bollinger et al.*). These results suggest that active pedagogical approaches that stimulate classroom interaction and curricula that attend to the histories and traditions of diverse groups would probably be fundamental features of colleges and universities that capitalize on the potential benefits of diversity. Indeed, after extensive analysis of a national, longitudinal cohort of students in 1985–1989, Astin (1993) concluded:

> The weight of empirical evidence shows that the actual effects on student development of emphasizing diversity and of student participation in diversity activities are overwhelmingly positive. . . . There are many developmental benefits that accrue to students when institutions encourage and support an emphasis on multiculturalism and diversity. (p. 431)

Evaluating the Impact of Diversity on Student Development

This study builds on the results of the preceding studies that have demonstrated the links between campus diversity, when appropriately supported, and educational benefits. It does so by analyzing the self-reported experiences of a national sample of students attending college in the early

1990s. Specifically, the study examines how diversity-related campus activities such as exposure to diverse curricula and opportunities to study and interact with diverse peers—activities that are only possible when a college or university has diversified its faculty and student body (Hurtado, Milem, Clayton-Pederson, & Allen, 1999)—positively affect student development.

Many campuses were not prepared for the changes they would undergo as a result of including more women and racial/ethnic minorities in their student bodies. Rising minority enrollments were connected with major intellectual and social movements that raised important questions about the production and transmission of knowledge, as well as access to education. Diverse student enrollments produced pressures to make institutions more responsive to the issues that arose as a result. This led to the development of—often with corresponding institutional and individual resistance to—new academic support programs and student organizations, diversification of the faculty and staff, the establishment of ethnic and women's studies programs, and the revision of curricula to better reflect the diversity of experiences and perspectives. Many of these issues posed new challenges in the classroom. For instance, diversification of the student body dictated that faculty develop a more expansive repertoire of approaches to curriculum and pedagogy (AAC&U, 1995).

Given these widespread changes in institutions, the impact of diversity on the intellectual environment is actually quite broad, and one can focus on any number of issues. In addition, measuring the effects of diversity is complicated because they cannot always be observed directly and often are not truly visible until gauged by long-term outcomes such as career choices, personal beliefs, and friendship patterns. Indeed, both Astin (1993) and Chang (1996) suggest that the effects of diversity on student outcomes are likely to be indirect and complex. With these caveats in mind, this study focuses on three questions, the answers to which will at least advance our understanding of the consequences of a more diverse faculty and student body:

- Does the gender or the racial/ethnic background of a faculty member make a difference in the classroom through their attention to pedagogical strategies and curricular emphases that support diversity?
- Do opportunities to interact with someone from a different racial/ethnic background in a learning situation enhance students' assessments of their own learning?
- Does the diversity that faculty introduce into the curriculum make a difference in terms of students' assessments of their own learning?

Method

To address these questions, the study analyzes data from the 1989–1990 Faculty Survey administered by UCLA's Higher Educational Research Institute composed of responses from over 16,000 faculty at 159 medium and highly selective predominantly white institutions across the country. Predominantly black institutions were excluded from these analyses, as were low selectivity institutions, because the current controversy over the benefits of diversity is located in higher education's predominantly white selective institutions. These faculty data were used to examine racial and gender differences in the instructional techniques most commonly used in undergraduate courses. (Details regarding the conduct of the national survey are reported in Astin, Korn, & Dey, 1991.) In addition, longitudinal student data were examined to understand the link between activities associated with a diverse student body and student self-reported growth on twenty general educational outcomes. The student responses come from the 1987–1991 CIRP student survey, also administered by the UCLA Higher Education Research Institute.[1] A random sample of approximately 4,250 students attending 309 four-year, predominantly white colleges and universities provided responses.

Analyses. Chi-square tests were performed on the faculty data to determine significant gender and race differences in instructional techniques. Partial correlations were conducted on the student data, controlling for college selectivity (average freshmen SAT/ACT scores), student abilities (high school GPA, academic self-concept), and academic habits (hours per week spent studying/doing homework). Controlling for these factors provides a strong test of how students' diversity-related activities relate to reported growth in twenty general education outcome areas. These outcomes constitute an item set on the 1991 student follow-up survey that asks students, "Since entering college, how much have you changed in the following areas?" For presentation purposes, the outcomes were sorted into three distinct categories: *civic outcomes*, which speak to a student's capacity for engagement in a pluralistic democracy; *job-related outcomes*, which include skills that employers have deemed important (Bikson & Law, 1994); and *learning outcomes*, or key skills higher educators have come to expect students to acquire in college. The diversity-related activities included the frequency with which students reported studying with someone from a racial/ethnic background different from their own and whether the student enrolled in an ethnic or women's studies courses in 1990. All of the diversity-related activities are more likely to occur with either a diverse faculty to introduce curricular innovations or a diverse student body to provide opportunities for interaction.

The current study relies on student self-reports of growth in a number of general education areas. There are obvious disadvantages to using such data for this purpose, including the possibility that perceptions may not always be a true reflection of reality. Yet, the educational community lacks good, widely used measures of cognitive and affective development for college students on a national level. Current national postsecondary data also lack good measures of current teaching, learning, and assessment practices (Dey et al., 1997). Thus, postsecondary decisionmaking with regard to curricula and a host of academic policies has largely proceeded on assumptions as to what is best for college students, rather than actual empirical data regarding the benefits of any particular approach. Even the use of self-reported data, therefore, represents an improvement (i.e., the use of actual empirical evidence to gauge the effects of higher education policies across institutions), and may actually be the best data available.

In addition, much of the national data does not provide an adequate assessment of the social environments associated with diversity that would allow a fuller understanding of its implications. While there are numerous small-scale, single-institution studies that may show the impact of diversity, evidence across a broad range of institutions regarding the impact of diversity relies on only a few national surveys that have asked some diversity questions, and even these are not consistently pursued. The fact that this study shows any effects across various types of institutions, given the inadequacies and lack of attention to important measures in national data, is significant.

Gender and Race Differences in Instructional Techniques

The findings suggest that the gender of an instructor has a distinct impact on the educational experiences of undergraduates in terms of both how classes are taught and course content. Specifically, female faculty are much more inclined than male faculty to require cooperative learning, experiential learning or field studies, and group projects in some or most of their courses. Table 1 shows the proportion of male and female faculty who report using specific instructional techniques in some or most of the undergraduate courses taught at the colleges. There are significant gender differences ($p = .0001$) with regard to virtually all techniques reportedly used in the majority of courses taught. While a high proportion of faculty utilize extensive lecturing in comparison to other techniques, a lower proportion of women (76 percent) than men (89 percent) report using such a technique in some or most of their courses. The preceding findings relating to gender differences are echoed later in similar findings relating to

TABLE 1 *Instructional Techniques Required in Undergraduate Courses: Percent by Gender of Faculty at Medium and Highly Selective Four-Year Colleges and Universities*

Technique Required in Some or Most Courses	Women	(N)	Men	(N)	Chi-Square Significance
Cooperative Learning	80%	(4600)	63%	(11370)	p = < .0001
Experiential Learning/ Field Studies	59	(4585)	47	(11349)	p = < .0001
Group Projects	67	(4592)	56	(11365)	p = < .0001
Extensive Lecturing	76	(4597)	89	(11400)	p = < .0001
Readings on Racial/ Ethnic Issues	55	(4589)	36	(11345)	p = < .0001
Readings on Women/ Gender Issues	58	(4590)	36	(11340)	p = < .0001
Social Science Faculty Only:					
Readings on Racial/ Ethnic Issues	70	(2230)	54	(5066)	p = < .0001
Readings on Women/ Gender Issues	68	(2230)	53	(5065)	p = < .0001

ethnic/racial differences in reported pedagogical use. They lend substantial support to policies promoting faculty diversity, suggesting that a diverse faculty is more likely on average to utilize pedagogical approaches that capitalize on the diversity in their classrooms and that lead to favorable learning outcomes.

With regard to diversification of the curriculum, the findings similarly support faculty diversity. It is clear that women are significantly more likely than men to require readings on racial/ethnic or gender issues in their courses. Because inclusion of these types of readings may be influenced by the faculty member's discipline,[2] these data were analyzed controlling for field of study among faculty. Approximately 70 percent of female social scientists and 54 percent of male social scientists required readings on racial/ethnic diversity issues. Similarly, 68 percent of female and 53 percent of male social scientists required readings on gender issues in some or most of their courses.

The race/ethnicity of faculty members is also associated with the reported use of specific instructional techniques. Table 2 shows the specific instructional techniques utilized by faculty of different races/ethnicities

TABLE 2 *Instructional Techniques Required in Undergraduate Courses: Percent by Race/Ethnicity of Faculty at Medium and Highly Selective Four-Year Colleges and Universities*

Technique Required in Some or Most Courses:	White	African American	American Indian	Asian American	Latino	Other	Sig.*
Cooperative Learning	68	74	70	59	78	64	****
Experiential Learning/ Field Studies	51	53	62	42	51	46	***
Group Projects	60	66	64	54	63	58	**
Extensive Lecturing	86	82	89	92	87	85	****
Readings on Racial/ Ethnic Issues	41	69	53	23	66	43	****
Readings on Women/ Gender Issues	42	64	45	24	59	39	****
Social Science Faculty Only:							
Readings on Racial/ Ethnic Issues	57	78	68	44	78	50	****
Readings on Women/ Gender Issues	58	72	61	42	71	47	****

Note: *Chi-square significant at ** p = < .01; *** p = < .001; **** p = < .0001. Sample sizes for each tabulation is approximately 14,600 White, 271 African American, 91 American Indian, 433 Asian American, 94 Latino, and 316 Other Faculty at Predominantly White, Four-Year Colleges of Medium and High Selectivity. Social Science faculty sample sizes include 6,712 White, 166 African American, 41 American Indian, 148 Asian American, 55 Latino, and 122 Other faculty.

at selective four-year institutions. Latino and African American faculty are most likely to require cooperative learning techniques (78 percent and 74 percent, respectively), while Asian American faculty are least likely to require these techniques in the classroom. Native American faculty are most likely to use experiential learning/field studies techniques (62 percent), while Asian American and Other faculty are least likely to do so (42 percent and 46 percent, respectively). Less pronounced yet still significant (p = .01) differences were detected across racial/ethnic groups with regard to the reported use of group projects in class, ranging from a high of 66 percent among African American faculty to a low of 54 percent among Asian American faculty. Significant differences were detected in the reported use of extensive lecturing, with Asian American faculty most likely to report requiring this technique (92 percent) and African American faculty least likely to report engaging in this teaching practice (82 percent).

With regard to curriculum, African American faculty are most likely (69 percent) to report having required readings on race/ethnicity in their courses, and Asian American faculty are least likely (23 percent) to require these in some or most of their courses. A similar pattern across the race/ethnicity of the faculty was observed with the introduction of gender readings. The course content, or inclusion of readings on race/ethnicity and gender, is clearly influenced by the disciplines the different racial/ethnic groups teach. In controlling for social science disciplines, the proportion of faculty from different racial/ethnic groups who report introducing diversity into the curriculum rises. Approximately 78 percent of African American and Latino faculty and 68 percent of Native American faculty in the social sciences say they have required readings on racial/ethnic issues in some or most of their courses. These same racial/ethnic groups are also significantly more likely than the other social science faculty to report having required readings on women or gender in the curriculum.

These results strongly suggest that women and different racial/ethnic faculty have distinct teaching styles that influence both the content and delivery of knowledge in the classroom. Even when considering the limitations of self-reported data, one can at least assume that faculty believe in the pedagogical methods they report using, even if they do not actually use them in practice. If this is so, these findings at the very least suggest that a diverse faculty is more likely to implement or learn about pedagogical methods known to improve learning outcomes. Furthermore, if students experience their learning environments differently due to the gender or ethnicity of the faculty member, then engagement with a diverse student body and faculty is likely to be related to their cognitive and affective development during college. The next section discusses how the activities associated with a diverse student body and faculty are related to student educational outcomes.

The Relationship between Diversity-Related Activities and Student Educational Outcomes

Table 3 illustrates significant relationships between student self-reported growth on various educational outcomes and activities during college that are associated with having a diverse student body and faculty.[3] The most consistent finding is that students who report having had the opportunity during college to study with someone from a racial/ethnic background different from their own in 1990 also report growth in all areas in 1991. Specifically, the strongest effects were associated with civic out-

TABLE 3 *Partial Correlations: Student Self-Reported Growth on Various Educational Outcomes and Diversity-Related Activities, Predominantly White Four-Year Institutions (N=4,253)*

Student Educational Outcomes	Activities Associated with a Diverse Student Body and Diverse Faculty/Curriculum		
	Studied with Someone from a Different Racial/ Ethnic Background	Enrolled in an Ethnic Studies Course	Enrolled in a Women's Studies Course
Civic Outcomes			
Acceptance of People of Different Races/Cultures	.18***	.14***	.08***
Cultural Awareness	.16***	.19***	.14***
Tolerance of People with Different Beliefs	.14***	.11***	.09***
Leadership Abilities	.13***	.04*	.02
Interpersonal Skills	.09***	.05***	.06***
Public Speaking Ability	.07***	.04*	.01
Religious Belief and Conviction	.03*	.01	−.03
Job-Related Outcomes			
Ability to Work Cooperatively	.10***	.01	.01
Ability to Work Independently	.06***	.03*	.03
Job-Related Skills	.06***	.02	−.04*
Preparation for Graduate/ Professional School	.06***	.04**	.02
Competitiveness	.06***	−.04**	−.03
Learning Outcomes			
Critical Thinking	.10***	.07***	.06***
Problem-Solving Skills	.08***	.01	.02
General Knowledge	.07***	.08***	.05***
Foreign Language Ability	.07***	.11***	.05***
Knowledge of a Particular Field	.05**	.03	.03
Writing Skills	.05**	.09***	.10***
Mathematical Ability	.04**	−.12***	−.13***
Confidence in Academic Abilities	.04**	.03	.01

Note: Partial correlations controlling for Students' Academic Self-Concept, High School GPA, Hours/week Spent Studying, and College Selectivity. Significance levels: * $p = < .05$; ** $p = < .01$; *** $p = < .001$. Scale of measures: Students reported their growth to be 1 = much weaker to 5 = much stronger.

comes such as the acceptance of people of different races/cultures, cultural awareness, tolerance of people with different beliefs, and leadership abilities. These findings support research conducted on other longitudinal cohorts of college students in the areas of cultural knowledge/awareness and leadership (Antonio, 1998; Bowen & Bok, 1998; see also Orfield & Whitla in this volume), indicating that opportunities for interaction with diverse peers foster civic development among college students. Enrollment in ethnic studies courses is also positively associated with many civic outcomes, such as students' cultural knowledge and awareness. Significant but somewhat less impressive effects were associated with enrollment in women's studies courses. Self-reported growth in job-related skills is associated primarily with a key diversity-related activity that includes the opportunity to study frequently with students from a different racial/ethnic group. It should be noted that the effects of this activity were strongest with regard to growth in student ability to work cooperatively with others without detriment to their capacity to work independently or their competitiveness after four years of college. In contrast, curricular diversity (ethnic or women's studies courses) had either weak or negligible effects on job-related skills. Similarly, having studied with someone from a different racial/ethnic background appears to have more pronounced effects than curricular diversity on self-reported growth in critical thinking and problem-solving skills. This suggests that the opportunity to interact with a diverse group of peers is just as, if not more, important to the development of critical skills as is exposure to a curriculum that makes diversity its explicit focus. Thus, the presence of diverse peers, though probably insufficient on its own, may indeed be an important precondition of learning from any curriculum that emphasizes diverse perspectives.

Some findings pertaining to relationships between curricular diversity and specific academic skills deserve more cautious interpretation due to questions about the direction of causality.[4] Still, relationships that are revealed on this front are of keen interest, if only for the possibility that exposure to a more diverse curriculum affects student outcomes. For instance, curricular diversity appears to be positively related to students' perceptions of growth in foreign language skills, writing ability, and general knowledge after four years of college.[5] Perhaps most notable in terms of academic skill enhancement, however, is the positive association between taking ethnic or women's studies courses and self-reported improvements in critical thinking skills ($p = .001$). Students who took these courses were on average more likely to report improvement in their critical thinking skills—those which would conceivably enhance their learning in any academic course and throughout life.

All told, the student-reported outcomes strongly suggest that interacting with diverse peers, faculty, and curricula as an undergraduate has a substantial positive effect on the development of skills needed to function in an increasingly diverse society as well as other academic skills important to the learning process. Again, caveats about the limitations of self-reported data may be justified here, especially with regard to students' subjective assessments of their academic abilities. Yet, since key outcomes from this study coincide closely with the outcomes of other research studies of the effects of campus diversity (Antonio, 1998; Bowen & Bok, 1998; Orfield & Whitla in this volume), a case for the legitimacy of these findings is quite strong. With regard to questions about the validity of self-reported academic outcomes, these findings at least imply that students, on average, do not perceive that their acquisition of academic skills is compromised as a result of the diversity that exists at their colleges.

Diversity Linked with Educational Objectives

These results suggest that the diversity of the faculty and student body has an impact on classroom environment and student development during college. The empirical evidence suggests that it makes a difference whether students are in classrooms led by diverse faculty and have an opportunity to interact with diverse peers on an equal status basis that may depend on the types of pedagogy that diverse faculty introduce into the classroom. The results show that women and different racial/ethnic faculty report having distinct teaching styles that may influence both the content and delivery of knowledge in the classroom. Therefore, the gender and race/ethnicity of the instructor are likely to have an impact on the educational experiences of undergraduates in predominantly white selective institutions. While faculty can be trained to facilitate more active learning pedagogies through faculty development programs, it should be noted that few instructional programs at the college level actually address how to create the complex instructional activities that facilitate learning in a diverse environment. It appears that female, African American, and Latino faculty may naturally be more attentive to peer status differences in the classroom and be more likely to employ active learning pedagogies.

Perhaps the most compelling argument for a diverse student body rests on evidence showing that interaction across racial/ethnic groups, particularly of an academic nature, is associated with important outcomes that will prepare students for living in a complex and diverse society. Not only were effects associated with such civic outcomes as acceptance of people of different races/cultures, cultural awareness, tolerance of people with different beliefs, and leadership ability, but also with learning outcomes such as critical thinking and problem-solving skills. Students also report growth of important skills related to a diverse work force, including the ability to work cooperatively with others. It should be noted that interaction with diverse peers demonstrated positive effects on job-related skills more frequently than did curriculum exposure. While the curriculum may acquaint students with the cultural legacies that make up a pluralistic society, it may be that the college peer group provides the opportunity to experience this knowledge firsthand and learn how to negotiate differences. Thus, the *diversity of the peer group becomes a necessary part of the curriculum* in a learning environment that views diversity as central to the learning process. The educational benefits of diversity may accrue as a result of a combination of opportunities to engage in a diverse curriculum introduced by a diverse faculty and to study and interact with racial/ethnically diverse students inside and outside of the classroom.

Conclusion

In sum, the research shows that diversity of the faculty and student body is linked with the fundamental work of teaching and learning in higher education. These findings cast substantial doubt on the veracity of the Fifth Circuit Court of Appeals' *Hopwood* decision, which asserted that the ethnic and racial diversity of a student body or faculty is of no relative consequential value to the education offered by a college or university. To the contrary, this study strongly suggests that such diversity may contribute significantly to students' improvement on key learning outcomes that are associated with both academic development and the critical abilities needed to work in diverse settings—skills that will be increasingly important in the 21st century.

While external factors may exert pressure on institutions to develop, clarify, or revise their efforts regarding diversity, the educational imperative must take precedence in campus diversity policy and initiatives. Furthermore, proponents of higher education admissions policies that consider race must begin to articulate clearly the educational value of diversity to the learning we expect students to achieve. This and other research helps to explicate diversity's fundamental relationship to the educational imperative. Responsibly defending these diversity policies from threatening opposition, such as that recently witnessed in California and Texas, demands the use of empirical evidence to sway decisionmakers and provide legal and educational justification for the existence of such policies[6] in this changing and contentious legal and policy environment.

Institutions that have taken up the basic challenges of American pluralism have begun to make changes to their student bodies with a keen eye on the impact of this diversity in the classroom and the co-curriculum. As a recent Association of American Colleges and Universities report stated, today's college students "will need to grapple with a country that is not only diverse but divided. To do this, they must come to understand and respect peoples and ways of life that have been hidden from them" (AACU, 1995, p. 8). Higher education's role remains central to this process as institutions attempt to prepare college graduates for their future as participants in a pluralistic democracy by providing an appropriate education. Sustaining this role will necessitate continuing research efforts to prove what many college and university decisionmakers already intuitively know—that diversity is a prerequisite for such an education.

Notes

1. The Higher Education Research Institute, with the continuing sponsorship of the American Council on Education, administers surveys to faculty and students at institutions across the country through the Cooperative Institutional Research Program (CIRP). The CIRP is the nation's largest and longest-running empirical study of higher education. Since 1966, over seven million students and over 100,000 faculty from over 1,300 institutions have participated. These surveys are collected to document substantial areas of student and faculty experiences at an institution. For the student data, the surveys probe experiences both prior to beginning college and during their college experiences. The student data provide a broad range of statistical controls for dispositions and abilities in order to assess change on a variety of student outcomes, several of which were used for these analyses.
2. Social sciences, for instance, may lend themselves more readily to the inclusion of diversity content than other fields of study.
3. It should be noted that while the coefficients are small, these are not unlike other coefficients in survey data that incorporate analyses of a large sample of students in relation to pedagogical practices (Dey & Hurtado, 1993). The restricted ranges on the four- and five-point scales of the survey items prevent variation that would allow high coefficients. However, many of the effects were strongly significant ($p = < .001$) and consistent across a broad range of outcomes. In order to focus on the most important effects, only those that meet at least a .01 significance level will be discussed. Given the large sample size, those with a .05 significance level or higher will be considered a rather weak or negligible effect.
4. For instance, it is conceivable that students who have a greater facility for foreign languages may be more likely to take ethnic studies courses, as opposed to the alternate interpretation that taking ethnic studies courses improves students' foreign language skills.

5. The negative association between enrollment in ethnic/women's studies courses and mathematical ability is worth a quick explanation. Math is one area where undergraduates are generally less likely to develop during college, unless they continue to take mathematics-related courses (Hurtado, Astin, Korn, & Dey, 1988). Therefore, those students who enroll in ethnic or women's studies courses may report less growth because they are less likely to have pursued mathematics-related majors.

6. See Orfield and Whitla in this volume for an illustration of how to use evidence in this manner.

References

Allport, G. W. (1954). *The nature of prejudice*. Cambridge, MA: Addison-Wesley.

Antonio, A. (1998, April). *Student interaction across race and outcomes in college*. Paper presented at the annual meeting of the American Educational Research Association, San Diego.

Association of American Colleges and Universities. (1995). *American pluralism and the college curriculum: Higher education in a diverse democracy*. Washington, DC: Author.

Astin, A. W. (1977). *Four critical years*. San Francisco: Jossey-Bass.

Astin, A. W. (1993). *What matters in college? Four critical years revisited*. San Francisco: Jossey-Bass.

Astin, A. W., Korn, W. S., & Dey, E. L. (1991). *The American college teacher: National norms for the 1989–90 HERI Faculty Survey*. Los Angeles: Higher Education Research Institute.

Bikson, T. K., & Law, S. A. (1994). *Global preparedness and human resources*. Santa Monica, CA: RAND Institute.

Bowen, W., & Bok, D. (1998). *The shape of the river: The long-term consequences of considering race in college and university admissions*. Princeton, NJ: Princeton University Press.

Chang, M. (1996). *Racial diversity in higher education: Does a racially mixed student population affect educational outcomes?* Unpublished doctoral dissertation, University of California, Los Angeles.

Chickering, A., & Reisser, L. (1991). *Education and identity*. San Francisco: Jossey-Bass.

Cohen, E. (1994). *Designing groupwork: Strategies for heterogeneous classrooms* (2nd ed.). New York: Teachers College Press.

Cohen, E., Bianchini, J. A., Cossey, R., Holthuis, N. C., Morphew, C. C., & Whitcomb, J. A. (1997). What did students learn? 1982–1994. In E. G. Cohen & R. A. Lotan (Eds.), *Working for equity in heterogeneous classrooms*. New York: Teachers College Press.

Cross, K. P. (1987). Teaching for learning, *AAHE Bulletin, 40*, 3–7.

Dey, E. L., & Hurtado, S. (1993, May). *Promoting general education outcomes*. Paper presented at the annual meeting of the Association for Institutional Research (AIR), Chicago.

Dey, E. L., Hurtado, S., Kurotsuchi Inkelas, K., Rhee, B. S., Wimsatt, L., & Guan, F. (1997, May). *Improving research on student outcomes: A review of the strengths and limitations of national data*. Paper presented at the annual meeting of the Association for Institutional Research (AIR), Orlando, FL.

Gratz et al. v. Bollinger et al. No 97-75231 (E.D. Mich., filed 1997).

Grutter et al. v. Bollinger et al. No. 97-75928 (E.D. Mich., filed 1997).

Hurtado, S., Astin, A. W., Korn, W. S., & Dey, E. L. (1989). *The American college student, 1987: National norms for 1983 and 1985 college freshmen.* Los Angeles: Higher Education Research Institute.

Hurtado, S., Milem, J. F., Clayton-Pederson, A., & Allen, W. A. (1999). *Enacting diverse learning environments: Improving the climate for racial/ethnic diversity in higher education* (ASHE-ERIC Report Series, vol. 26, no. 8). Washington, DC: George Washington University.

Justiz, M. J. (1994). Demographic trends and the challenges to American higher education. In M. J. Justiz, R. Wilson, & L. G. Bjork (Eds.), *Minorities in higher education.* Phoenix, AZ: ACE/Oryx Press.

Muss, R. E. (1988). *Theories of adolescence* (5th ed.). New York: Random House.

Pascarella, E. T., Edison, M., Nora, A., Hagedorn, L. S., & Terenzini, P. T. (1996). Influences on students' openness to diversity and challenge in the first year of college. *Journal of Higher Education, 67*(2), 174–195.

Perry, W. (1970). *Forms of intellectual and ethical development in the college years: A scheme.* New York: Holt, Rinehart & Winston.

Piaget, J. (1975). *The equilibration of cognitive structures: The central problem of intellectual development.* Chicago: University of Chicago Press.

Selman, R. L. (1980). *The growth of interpersonal understanding: Developmental and clinical analyses.* New York: Academic Press.

Slavin, R. (1995). Cooperative learning groups and intergroup relations. In J. A. Banks & C. A. McGee Banks (Eds.), *Handbook of research on multicultural education.* New York: MacMillan.

Smith, D. (1996). *Achieving faculty diversity: Debunking the myths.* Washington, DC: Association of American Colleges and Universities.

Wolfe, C. T., & Spencer, S. J. (1996). Stereotypes and prejudice: Their overt and subtle influence in the classroom. *American Behavioral Scientist, 40,* 176–185.

CHAPTER 9

The Impact of Affirmative Action on Medical Education and the Nation's Health

TIMOTHY READY

Introduction

Political and judicial assaults on the use of race-conscious affirmative action in higher education admissions have created a crisis for those of us concerned with diversity in the medical profession. The purpose of this paper is to summarize the history of affirmative action in U.S. medical education and the impact of that policy on medical schools and on the nation as a whole. That impact has been both dramatic and overwhelmingly positive.

The Origins of Affirmative Action in U.S. Medical Schools

It was not long ago that medical schools, like most other institutions in U.S. society, were highly segregated and overwhelmingly white. The progress of desegregation has been such that we tend to forget how recently the laws and customs that enforced racial stratification and injustice in this country were dismantled.

The military was the first major American institution to desegregate, after the Korean War in the 1950s. The last vestiges of segregation in the armed forces were not eliminated until 1965.[1] The segregation of public schools and colleges—perhaps the most insidious form of racial discrimination—has been illegal since the 1954 U.S. Supreme Court decision in *Brown v. Board of Education,* but widespread desegregation of schools did not occur until the 1960s. Substantial progress was made in the 1970s, yet segregation in elementary and secondary schools continues to this day, accompanied by gross inequalities in the availability of educational resources, including overall levels of funding, quality of the curriculum, and availability of skilled teachers.[2]

The G.I. Bill of 1944 opened the door to higher education for the first time for many low-income and minority veterans, although black veterans from the South still were barred from all but historically black colleges. G.I. Bill funds enticed many northern universities to admit minority veterans; often they waived or lowered admission requirements to accommodate soldiers returning from the war, and the newly enrolled veterans generally performed well academically.[3] Thus this intervention by the federal government, though not specifically racially targeted, gave many black, Latino, and Native American students the opportunity to enter professions generally associated with a middle-class standard of living.

President Kennedy coined the term "affirmative action" in 1961, but affirmative action itself did not play a major role in federal policy until 1965, when President Johnson issued Executive Order 11246. This order required institutions doing business with the federal government to develop plans to seek out and employ qualified underrepresented minorities. Reginald Wilson argues that affirmative action had its greatest impact on higher education between 1965 and 1975, and the record of diversity at U.S. medical schools confirms his observation.

As was true elsewhere in higher education, medical schools began to take affirmative actions during the late 1960s to correct policies and practices that had perpetuated a system of quasi-apartheid in medical education. Only 2.2 percent of all medical students in 1964 were black, and 76 percent of all black medical students were enrolled at either Howard or Meharry—the nation's two historically black medical schools.[4] The other eighty-one medical schools enrolled, on average, one black student every two years. In 1968, the first year that the Association of American Medical Colleges (AAMC) began systematically to collect data on minority[5] students, only three Native Americans, twenty Mexican Americans, three mainland Puerto Ricans, and 266 blacks were among the 9,963 students enrolled in first-year classes; Meharry and Howard were still enrolling 50 percent of all black medical students.

Between 1968 and 1974, the number of black students enrolled in first-year medical classes increased from 266 (2.7 percent of the total) to 1,106 (7.5 percent). In the same period, the number of Native American students increased from 3 to 71; Mexican Americans, from 20 to 227; and mainland Puerto Ricans, from 3 to 68. Between 1964 and 1974, the per-

TABLE 1   *Average Annual Total and Excess Death in Blacks from Six Leading Causes of Mortality, U.S., 1979–1981*

Cause of Death	Excess Deaths, Males and Females, Cumulative to Age 70	
	Number	Percent
Heart disease and stroke	18,181	30.8
Homicide and accidents	10,909	18.5
Cancer	8,118	13.8
Infant mortality	6,178	10.5
Cirrhosis	2,154	3.7
Diabetes	1,850	3.1
Subtotal	47,390	80.4
All other causes	11,552	19.6

centage of all black students enrolled in the two historically black medical schools plummeted from 76 percent to 18 percent.[6]

The period from 1968 to 1974 brought significant integration in medical education. Why did this transformation happen so quickly? The assassination of Dr. Martin Luther King Jr. in 1968 was a catalytic event. It markedly heightened awareness of racial injustice in medical education and led to dramatic action. Despite the passage of civil rights laws prohibiting discrimination, medical schools had made little progress toward diversity. Beginning in 1968, they moved from a stance of race-neutral "receptive passivity" regarding minorities toward affirmative action to increase minority student outreach and enrollment.[7]

Awareness of racial and class disparities in the health of the American people also spurred medical educators, the federal government, and, to some extent, the public at large to support efforts to increase the number of minority doctors. For example, the difference in life expectancy between blacks and whites in 1970 was 7.6 years.[8,9] Although differences in socioeconomic status account for some of this gap, morbidity and mortality rates for blacks remain higher even after controlling for income. According to a landmark 1985 report by the Department of Health and Human Services, six causes of mortality accounted for more than 80 percent of the excess deaths for black Americans (see Table 1).[10]

Medical student activism after the assassination of Dr. King contributed to the heightened awareness of the injustice of maintaining policies and practices that excluded blacks and other minorities from the medical profession. There was growing recognition as well that the same minority groups that had borne the brunt of discriminatory treatment throughout U.S. history had the most acute medical needs and the least access to medical care. It was believed that minority doctors would be more likely to practice in underserved communities and to understand the cultures, beliefs, and concerns of minority patients.

Other arguments for increasing minority enrollment in medical schools have more recently emerged:[11]

- Student diversity enhances the teaching and learning of medicine for all students.
- Diversity is needed to set an appropriately comprehensive research agenda. As noted by AAMC President Jordan Cohen,

> Our society as a whole is plagued by many unsolved health problems, many of which swirl disproportionately around our minority populations. Our country's research agenda is, in large measure, set by those who have chosen careers in investigation. Individual investigators, in turn, tend to do research on problems that they "see." And what people see and what tickles their fancy depends, to a great extent, on their particular cultural and ethnic filters. Recognizing all of these truths leads to the reality that finding solutions to our country's most recalcitrant health problems, even being able to conceptualize what those problems are, will require a research work force that is much more diverse racially, ethnically, and by gender than we have now. Creating that work force begins with ensuring diversity among those admitted to our M.D. and Ph.D. educational programs.[12]

- The need for minority representation in the leadership of the health-care industry. Health care accounts for one-seventh of the gross domestic product. Racial and ethnic diversity in medical schools is needed to ensure that minorities are not excluded from leadership positions in this major industry.
- Diversity in the leadership of the health-care industry is essential to delivering high-quality care. Recent studies have found that minority patients often receive care that is different from and often inferior to that received by other patients. These differences are found even when the economic circumstances, including insurance coverage, of minority and nonminority patients are similar.[13]

Government and Foundation Support for Diversity[14]

Both the federal government and private foundations helped medical schools' efforts to support the academic preparation of prospective minority medical students, as well as their recruitment to and retention in medical school. The Josiah M. Macy Foundation was a pioneer in these efforts. In 1966 it funded postbaccalaureate programs for minority college graduates who were interested in medicine but needed extra academic preparation to qualify. The following year, the Macy Foundation sponsored a series of influential conferences for medical educators.

The first major financial support ($5 million) for minority recruitment, enrichment, and retention activities came in 1967 from the U.S. Public Health Service through its Special Health Career Opportunity Grant Program. In 1971, this program would be renamed the Health Careers Opportunity Program. This and other Public Health Service programs continue to support efforts to increase enrollment of minority and disadvantaged students in medical schools and the health professions.

In 1969, the federal Office of Economic Opportunity allocated $1.5 million to establish offices of minority affairs at the AAMC and at fifty-six health professional schools—mostly schools of medicine. In 1970, an AAMC task force called for a short-term goal that 12 percent of all medical students be from racial and ethnic groups underrepresented in medicine. This goal was set in relation to the broader objective of having minority students' numbers in medical schools reflect their representation in the population at large. To achieve this goal, medical schools were to work closely with undergraduate colleges to ensure that minority college students knew about opportunities in U.S. medical schools. Schools also were to address the financial issues that prevented many minority students from studying medicine. Medical schools also were asked to ensure that their minority students had mentors and were tied into a system of social and academic support that would enable them to persist in their studies and to graduate.

The AAMC Executive Council's endorsement of the Minority Task Force report included the following statement:

> In developing new and modifying existing educational programs, medical school faculties should be aware that minority students, while not always as well prepared in the traditional sciences basic to medicine, bring to the profession special talents and views which are unique and needed. Educational programming for all medical students should be sufficiently flexible to allow individual rates of prog-

ress and individualized special instruction. With such programming, the opportunity for minority student success will be maximized.[15]

Since the late 1960s and early 1970s, the National Institutes of Health and the Robert Wood Johnson, Kellogg, and Kaiser foundations also have supported minority student recruitment, academic enrichment, or retention activities in medical schools.

Affirmative Action in Medicine Has Worked

There is no question that the affirmative action initiatives of U.S. medical schools begun in the 1960s have been successful, in three interrelated ways. First, these racially targeted programs and policies were in fact responsible for dramatically increasing minority student enrollment in medical school. Second, the minority students who entered medical school through these programs performed academically at levels comparable to those of other students admitted in traditional ways. Finally, those admitted to the medical profession through affirmative action have proved to be more likely to address the health-care needs of minority and disadvantaged patients than other doctors.

Racial targeting increased minority enrollment significantly. As noted above, minority enrollment in medical school increased dramatically from the mid-1960s to 1974, when it reached 9 percent of the first-year class. These gains occurred because of direct affirmative action, both by medical schools and by undergraduate colleges that took similar measures to increase minority enrollment. Thus the number of well-prepared minority applicants to medical schools also was increasing. Medical schools actively recruited minority students, sponsored educational enrichment programs for minorities, and broadened the criteria for admissions decisions.

On average, the Medical College Admission Test (MCAT) scores and grades of minority medical students of that era were not as high as those of white students, as is the case today.[16] Nevertheless, medical schools recognized the social and moral imperative of making medical education accessible to students from racial and ethnic groups that were both underrepresented and disadvantaged. Besides sponsoring educational enrichment programs for minority premedical students and providing support services for enrolled students to enhance retention, medical schools began to examine the importance of noncognitive variables to students' success. The AAMC developed and implemented the Simulated Minority Admission Exercise[17] to help admissions committees recognize factors such as positive self-concept, ability to set long-term goals, realistic self-appraisal, and commitment to community service.

The rapid increase in minority enrollment between 1968 and 1974 leveled off in 1975. The numbers remained stagnant for the next fifteen years. Despite the continuation of most of the programs and policies from the previous era, minorities were more underrepresented in medical schools in 1990 than they were in 1974. Recognizing this pattern early on, the AAMC convened a second task force in 1978. Among its members was Louis Sullivan, dean of the newly created Morehouse School of Medicine, who in 1988 would become secretary of the Department of Health and Human Services under President Bush.

The 1978 task force found that the primary cause of the stagnation in minority enrollment was the small number of qualified minority applicants. It also noted that the goal of reaching 12 percent minority enrollment by 1975 was based on an

> overly optimistic assumption by the [1970] Task Force concerning the rate at which minority students would continue to be accepted from the minority applicant pool. The estimated admission rate of 75 percent for blacks in 1969–70 was never again achieved. The highest subsequent rate for black students was 57 percent in 1971. This rate dropped gradually to 38 percent in 1976, a figure essentially equivalent to that year's rate for majority students.[18]

Commenting on the adverse political and legal climate for affirmative action in 1978, the task force noted that

> although medical schools have not completely backed away from their efforts to increase the participation of minority students, many which had developed positive programs have appeared to modify their admissions programs and are awaiting the Supreme Court's [still pending] decision in the Bakke case.

The primary conclusion of the 1978 task force was that the size and quality of the applicant pool were two of the most critical factors affecting the number of minority students admitted. Its primary recommendation was that medical schools work with high schools and undergraduate colleges to increase the supply of academically well-prepared minority students interested in medicine.[19]

The 1978 task force made two other important recommendations. First, it increased the minority student enrollment goal, set at 12 percent in 1970, to 16 percent. This reflected a rapid increase in the minority population during those years, as well as the previously unaccounted-for presence of underrepresented minority groups other than blacks. Second, the task force recommended that medical schools work to increase the number of minority students in the applicant pool to 16 percent. Medical schools did not immediately act on these recommendations, but they would become the cornerstone of Project 3000 by 2000 in the 1990s (see below).[20]

The record of minorities in medical school has been good. Despite having lower average MCAT scores and undergraduate grades than whites, minority students have done well in medical school. They take slightly longer to graduate, but very few minority students drop out for academic reasons. According to AAMC enrollment statistics, 95 percent of 1992 matriculants from underrepresented minorities had either graduated or were still enrolled in 1996. Only 1.1 percent had been dismissed and 1.2 percent had withdrawn voluntarily. By comparison, 97 percent of nonminority matriculants had graduated or were still in school; 0.2 percent had been dismissed and 0.9 percent had withdrawn voluntarily.[21]

A national study of 1994 medical school graduates found that 88 percent of blacks, 95 percent of Hispanics, 97 percent of Asians, and 99 percent of whites had passed both Part 1 and Part 2 of the U.S. Medical Licensing Examination (USMLE) of the National Board of Medical Examiners six years after entering medical school.[22]

Another study published in 1997 in the *Journal of the American Medical Association* compared former students at the University of California at Davis School of Medicine who entered that school between 1968 and 1987 through affirmative action with other students from the same period. The study found that 94 percent of the affirmative action students had graduated, compared to 97 percent of all others. Although regular admission students scored slightly higher on their USMLE tests, there was no difference between the two groups in completion of residency training or evaluation of performance by residency directors. The authors of the study concluded that the affirmative action program at Davis had increased the diversity of the student population while producing no evidence of diluting the quality of graduates.[23]

Minority physicians disproportionately serve disadvantaged patients. A growing number of studies have reported essentially similar findings about minority physicians' impact on the health of the nation. One of the earliest studies, by Keith and others,[24] looked at the experiences of doctors who graduated from medical school in 1975. The authors found that minority physicians were more likely to practice in federally designated health-manpower shortage areas (12 percent versus 6 percent) and had more Medicaid recipients in their patient populations (31 percent for blacks, 24 percent for Hispanics, and 14 percent for whites). Physicians from each racial or ethnic group disproportionately served patients from their own group.

Relying on survey data from a national sample of 15,000 patients rather than data provided by physicians, Moy and Bartman found that minority physicians were more likely than white doctors to provide care for patients who are minorities, are indigent, or have more serious health problems.[25]

A study by Xu and others of a random sample of 2,600 generalist physicians (general internists, pediatricians, and family practitioners) who graduated from medical school in 1983 or 1984 also found that black, Hispanic, and Native American doctors were much more likely than those of other races to provide care for medically indigent patients. This study statistically controlled for other variables, such as gender; the income of the physician's family of origin; whether the doctor grew up in an inner city, suburban, or rural area; and the doctor's level of indebtedness from student loans. The authors found that race and ethnicity were the most important predictors that a physician would provide care to minority and medically underserved populations.

The authors concluded that

> these findings corroborate the assumptions of those concerned with strategies for recruiting underrepresented minority students. . . .
>
> One could speculate that underrepresented minority physicians are more willing to care for underserved patients because they are sensitive to the unmet needs of the population. . . . Conversely, underrepresented minority patients may prefer to seek out physicians with similar backgrounds. In either case, medical schools might wish to implement specific strategies to recruit underrepresented minority students, as well as to encourage all students to serve underserved populations.[26]

The authors also raise the possibility that minority physicians may be more likely to provide care to poor and minority patients because they cannot establish more "desirable" practices. Findings from an AAMC survey of U.S. medical students just before their graduation in 1996 do not support this hypothesis, however. Two-thirds of underrepresented minority graduates indicated a preference to locate in a socioeconomically deprived area compared to only 16 percent of all other graduates.[27]

Joel Cantor and colleagues studied findings from a survey that asked doctors who graduated from medical school in the 1980s about their practices. The authors examined whether minority physicians were more likely to provide care to minority patients and to the medically underserved (as has been found in virtually every other study), even after controlling for other factors such as the physician's gender and socioeconomic status. They found that doctors of all races who were from low-income backgrounds were more likely than others to provide care to disadvantaged populations, but that race, ethnicity, and gender of the physician were much more powerful predictors of care to the disadvantaged.

Discussing their findings in relation to the elimination of affirmative action in California, Cantor and colleagues wrote:

> Some in the affirmative action debate have advocated a shift from using race and ethnicity to define groups for special recruitment to using "disadvantage" as the defining characteristic. Our findings do not support such a substitution.[28]

A 1996 study of black and Latino physicians in California by Komaromy and others found that communities with high concentrations of black and Hispanic residents were four times as likely as others to have a shortage of doctors, regardless of the community's income. They also found that black physicians were much more likely than others to locate in communities with a high concentration of black residents, and Latino physicians were much more likely than others to practice in largely Hispanic communities. Black physicians were more likely to provide care to Medicaid patients, and Hispanic doctors provided a disproportionate amount of care to uninsured patients. The authors concluded:

> Black and Hispanic physicians have a unique and important role in caring for poor, black and Hispanic patients in California. Dismantling affirmative action programs, as is currently proposed, may threaten health care for both poor people and members of minority groups.[29]

Project 3000 by 2000

Project 3000 by 2000 is a campaign of U.S. medical schools to increase minority enrollment. Its goal is that 3,000 underrepresented minority students will matriculate annually at U.S. medical schools.[30] The number 3,000 is based on population parity for underrepresented minorities in the United States, as were the earlier goals set by the AAMC minority task forces. Project 3000 by 2000 recognizes that aggressive recruitment, affirmative action in admissions, and maintaining an environment in medical schools that is hospitable to minorities are necessary strategies to achieve diversity. These strategies alone, however, have proved insufficient to reach the profession's goals for diversity.[31]

For many years, the percentage of minorities in the medical school applicant pool has remained approximately the same as their percentage among matriculants. In 1998, for example, minorities made up 11 percent of all applicants and 11.6 percent of all matriculants. To achieve population parity among matriculants—approximately 20 percent—without a comparable increase in the percentage of minorities in the applicant pool would require changes in admission policies and practices that would dramatically favor minority applicants. This seems unlikely, to say the least, in the political and legal climate of the 1990s. For this reason, Project 3000 by 2000 has called on medical schools to work in partnership with feeder high schools and colleges to increase the number of academically well-prepared minority applicants. Medical schools have responded to this call by dramatically increasing their involvement in education partnerships with minority-serving schools and colleges.[32]

After Project 3000 by 2000 was launched, the number of underrepresented minority students entering medical school increased 36 percent, from 1,485 in 1990 to 2,024 in 1994, and remained virtually unchanged in 1995. The number of minority matriculants fell substantially in 1996 and 1997, primarily because of declines in the states of California, Texas, Louisiana, and Mississippi—states where new prohibitions against affirmative action had gone into effect. Minority enrollment increased slightly in 1998 with the result that the number of minority matriculants was still 26 percent higher than in 1990.

The enrollment gains that were achieved during Project 3000 by 2000 were made possible by a 65 percent increase in minority applicants between 1990 and 1995. While we do not know exactly why the minority applicant pool rose so quickly, it is likely related to the rising popularity of medicine as a career among both minority and nonminority students, as well as to substantial science education reform efforts, including minority targeted programs of the National Science Foundation, the National Institutes of Health, medical schools, and others.

Affirmative Action in Medical School Remains Imperative

The studies summarized above document the unique role that minority physicians play in addressing the health-care needs of minorities and the poor. Critics of affirmative action ask whether medical schools can't find other ways to address these needs without explicitly considering race and ethnicity in admissions.

There is little if any disagreement that educational reforms leading to the continued development of the minority applicant pool must be the foundation of any long-term solution to this problem. Now, and for the foreseeable future, however, large differences still exist between minorities and others on virtually all standardized tests,[33] including the MCAT.[34] To the extent that courts and politicians continue to cite the lower test scores of minorities as legitimate evidence that they are less "deserving" of educational opportunities, it is hard to imagine any short-term strategy other than race-conscious affirmative action that will be effective in producing diversity in medical schools.[35,36]

The MCAT may predict students' performance in basic science courses and on other standardized tests. But leading medical educators have long argued that there is no evidence that the MCAT predicts who will provide the kind of medical care that meets the most pressing needs of our communities.[37] "No one in their right mind would argue for admitting anyone to medical school who did not evidence the academic skills and personal qualities necessary for completing the M.D. degree," points out Jordan Cohen, president of the AAMC. However, once you move beyond the very low test scores that are predictive of academic risk, performance on the MCAT is essentially unrelated to the likelihood of successfully completing medical school.[38]

The students with the highest scores will not necessarily make the best doctors. Medical schools therefore do not consider the admissions process to be a contest among applicants for the highest test scores.

The AAMC's Jordan Cohen writes:

> Academic medicine (including the medical school admissions process) is, after all, largely about the future. It's about improving the health of future generations by educating physicians who will care for tomorrow's children, and by discovering better ways to keep tomorrow's children healthy. Given that our primary obligation to society is to furnish it with a physician work force appropriate to its needs, our mandate is to select and prepare students for the profession who, in the aggregate, bear a reasonable resemblance to the racial, ethnic, and, of course, gender profiles of the people they will serve.[39]

More than fifty professional organizations related to medicine have formed a coalition called Health Professionals for Diversity to express their support for affirmative action. Its members include the American

Medical Association, the American College of Physicians, the American College of Surgeons, the American Public Health Association, the American Academy of Pediatrics, the American Psychological Association, and the National Dental Association. Concerned about the continued ability of the medical profession to meet the nation's health-care needs, these leaders of American medicine have summed up their position as follows:

> Racial/ethnic diversity in the health professions work force is essential for the delivery of quality health care. At least for the short term, preserving the prerogative of health professions schools to consider race/ethnicity among the many factors they examine in admissions decisions is indispensable for the training of a diverse health professions work force.

Notes

1. National Research Council, *A Common Destiny: Blacks and American Society* (Washington, DC: National Academy Press, 1989), p. 67.
2. See Gary Orfield, Mark Bachmeier, David R. James, and Tamela Eitle, "Deepening Segregation in American Public Schools" (Cambridge, MA: Harvard Project on School Desegregation, April 5, 1997); James S. Coleman et al., "Equality of Educational Opportunity" (Washington, DC: Office of Education, 1966).
3. Reginald Wilson, "Affirmative Action in Higher Education," in *Minorities in Higher Education, 1995–96,* ed. Deborah J. Carter and Reginald Wilson (Washington, DC: American Council on Education, 1996), p. 37.
4. Herbert W. Nickens, Timothy Ready, and Robert G. Petersdorf, "Project 3000 by 2000: Racial and Ethnic Diversity in U.S. Medical Schools," *New England Journal of Medicine, 331* (1994), 472–476.
5. The term *minority,* when used in this paper in relation to medical education, is synonymous with *underrepresented minority.* Racial and ethnic groups recognized by the AAMC as underrepresented include blacks, Mexican Americans, mainland Puerto Ricans, and Native Americans. Individual medical schools may recognize other racial or ethnic groups as also being underrepresented.
6. Charles E. Odegaard, *Minorities in Medicine: From Receptive Passivity to Positive Action, 1966–76* (New York: Josiah Macy, Jr. Foundation, 1977), pp. 29–41.
7. See Roy K. Jarecky, "Medical School Efforts to Increase Minority Representation in Medicine," *Journal of Medical Education, 44* (1969), 912–918; Odegaard, *Minorities in Medicine,* pp. 22, 41.
8. U.S. Department of Health and Human Services, *Health Status of Minorities and Low Income Groups,* DHHS Publication No. (HRSA) HRS-P-DV 85-1 (1985), p. 41.
9. Since 1970, life expectancy at birth has increased for both blacks and whites. However, the 7.6-year racial gap that existed then had decreased only slightly to 6.6 years by 1996. *National Vital Statistics Report, 47,* No. 13 (1998).
10. Department of Health and Human Services, *Report of the Secretary's Task Force on Black and Minority Health, Vol. I: Executive Summary* (Washington, DC: Author, 1985), p. 5.
11. See Herbert W. Nickens, "The Rationale for Minority Targeted Programs in Medicine in the 1990s," *Journal of the American Medical Association, 267* (1992), 2390–

2395; Herbert W. Nickens and Jordan J. Cohen, "On Affirmative Action," *Journal of the American Medical Association, 275* (1996), 572–574.

12. Jordan J. Cohen, "Finishing the Bridge to Diversity," *Academic Medicine, 72* (1997), 105.

13. See Kenneth C. Goldberg, Arthur J. Hartz, Steven J. Jacobson, Henry Krakauer, and Alfred A. Rimm, "Racial and Community Factors Influencing Coronary Artery Bypass Graft Surgery Rates for All 1986 Medicare Patients," *Journal of the American Medical Association, 267* (1992), 1473–1477; Mark B. Wenneker and Arnold M. Epstein, "Racial Inequalities in the Use of Procedures for Patients with Ischemic Heart Disease in Massachusetts," *Journal of the American Medical Association, 261* (1989), 253–257; Edward L. Hannan, Harold Kilburn Jr., Joseph O'Donnell, Gary Lukacik, and Eileen P. Shields, "Interracial Access to Selected Cardiac Procedures for Patients Hospitalized with Coronary Artery Disease in New York State," *Medical Care, 29* (1991), 430–441; Marian E. Gornick, Paul W. Eggers, Thomas W. Reilly et al., "Effects of Race and Income on Mortality and Use of Services Among Medicare Beneficiaries," *New England Journal of Medicine, 335* (1996), 791–799; Kevin A. Schulman, Jesse A. Berlin, William Harless et al., "The Effect of Race and Sex on Physicians' Recommendations for Cardiac Catheterization," *New England Journal of Medicine, 340* (1999), 618–625.

14. For a more detailed discussion of the issues in this section, see Timothy Ready and Herbert W. Nickens, "Programs That Make a Difference," in *More Minorities in Health,* ed. Barbara H. Kehrer and Hugh C. Burroughs (Menlo Park, CA: Henry J. Kaiser Family Foundation, 1994), pp. 29–90, 143–145.

15. Odegaard, *Minorities in Medicine,* p. 26.

16. Association of American Medical Colleges, *Minority Students in Medical Education: Facts and Figures, Tenth Edition* (Washington, DC: Lois Bergeisen, 1997), pp. 70–71.

17. William E. Sedlacek and Dario O. Prieto, "Predicting Minority Students' Success in Medical Schools," *Academic Medicine, 65* (1990), 161–166.

18. *Report of the Association of American Medical Colleges Task Force on Minority Student Opportunities in Medicine* (Washington, DC: AAMC, 1978), p. 14.

19. *Report of the Association of American Medical Colleges Task Force,* p. 21.

20. Robert G. Petersdorf, Katherine Turner, Herbert W. Nickens, and Timothy Ready, "Minorities in Medicine: Past, Present and Future," *Academic Medicine, 65* (1990), 633–670.

21. Association of American Medical Colleges, *Minority Students in Medical Education,* p. 77.

22. Stephen Case, David Swanson, Donna Ripkey et al., "Performance of the Class of 1994 in the New Era of USMLE," *Academic Medicine, 71,* No. 10 (1996), S91–S93.

23. Robert C. Davidson and Ernest L. Lewis, "Affirmative Action and Other Special Consideration Admissions at the University of California, Davis, School of Medicine," *Journal of the American Medical Association, 278* (1997), 1153–1158.

24. Stephen N. Keith, Robert M. Bell, August G. Swanson, and Albert P. Williams, "Effects of Affirmative Action in Medical Schools: A Study of the Class of 1975," *New England Journal of Medicine, 313* (1985), 1519–1525.

25. Ernest Moy and Barbara Bartman, "Physician Race and Care of Minority and Medically Indigent Patients," *Journal of the American Medical Association, 273* (1995), 1515–1520.

26. Gang Xu, Sylvia Fields, Christine Laine, J. Jon Voloski, Barbara Barzansky, and Carlos J. Martini, "The Relationship between Race/Ethnicity of Generalist Physicians and Their Care for Underserved Populations," *American Journal of Public Health, 87* (1997), 817–822.

27. Association of American Medical Colleges, *Minority Students in Medical Education,* pp. 36–37.

28. Joel Cantor, Erika L. Miles, Laurence C. Baker, and Dianne C. Baker, "Physician Service to the Underserved: Affirmative Action in Medical Education," *Inquiry, 33* (1996), 167–180.

29. Miriam Komaromy, Kevin Grumbach, Michael Drake et al., "The Role of Black and Hispanic Physicians in Providing Health Care for Underserved Populations," *New England Journal of Medicine, 334* (1996), 1305–1310.

30. Nickens, Ready, and Petersdorf, "Project 3000 by 2000," 472–476.

31. Robert G. Petersdorf, "Not a Choice, an Obligation," *Academic Medicine, 67* (1992), 73–79.

32. William T. Butler, "Project 3000 by 2000: Progress during Tumultuous Times," *Academic Medicine, 74* (1999), 308–309.

33. L. Scott Miller, *An American Imperative: Accelerating Minority Educational Achievement* (New Haven, CT: Yale University Press, 1995), pp. 1–83.

34. Association of American Medical Colleges, *Minority Students in Medical Education: Facts and Figures, Eleventh Edition* (Washington, DC: Lois Bergeisen, 1998), pp. 55, 57, 59.

35. *Questions and Answers on Affirmative Action in Medical Education* (Washington, DC: Association of American Medical Colleges, 1998).

36. William G. Bowen and Derek Bok, *The Shape of the River: Long-Term Consequences of Considering Race in College and University Admissions* (Princeton, NJ: Princeton University Press, 1998), pp. 15–52.

37. Nickens and Cohen, "On Affirmative Action," pp. 572–574.

38. Nickens and Cohen, "On Affirmative Action," pp. 572–574.

39. Cohen, "Finishing the Bridge to Diversity," pp. 103–109.

CHAPTER 10

Racial Differences in the Effects of College Quality and Student Body Diversity on Wages

KERMIT DANIEL
DAN A. BLACK
JEFFREY SMITH

In recent years, the advent of affirmative action programs at colleges and universities in the United States has generated widespread controversy. Bowen and Bok (1998) and Trow (1999) provide recent examples on either side of the issue. One of the most notable aspects of this controversy is that, until very recently, empirical evidence has played a very small role in it. In this chapter, we contribute to the discussion by providing empirical evidence on two related questions that underlie the debate. Our study finds that there may be substantial earning gains related to diversity, gains that may extend to white as well as black students.

Diversity programs have the effect of raising the average quality of the university that students in the minority group favored by the program attend, relative to what their other characteristics would imply.[1] Such programs have a wide variety of potential justifications, but we focus only on two possible economic rationales for these programs. The first is that the return to college quality may be higher for the group helped by the program. If so, to the extent that the taxpayers rather than the students provide the funds for higher education, it makes sense for colleges, acting as the taxpayers' agents, to spend those funds where their return is highest.

The second is that a racially diverse student body may have direct benefits to students in either the minority or the majority group. A diverse student body may provide minority students with access to wider social networks, which in turn could lead to better jobs and higher earnings. At the same time, being able to interact with individuals from other racial (and, in many cases, family income) backgrounds may be a skill that the market values; majority students who attend universities with racially diverse student bodies may be more likely to learn this skill. In either case, affirmative action programs might then be justified on the grounds that they increase the value of the education provided by the university.

In this chapter we use data from the National Longitudinal Survey of Youth (NLSY)—a random sample of young people in the United States—to provide basic evidence on both of these questions. First, using information on college quality collected from two sources, matched to information on the colleges attended by members of our sample, we estimate the effect of college quality on wages separately for blacks and nonblacks.[2] Second, using information on the fraction of black students at each college, we estimate the effect on later wages of attending a college with a more diverse student body.[3]

The NLSY is ideal for this purpose, for two reasons. First, selection bias is a major risk when estimating the effect of college quality on wages. We expect students at high-quality universities to differ in important ways from students at low-quality universities because the selection of colleges by students (and vice versa) is not random. For example, students at higher-quality colleges may be there largely because they have higher ability, more motivation, better-educated parents, or have attended better primary and secondary schools. These characteristics also increase later wages, so failure to control for them in estimating the effect of college quality leads one to overstate its effect. Unfortunately, these characteristics, while obvious to college admissions officers, are often hidden from researchers trying to understand wages.

The NLSY contains a rich set of observable characteristics that, taken together, reveal some of the differences across students that remain hidden in other data sets. The data include an ability measure, geographic location, characteristics of the parents and of the student's home environment as a child, high school characteristics, and detailed labor market histories before, during, and after college. Because many colleges use test scores and high school grades as major determinants of admissions, it is particularly important that data contain a well-regarded measure of academic ability. This measure is based on the Armed Services Vocational Aptitude Battery (ASVAB). Numerous authors, including O'Neill (1990), Blackburn and Neumark (1992), and Neal and Johnson (1996), have used these ASVAB scores to control for otherwise unobserved differences in ability. By controlling for all of these characteristics, we can reduce (or eliminate) the selection bias in our estimates of the effect of college quality.

The second reason for making use of the NLSY in this context is that it represents the most recent panel with several years of available post-college wage data. Thus, we can look at the effect of college quality or of student body racial composition in college on wages after most of the respondents have had a few years to get established in their careers.

The NLSY data provide a strong answer to one of the questions we address and mixed findings on the other. The mixed findings concern the question of whether or not the racial diversity of the college student body (here proxied by the percentage of students who are black) has an effect on later wages. We find a positive effect for men who are not black of attending a college with at least 5 percent black students. The data suggest a hill-shaped pattern with the largest positive wage effect on nonblacks attending colleges with 8 to 17 percent black students. We cannot reject the hypothesis that the effects of the percentage of black students on later wages do not differ between black and nonblack men. In contrast, Daniel, Black, and Smith (1995) find no evidence of an effect on white women and only modest evidence of an effect for black women. For the latter group, the largest effect is associated with colleges with from 5 to 7 percent black students, rather than from 8 to 17 percent as for black men.

Our data provide stronger evidence regarding the other question we address, whether and how much college quality affects later wages. We find that the effect of college quality on the later wages of black men is roughly triple that for nonblack men. We report a similar finding for women in Daniel, Black, and Smith (1995). For both men and women, this result is not sensitive to alternative ways of specifying the wage equation. It is consistent with Loury and Garman's (1995) finding of larger effects of college quality for black men in their study using the National Longitudinal Survey of the High School Class of 1972. The benefit to attending a higher-quality college or university is apparently much greater for black students than for others.

In the next section we describe our data. In section three, we describe the construction of our index of college quality. Section four presents our empirical findings. Finally, in section five we draw some conclusions from our findings and offer some important caveats regarding their interpretation.

Data

Our data come from three sources. Our primary source is the NLSY, a panel data set based on annual surveys of a sample of men and women who were ages 14–21 on January 1, 1979. Respondents were first interviewed in 1979 and have been reinterviewed each year since then. Of the five subsamples that comprise the NLSY, we use only the representative cross-section and the minority oversamples.

The NLSY provides the identity of the colleges that respondents attended. For each respondent who attended college, we attach his or her college's characteristics. Our data on college characteristics come from the U.S. Department of Education's Integrated Postsecondary Education Data System (IPEDS) for 1990 and *U.S. News and World Report*'s Directory of Colleges and Universities (1991). The former source provides most of the information about the colleges' finances and faculties; the latter provides most of the summary information about the colleges' students. Because data are available on college characteristics only for a limited number of two-year colleges, we only include information on four-year colleges in our data.[4]

The College Quality Index

Our data include seventeen different college characteristics. Empirically, we find in Daniel, Black, and Smith (1995, 1997) that for both men and women, these characteristics positively correlate with one another.[5] Related to this, each one entered separately has a positive effect on later wages (when coded so that higher values correspond to higher "quality"). To simplify the interpretation and exposition of our analysis, and because we view each of these characteristics as a noisy measure of some underlying true notion of quality, we construct a quality index based on a subset of these variables.[6]

In this chapter, we use the indices we constructed in Daniel, Black, and Smith (1995, 1997). Because not all of the college characteristics are available for every college, we faced a trade-off in constructing the indices between the number of variables used in the index and the number of colleges for which the index could be calculated. We found empirically that indices based on at least three characteristics tended to be highly correlated with one another, while indices constructed with only two characteristics sometimes were not. We carefully examined the correlations across indices constructed using different characteristics and the number of colleges for which we could construct each index. Based on this examination, we use the first factor of spending per student, the rejection rate, and the average SAT score of the entering class as our index for men. For women, we use the first principal component[7] of spending per student, the faculty/student ratio, the rejection rate, the average SAT of the entering class, and the fractions of the entering class in the top 10 and top 25 percent of their high school class.

While our choice of characteristics to use in constructing the indices is somewhat ad hoc, they appear to do a good job of capturing what we mean by college quality. The rankings of the colleges implicit in our indices correspond well to a priori notions of quality. For example, for men the top five colleges are Stanford, MIT, Yale, Harvard, and Columbia. Visual inspection of the entire rankings for both men and women suggest that the indices produce a reasonable ordering of colleges. Finally, the results presented in the next section are robust to variation in the particular characteristics included in the indices.

Empirical Findings

In this section we present our findings regarding the effect of university quality and racial composition of the college student body on later wages for both blacks and nonblacks. Table 1 presents our estimates for men in the NLSY. For reasons of space, we discuss but do not present results for women.[8] For each specification in Table 1 we report selected coefficients of interest from a regression, with the natural log of the real wage for the year ending in the 1987 interview as its dependent variable. Each column in the table corresponds to a different set of conditioning variables; a complete list of the variables in each specification appears in the notes to the table. With the exception of the final column, the set of conditioning variables becomes richer, moving from left to right in the table. Surprisingly, our substantive results do not depend on the set of conditioning variables used.

The first pair of rows in Table 1 shows the estimates from regressions that include the fraction black of the student body at each respondent's college, along with an interaction term between the fraction black and whether or not the respondent himself is black. The estimated effect for nonblacks consists of the coefficient on the fraction black variable, while the estimated effect for blacks consists of the sum of the coefficient on the fraction black and that on the interaction term. For example, in the first column the estimated effect for nonblacks is 0.431, while that for blacks is –0.102 (= 0.431–0.533). These estimates indicate a small and marginally statistically significant impact of the fraction black on the wages of nonblack men, and no effect, or a small negative effect, on the wages of black men.

The next three rows present the estimated coefficients from adding our college quality index to the specification just considered. To the extent that college quality is correlated with the fraction of black students, omitting it may bias the coefficient on the fraction of black students. We find that including the quality index reduces the standard errors on the fraction black variable, so that the positive effect for nonblacks is now consistently statistically significant. The point estimates of the fraction black coefficient also increase somewhat in all of the specifications. Overall, however, the key substantive findings remain unchanged.

The final set of four rows presents the coefficient estimates from a specification that adds an interaction between the college quality index and whether or not the respondent is black. This interaction term allows us to obtain separate estimates of the effect of the quality of college on the later wages of blacks and nonblacks. We consider the estimated quality effects shortly; first, note that adding this additional interaction term has almost no effect on the estimated coefficients for the fraction black variable or its interaction with whether the respondent is black.

The specifications presented in Table 1 allow only a linear effect of the fraction of black students at the respondent's college on his wage. To check for potential non-linear effects, Daniel, Black, and Smith (1997) divide the fraction black into categories and include categorical indicators in the log wage equation in place of the fraction black variable (see their Table 4). Because of the very different distributions of the fraction black variable among black and nonblack NLSY respondents, choosing categories such that each category includes a reasonable number of blacks and nonblacks is somewhat difficult. In the NLSY, for nonblack men, the 25th percentile is 2 percent black; the 50th percentile is 5 percent; the 75th percentile is 8 percent. For black men, the 25th, 50th, and 75th percentiles are 7, 16, and 83 percent black, respectively.

After careful examination of the available data, Daniel, Black, and Smith (1997) use categories of 0–4 percent black, 5–7 percent black, 8–17 percent black, and more than 17 percent black. They include indicators for the latter three categories both by themselves and interacted with an indicator for whether or not the respondent is black. For specifications without the interaction terms, those attending colleges with between 5 and 7 percent black students earn more than those attending colleges with fewer than 5 percent black students. In addition, men attending colleges with between 8 and 17 percent black students earn more than men

TABLE 1 *Wages and Racial Composition of Student Body*

	(1)	(2)	(3)	(4)	(5)	(6)	(7)
Race							
Fraction black	.431**	.402*	.305	.304	.357*	.346	.443**
	(.213)	(.210)	(.216)	(.216)	(.215)	(.214)	(.206)
Fraction black interacted with black indicator	−.533**	−.506**	−.427*	−.431*	−.491**	−.475**	−.556**
	(.228)	(.226)	(.231)	(.231)	(.230)	(.230)	(.222)
Fraction black	.498**	.468**	.379*	.376*	.429**	.422**	.514**
	(.218)	(.214)	(.217)	(.218)	(.216)	(.214)	(.209)
Fraction black interacted with black indicator	−.542**	−.517**	−.440*	−.444*	−.502**	−.487**	.566**
	(.229)	(.227)	(.231)	(.230)	(.229)	(.228)	(.222)
College quality index	.068**	.071**	.070**	.069**	.066**	.066**	.069**
	(.022)	(.021)	(.021)	(.021)	(.020)	(.020)	(.021)
Fraction black	.497**	.468**	.380*	.376*	.431**	.424**	.517**
	(.218)	(.214)	(.217)	(.217)	(.215)	(.214)	(.209)
Fraction black interacted with black indicator	−.483**	−.454*	−.386*	−.389*	−.444*	−.431*	−.501**
	(.233)	(.231)	(.234)	(.234)	(.232)	(.231)	(.226)
College quality index	.050**	.052**	.053**	.053**	.048**	.048**	.048**
	(.024)	(.024)	(.023)	(.023)	(.022)	(.023)	(.024)
College quality index interacted with black indicator	.099**	.109**	.095*	.095*	.103*	.101*	.117**
	(.057)	(.055)	(.056)	(.056)	(.057)	(.056)	(.055)

[1] "**" indicates statistical significance at the 5 percent level; "*" indicates statistical significance at the 10 percent level.

[2] The sample size is 2,834 in each column.

[3] White (1980) heteroskedasticity-consistent standard errors appear in parentheses.

[4] The dependent variable is the natural log of the wage for the year ending in the 1987 interview. All specifications include a constant, a variable indicating whether or not the respondent had any postsecondary schooling, ability controls in the form of the first two principal components of the respondent's age-adjusted ASVAB scores and these two variables squared, years of schooling completed, years of postsecondary schooling completed, quartics in age, tenure, pre–college-graduation labor market experience and postcollege-graduation labor market experience, and indicators for race and ethnicity, Census region, urban residence and receipt of a bachelor's degree. Specification (2) adds indicators for college major. Specification (3) adds indicators for industry of employment in 1987 and union status to specification (2). Specification (4) adds variables capturing characteristics of the respondent's home environment while growing up to specification (3). Specification (5) adds characteristics of the respondent's parents to specification (4). Specification (6) adds characteristics of the respondent's high school to specification (5). Specification (7) repeats specification (6) but drops the industry of employment and union status variables. Daniel, Black, and Smith (1995, 1997) describe the construction of the variables in detail.

[5] In all cases, with the exception of the dependent variable, we include indicators for values missing due to item nonresponse rather than performing list-wise deletion.

attending schools with fewer than 8 percent black students and more than 17 percent black students.

Daniel, Black, and Smith (1997) report similar findings when they include interactions between the fraction black categories and the indicator for whether or not the respondent is black. In particular, formal statistical tests do not reject the null hypothesis that the coefficients on the interaction terms for the fraction black categories are zero. This evidence suggests that the relationship for men between the fraction of black students at their college and later wages is hill-shaped for both groups. The signs of the coefficients in Table 1 on the fraction black variable result from the differing distributions of the fraction black variable among blacks and nonblacks in the data. The nonblack data are concentrated in the upward sloping part of the hill at low levels of the fraction black, while the black data are concentrated on the downward-sloping part of the hill at higher levels of the fraction black. The result is a positive coefficient for nonblacks and a negative coefficient for blacks when estimating a linear specification like that in Table 1.

Our findings for women, reported in Daniel, Black and Smith (1995), reveal much less evidence of an effect of the fraction of black students in college on later wages. We find no effect for white women in any of the specifications we examine. In every specification we examine for this group, we estimate small positive coefficients with relatively large standard errors. For black women, we find evidence that attending a college with 5 to 7 percent black students is associated with higher wages later on, compared to colleges with a higher or lower percentage black. The magnitude of the effect is about twice what we found for men.

In sum, even after controlling for college quality and student characteristics, we find evidence that attending a college with a moderately diverse student body, as measured by the fraction of black students, raises earnings for both black and nonblack men. In contrast, for women we report evidence of a weaker effect that appears to apply only to black women.

We now turn to the effects of college quality on black and nonblack students. For this question, the results for men and women stand in complete agreement. The estimates in the final row of Table 1 imply an effect of college quality on black male students from three to four times as large as that for nonblack male students. These estimates represent a substantively important effect: for nonblack men they imply around a 10 percent increase in wages when going from the bottom quintile to the top quintile of the distribution of college quality in our sample. Similar estimates emerge in specifications without the fraction black variable or its interaction with whether the respondent is black. As noted earlier, Loury and Garman (1995) report a similar finding using different data on men in an earlier cohort. Daniel, Black, and Smith (1995) find a similar ratio in their estimated effects of college quality for black and white women, although the results are somewhat less robust for women than for men.

Conclusion

In this chapter we provide empirical evidence from a recent cohort of American youth on two fundamentally empirical questions that underlie the policy debate surrounding diversity programs that favor minority groups in college admissions. In regard to the first question, the different effects of attending a higher-quality college on black and nonblack students, we find strong evidence of a much larger effect of college quality on the later wages of blacks than of nonblacks. This finding is consistent with that found by other authors using different data sets. The larger effect for blacks provides an efficiency justification for diversity programs at good colleges. Our analysis does not distinguish effects of college quality resulting from increased productivity from those resulting from the value of college quality as a signal in the labor market. That topic remains for future work.

We regard our findings on the effects of a racially diverse student body on later wages as provocative but at the same time merely suggestive. Policy should not be based upon them but, we argue, future research should be. The reasons for thinking the results provocative hardly need stating. If the relationship we find in the data really is causal, so that male students (and black female students) at more racially diverse colleges have higher wages later in life, then this has important implications for policy in this area.

At the same time, there are empirical and theoretical reasons for being cautious about basing policy on these results. First, we cannot ignore the possibility that the fraction black variable may proxy for some other dimension of college quality not well captured by our quality index. In this case, the observed relationship results from omitted variable bias, not from a causal effect of the fraction of black students in college on later wages. Second, our diversity measure is not ideal and corresponds to only one part of what most college diversity programs do. Such programs typically seek to increase the representation of many minority groups in addition to blacks. Our results, obviously, have nothing to say about the other aspects of these programs.

Third, the lack of a consistent effect across groups of the fraction black variable may be a red flag. We find no effect for white women and a different relationship in terms of the optimal fraction black for black women than we find for black men. We can think of no theoretical reason why a causal effect would differ between men and women, so the differences are troubling. They suggest that we have uncovered something other than a causal relationship. Fourth, we hesitate to push the view that this relationship is causal in the absence of what economists call "microfoundations." That is, we would like to see a well-developed theory of how the fraction of students who are black can affect later wages, and to see some empirical evidence at the micro level consistent with that theory. In the absence of a convincing story at the micro level, a strong interpretation of our estimates awaits further research.

Finally, we note that in a complete cost-benefit analysis of college diversity programs, many other factors must weigh in beyond just later wage effects, should our results turn out to reflect a causal impact. These other factors include the dissension and acrimony observed on some campuses over unequal entrance requirements across groups. At the same time, our results regarding the racial composition of the college student body are surprising and highly provocative. Further research could shed additional light on the extent to which the estimated effects are causal, on the reasons for the different effects found for men and women, and on the individual-level behavior that accounts for the measured effects at the group level.

Notes

1. For the remainder of the chapter, we use the term *diversity program* or just *program* to refer to the full range of programs from affirmative action as originally conceived right up through explicit numerical quotas.
2. We are unable to examine the effect of college quality on later wages separately for members of other racial and ethnic groups due to sample size limitations. Our combining African Americans with other black ethnic groups was similarly driven by sample size considerations. The vast majority of the respondents we characterize as "black" identify themselves in the NLSY as "African American."
3. While we would prefer to examine multiple measures of racial and ethnic diversity, including in particular measures that included groups other than just blacks, the available data limit us to this single measure.
4. For a more detailed description of the data, see Daniel, Black, and Smith (1995, 1997).
5. All of the variables were coded so that higher values correspond to higher quality.
6. Daniel, Black, and Smith (1997) provide a theoretical justification for our procedure for constructing the indices based on the idea that the individual characteristics constitute noisy signals of a latent unobserved quality variable.
7. In both samples, quality indices constructed using factor analysis or principal components analysis on the same set of variables have a correlation of 0.99. Our theoretical justification corresponds more closely to factor analysis.

8. Daniel, Black, and Smith (1997) present a full set of results for men, while Daniel, Black, and Smith (1995) present a full set of results for women.

References

Blackburn, M., & Neumark, D. (1992). Unobserved ability, efficiency wages and interindustry wage differentials. *Quarterly Journal of Economics, 107*, 1421–1436.

Bowen, W., & Bok, D. (1998). *The shape of the river: Long-term consequences of considering race in college and university admissions.* Princeton, NJ: Princeton University Press.

Daniel, K., Black, D., & Smith, J. (1995). *College characteristics and the wages of young women.* Unpublished manuscript, University of Western Ontario.

Daniel, K., Black, D., & Smith, J. (1997). *College quality and the wages of young men.* University of Western Ontario Department of Economics, Working Paper No. 9707.

Loury, L., & Garman, D. (1995). College selectivity and earnings. *Journal of Labor Economics, 13*, 289–308.

Neal, D., & Johnson, W. (1996). The role of premarket factors in black-white wage differences. *Journal of Political Economy, 104*, 869–895.

O'Neill, J. (1990). The role of human capital in earnings differences between black and white men. *Journal of Economic Perspectives, 4*, 25–45.

Trow, M. (1999). *California after racial preferences. Public Interest, 135*, 64–85.

U.S. News and World Report. (1991). *1992 College Guide.* Washington, DC: Author.

CHAPTER 11

Increasing Diversity Benefits: How Campus Climate and Teaching Methods Affect Student Outcomes

JEFFREY F. MILEM

Affirmative action to increase the numbers of minority students and faculty at selective colleges rests on the U.S. Supreme Court's 1978 finding, in *Regents of the University of California v. Bakke,* that diversity is important to the core functions of a university. The current challenge to *Bakke* includes the claim that diversity does not, in practice, have the positive effects attributed to it by most educators. Critics often cite, for example, the lower retention rates and lower grades of minority students at selective colleges. But the relationship between campus diversity and such student outcomes is not as simple as these critics imply. Bowen and Bok (1998) offer compelling evidence that challenges this assertion. Moreover, these criticisms of affirmative action suggest that the persistence and academic achievement of students can only be ascribed to the characteristics and attributes of individual students. This assertion completely ignores the role that institutions have in encouraging (or discouraging) persistence and other indicators of academic success.

Studies of public school desegregation clearly demonstrate that the benefits of student diversity depend on the responses of the institution to its changing make-up.[1] Janet Ward Schofield writes in this volume that "desegregation and student diversity is just the first step in a long process, and . . . attention to the many specifics of that process is absolutely vital if one wants to maximize the potential benefits and minimize the potential problems." Therefore, in assessing the success or failure of affirmative action in higher education it is essential to pay attention not only to admissions practices but also to campus climate, the content of the curriculum, and the ability of faculty to adapt their teaching methods to the needs of students.

This study explores the relationship between student diversity, campus climate, faculty composition, and the content of research and teaching. It finds that the institutions that have made the most progress in increasing the enrollment of minority students—the selective research universities—are in many respects the least flexible and least adaptive in responding to changing student needs. These institutions are dominated by faculty oriented to specialized research, not to flexible approaches to teaching.

This study also finds that simply admitting more minority students does not produce the substantial changes in teaching approaches or content necessary to realize the full benefits of diversity. Such changes do take place, however, where there is increased faculty diversity and leadership that alters the campus climate. These findings suggest that the value of diversity in practice depends on the kind of institution minority students gain access to and the degree to which those schools adapt. In particular, it is enhanced by faculty who build diversity into the teaching and research missions of the university.

Conceptualizing the Campus Climate

Hurtado, Milem, Clayton-Pedersen, and Allen (1998, 1999) suggest a four-dimensional framework for describing the campus racial climate. These dimensions consist of: 1) an institution's historical legacy of inclusion or exclusion of various racial or ethnic groups; 2) structural diversity, or the numerical and proportional representation of diverse groups on campus; 3) the psychological climate, including perceptions and attitudes between groups; and 4) and the behavioral climate, or nature of intergroup relations on campus. The institutional climate for diversity on campus is a product of these four dimensions. Hurtado et al. (1998, 1999) argue that campus climate has been examined almost exclusively from a structural perspective. When structural diversity is increased without considering the other dimensions of climate, problems are likely to result. Support for this assertion can be found in the work of race relations theorists who assert that the larger the relative size of a minority group, the more likely minority individuals will come into conflict with members of the majority (Blalock, 1967). A number of studies of the impact of structural diversity on campus document this finding (Hurtado et al., 1998, 1999).

However, conflict need not be a destabilizing force in higher education institutions. Conflict, after all, is an essential part of research and education. In fact, some kinds of conflict are probably a necessary precondition for real changes in campus race relations and for serious intellectual
exchanges. Palmer (1987) argues that a "primary virtue" of a university is
a "capacity for creative conflict" and that "healthy conflict is possible
only in the context of supportive community" (p. 25). Students are generally unable to bring such creative conflict to classrooms for fear of being
exposed, appearing ignorant, or being called stupid.

Factors That Influence How Faculty Teach

A large body of research indicates that active forms of learning enhance
student learning and development when they are used in the classroom
(e.g., see Astin, 1993; Johnson & Johnson, 1985, 1986a, 1986b; Johnson,
Johnson, & Smith, 1988; Milem & Wakai, 1996a, 1996b; Slavin, 1987,
1988). Active learning methods include the use of cooperative learning,
student presentations, group projects, experiential learning, student eval-
uations of others' work, independent learning projects, student-selected
course topics, class discussions, student-designed learning activities, and
the absence of extensive lecturing as pedagogical techniques in classrooms (Astin, 1993). These more "active" techniques enable students to
exercise initiative and assume responsibility for their own learning. Moreover, the use of these teaching methods in the classroom gives students
opportunities to come together to communicate across communities of
difference—essential activities in efforts to build a more supportive campus racial climate (Hurtado et al., 1998, 1999).

Research on teaching methods indicates that faculty characteristics
have a strong influence on learning (Easton & Guskey, 1983; Kozma,
Belle, & Williams, 1978). Studies show that women and faculty from historically underrepresented racial and ethnic groups are more likely to report using student-centered approaches to teaching and "active learning"
techniques such as class discussion (Milem & Wakai, 1996a, 1996b;
Milem & Astin, 1992). One study found female professors more likely
than males to encourage students' input and independence, and to view
students as active collaborators in learning (Statham, Richardson, &
Cook, 1991).

Merton (1973) looked at institutional "outsiders"—those having
lower social status—and asserted that they gain special perspective and
insight that may lead them to inquire into problems relevant to their
groups and to develop unique solutions. As teachers, racial and ethnic

outsiders may be more likely to be sensitive to classroom dynamics that are taken for granted by insiders.

Institutional characteristics also influence teaching practice. Faculty at research universities have consistently been shown to spend less time teaching and advising students and more time on their own research and publications (Astin 1993; Astin & Chang, 1995; Bayer, 1973; Ladd, 1979). Research evidence also indicates that the size of an institution influences faculty teaching practices. Smaller institutions tend to provide educational advantages to students that include more effective teaching practices (Astin, 1993; Bowen, 1977; Chickering, 1971; Feldman & Newcomb, 1969).

The climate of an organization can influence people's behavior, and thus may be linked to teaching practices. A school's administration can help create a climate that promotes high faculty morale, according to Baldwin and Krotseng (1985), by being responsive to faculty needs and allowing teachers to feel autonomous and in control of their work. Guskin and Bassis (1985) assert that faculty are more motivated and committed to their work at institutions where the administration encourages them to take part in decisionmaking. Altschuler and Richter (1985) suggest that administrators working to prevent burnout should encourage faculty to learn new skills, including new teaching practices. Finally, Kozma, Belle, and Williams (1978) argue that institutional climates with high tolerance for deviation and desirability for change facilitate quality teaching by supporting innovative efforts for improvement.

Data, Methodology, and Outcome Measures

This chapter studies the effect different levels of student diversity (defined as the proportions of African American, American Indian, Asian American, and Latino students on campus) have on university faculty. The data come from three primary sources: 1) the 1992–1993 survey of college and university faculty conducted by the Higher Education Research Institute (HERI) at the University of California, Los Angeles, which provided normative data for full-time faculty at 344 institutions;[2] 2) the Higher Education Governance Institutional Survey (HEGIS) database, which provided data on the racial composition of student bodies at 244 of the institutions included in the HERI survey; and 3) the Carnegie Foundation, which provided data from their classification system for colleges and universities.

Exploratory factor analysis was employed first to examine the patterns of relationship among a group of items from the HERI survey that assess faculty perceptions of institutional climate. A set of descriptive analyses depicted key independent variables and their relationships to the dependent variables. Finally, blocked hierarchical regression analyses were used to determine the predictors of each of four selected dependent variables.

Three sets of items were analyzed to construct the climate scales. The first set consisted of thirteen items in which faculty assessed the priorities of their institutions on a four-point scale. The second consisted of fourteen items in which faculty rated their campus environments. The third asked faculty to respond to a set of institutional descriptions. Eight factors were ultimately selected as the most useful for this study. Those factors, the individual items that compose them, their factor loadings, and their reliability coefficients are summarized in Table 1.

Civic Responsibility, the first of the eight factors, encompasses the notion of building community on campus while helping students examine their values, develop leadership skills, and become involved in community service. *Student-Centeredness* describes the degree to which faculty and staff are committed to helping students both in and out of the classroom. *Structural Diversity* covers efforts to increase the representation of people of color and women on the faculty, to increase the numbers of underrepresented minority students, and generally to create a diverse campus. *Collegial Relations* includes faculty perceptions of the working atmosphere on campus.

Active Multicultural Support relates to aspects of the racial climate other than structural diversity—for example, the behavioral and psychological dimensions of climate. This construct characterizes a campus's general level of racial harmony and trust, and the faculty's level of attention to minority issues. *Curricular Inclusion* refers to faculty perceptions of the level of multicultural perspective in the curriculum. *Institutional Prestige* describes the level of emphasis placed on the national reputation of the campus. *Academic Ability* incorporates faculty perceptions of students and their preparation for academic work.

This study considers four outcomes related to maximizing the benefits of racial diversity in teaching and learning. They are 1) teaching practices associated with active learning; 2) inclusion in the curriculum of readings on the experiences of diverse racial and ethnic groups; 3) faculty participation in research on race, ethnicity, or gender; and 4) faculty attendance at workshops on racial awareness or curriculum inclusion. Each of these outcomes is significant as a direct or indirect measure of the faculty's willingness and/or ability to be innovative in their teaching practices.

TABLE 1   *Factor Loadings and Alpha Reliabilities for Institutional Climate Scales*

Item	Factor Loading
Factor One – Civic Responsibility Orientation	
INSPRI05 – Develop leadership among students	.78
INSPRI08 – Help students change American society	.75
INSPRI02 – Help students examine personal values	.72
INSPRI07 – Facilitate student involvement in community service	.72
INSPRI04 – Develop community among students and faculty	.71
Alpha reliability	.83
Factor Two – Student-Centered Emphasis	
INSOPN09 – Faculty interested in students' academic problems	.69
INSOPN01 – Faculty interested in student problems	.66
INSDSC01 – Easy to see faculty outside office hours	.62
INSOPN06 – Faculty committed to welfare of the institution	.58
INSDSC06 – Students (not) treated like numbers in a book	.55
INSDSC08 – (Much) student/faculty contact	.51
INSDSC12 – Faculty rewarded for being good teachers	.26
Alpha reliability	.78
Factor Three – Structural Diversity Emphasis	
INSPRI03 – Increase minority representation in faculty	.88
INSPRI11 – Recruit more minority students	.82
INSPRI06 – Increase women's representation in faculty	.81
INSPRI13 – Create diverse multicultural campus environment	.72
Alpha reliability	.86
Factor Four – Collegial Relations	
INSDSC04 – Faculty (not) at odds with administration	.72
INSOPN14 – Administrators act in good faith	.70
INSOPN03 – People (do) respect each other	.55
INSDSC05 – Faculty respect each other	.49
INSOPN05 – Student affairs staff supported by faculty	.37
Alpha reliability	.71
Factor Five – Active Multicultural Support	
INSOPN12 – Faculty of color treated fairly	.72
INSOPN10 – (Not much) racial conflict here	.70
INSOPN13 – Women faculty treated fairly	.64
INSOPN08 – (Much) trust between minorities and administration	.63
INSDSC09 – Institution committed to help minorities	.43
INSOPN02 – Faculty attentive to minority issues	.36
Alpha reliability	.76

TABLE 1   *Factor Loadings and Alpha Reliabilities for Institutional Climate Scales (continued)*

Item	Factor Loading
Factor Six – Curricular Inclusion	
INSOPN11 – Courses include feminist perspectives	.81
INSOPN07 – Courses include minority perspectives	.79
Alpha reliability	.74
Factor Seven – Institutional Prestige Orientation	
INSPRI12 – Enhance institution's national image	.87
INSPRI09 – Increase/maintain institutional prestige	.86
INSPRI10 – Hire faculty "stars"	.70
Alpha reliability	.76
Factor Eight – Academically Able Students	
INSDSC03 – Most students are very bright	.82
INSOPN04 – Students are well prepared academically	.80
Alpha reliability	.68
Other items not loading	
INSDSC07 – Social activities overemphasized	
INSDSC10 – Intercollegiate sports overemphasized	
INSDSC02 – Great deal of student conformity	
INSDSC11 – Students don't socialize regularly	
INSPRI01 – Promote intellectual development of students	

A Summary of Key Findings from the Descriptive Analyses

Levels of student diversity on campus in the following analyses were computed by adding the percentages of full-time African American, American Indian, Asian American, and Hispanic/Latino students. Research institutions were found to be most diverse, with 13.9 percent students of color. At doctoral institutions, the figure was 12.5 percent; at comprehensive institutions, 9.1 percent; and at liberal arts institutions, 7.7 percent.

The underrepresentation of faculty of color is dramatic at all levels of higher education. The proportion of African American faculty varies from 1.3 to 1.9 percent in the different Carnegie classifications of institutions; the totals of Hispanic and Latino faculty are similar (see Table 2).

TABLE 2   *Racial Diversity of Faculty by Campus Type*

	All (N=35,061)	Research (N=8,960)	Doctoral (N=4,067)	Compre- hensive (N=14,401)	Liberal Arts (N=7,633)
African American	1.8	1.9	1.3	1.7	1.3
American Indian	1.0	0.7	0.8	1.4	0.9
Asian/Asian American	3.2	4.8	3.6	3.1	2.6
Chicano/Mexican American	0.5	0.4	0.3	0.7	0.3
Puerto Rican	0.2	0.2	0.2	0.2	0.3
Other Latino	0.9	0.9	1.0	0.8	0.8
White	89.5	89.1	89.8	89.6	90.9

Methods of Teaching

Reliance on the lecture is one important measure of teaching practice; the greater the reliance, the less likely that the teacher uses active learning and student-centered methods. More than half of all faculty report that they use extensive lecturing in all or most classes, but the proportion is clearly related to the size and mission of the institution. Faculty at research institutions are most likely to use extensive lecturing (66.0 percent), followed by faculty at doctoral institutions (60.4 percent), comprehensive institutions (52.6 percent), and liberal arts institutions (43.2 percent). Women are less likely than men to report the use of extensive lecturing—42.7 percent compared to 60.3 percent.

Only about one faculty member in seven (14 percent) reports incorporating readings on race or ethnicity in all or most of their classes. There is considerable variation in this measure by racial background of the faculty. African American (28.5 percent), Chicano and Latino (30.7 percent), and American Indian (26.3 percent) faculty are all at least twice as likely as white faculty (13.7 percent) to integrate their curricula in this way. Asian American faculty are the least likely to do so (6.2 percent). Women are twice as likely as men to report that they incorporate readings on racial issues into their classes (21.7 percent for women as compared to 10.1 percent for men).

Only one faculty member in five reports having conducted research on race or ethnicity. African American (61 percent) and Chicano/Latino (65 percent) faculty are far more likely than white (19 percent) or Asian American (18 percent) faculty to have done so. These findings are fairly consistent across the four Carnegie classifications of research and teaching campuses.

Only about one in three faculty members reports having attended a racial or cultural awareness workshop. Again, whites and Asian Americans are least likely to have done so. Considered in the aggregate, faculty at liberal arts institutions are twice as likely to have attended such workshops as faculty at research institutions.

Student diversity is correlated only weakly, if at all, with the four dependent variables in this study. There are weak correlations between the variables and campus type: research institutions are negatively correlated with active learning, curriculum inclusion, and participation in diversity workshops. Being a faculty member at a comprehensive or liberal arts institution is positively correlated with all four dependent variables, though only weakly.

Stronger patterns of relationship emerge between the eight measures of institutional climate and the campus types. Faculty at research universities, for example, are less likely to perceive their institutions as student centered ($r = -.27$) or as emphasizing civic responsibility ($r = -.17$), while faculty at liberal arts colleges are more likely to perceive their institutions to be student centered ($r = .25$) and to emphasize civic responsibility ($r = .15$). Research institutions are likely to be seen by faculty as placing greater emphasis on institutional prestige ($r = .25$).

These simple correlations suggest that faculty perceive institutional climates to be most supportive of diversity at those universities that have the lowest representation of students of color (the liberal arts and comprehensive institutions) and least supportive at those with the largest representation (research and doctoral institutions).

Predicting the Likelihood of Faculty Innovation

Four multiple regression analyses were conducted using six "blocks" of independent variables, assigned to each block according to how they were believed to fit in the study model. The first block measures faculty characteristics, including race, gender, and age. The second block measures institutional type as defined by the Carnegie classification system: research, doctoral, comprehensive, and liberal arts. Community colleges and specialized schools are characterized as "other" in these analyses. The third block measures faculty job characteristics, including discipline type (hard-applied, hard-pure, soft-applied, soft-pure), academic rank, and tenure. The fourth block measures faculty job activity, including primary interest in teaching or research and whether research is primarily collaborative. The fifth block measures student diversity on campus. The last block comprises the eight institutional climate factors described above. The results of the regression analyses are summarized in Table 3.

Factors predicting active learning. The following factors are associated with a significantly higher likelihood of active learning techniques being used in the classroom: faculty who perceive their institutions as oriented to civic responsibility (ß = .13), women faculty (ß = .12), faculty who perceive their institutions as having highly able students (ß = .09), faculty who perceive their institutions as emphasizing curricular diversity (ß = .07), faculty in soft-applied disciplines (ß = .06), faculty who report that they are more likely to collaborate with others in their research (ß = .05), faculty who perceive their institutions as student centered (ß = .03), American Indian faculty (ß = .03), and Puerto Rican faculty (ß = .02).

These factors are associated with a significantly lower likelihood of the use of active learning techniques: faculty in hard-pure disciplines (ß = −.19), faculty at research institutions (ß = −.08), faculty who perceive their institutions to have high levels of multicultural support (ß = −.07) and collegial relationships (ß = −.07), tenured faculty (ß = −.06), faculty on more diverse campuses (ß = −.05), faculty in soft-pure disciplines (ß = −.04), Asian American faculty (ß = −.04), faculty at doctoral institutions (ß = −.03), and older faculty (ß = −.02).

Factors predicting curriculum inclusion. The following factors are associated with a significantly higher likelihood of including readings on race, ethnicity, or gender in the curriculum: faculty in soft-pure disciplines (ß = .16), women faculty (ß = .14), faculty who perceive their institutions to have a high level of curricular diversity (ß = .13) and to emphasize civic responsibility (ß = .05) and student diversity (ß = .05), faculty at higher ranks (ß = .04), faculty whose interests are more in research than teaching (ß = .03), American Indian faculty (ß = .03), African American faculty (ß = .02), and Mexican American/Chicano faculty (ß = .02).

These factors are associated with a significantly lower likelihood of including readings on race, ethnicity, or gender in the curriculum: faculty in hard-pure disciplines (ß = −.21), faculty who perceive their institutions to have high levels of multicultural support (ß = −.15), faculty in hard-applied disciplines (ß = −.13), faculty at research institutions (ß = −.05),

TABLE 3 Results of Blocked Hierarchical Regression for all Institutions in the Sample (N=26775)

Unstandardized and Standardized Coefficients for Regression Predicting

Variable	Active Learning b	Beta	Sig	Curriculum Inclusion b	Beta	Sig	Research on Diversity b	Beta	Sig	Attendance at Diversity Workshops b	Beta	Sig
Background Characteristics												
Age	-.05	-.02	**	.01	.01		.01	.03	**	-.00	-.01	
Political View: Liberal	.37	.08	**	.34	.17	**	.11	.13	**	.09	.10	**
Father's Education	.00	.00		-.00	-.00		.00	.00		-.00	-.01	
Race: African American	-.21	-.01		.21	.02	*	.19	.03	**	.19	.03	**
Race: American Indian	1.13	.03	**	.53	.03	**	.22	.03	**	.14	.02	**
Race: Asian American	-.84	-.04	**	-.46	-.05	**	-.29	-.07	**	-.18	-.04	**
Race: Mexican American/Chicano	.29	.01		.38	.02	**	.30	.03	**	.29	.03	**
Race: Puerto Rican	1.61	.02	**	.14	.00		.05	.00		-.04	-.00	
Race: Other Latino	.12	.00		-.05	-.00		.05	.01		.05	.01	
Race: White	-.12	-.01		-.12	-.02		-.21	-.08	**	-.17	-.06	**
Sex: Female	1.07	.12	**	.52	.14	**	.24	.15	**	.20	.12	**
	R^2 = .056** R^2Ch = .056**			R^2 = .136** R^2Ch = .136**			R^2 = .118** R^2Ch = .118**			R^2 = .060** R^2Ch = .060**		
Institutional Type												
Research	-.74	-.08	**	-.18	-.05	**	-.02	-.01		-.29	-.17	**
Doctoral	-.42	-.03	**	-.07	-.01		.03	.02		-.22	-.09	**
Comprehensive	.09	.01		-.04	-.01		.04	.03	*	-.13	-.08	**
Liberal Arts	-.10	-.01		.03	.01		.05	.03	*	-.09	-.05	**
	R^2 = .066** R^2Ch = .010**			R^2 = .144** R^2Ch = .008**			R^2 = .124** R^2Ch = .006**			R^2 = .080** R^2Ch = .020**		

TABLE 3   Results of Blocked Hierarchical Regression for all Institutions in the Sample (N=26775) (continued)

Unstandardized and Standardized Coefficients for Regression Predicting

Variable	Active Learning			Curriculum Inclusion			Research on Diversity			Attendance at Diversity Workshops		
	b	Beta	Sig	b	Beta	Sig	b	Beta	Sig	b	Beta	Sig
Job Characteristics												
Academic Rank	.05	.01		.06	.04	**	.06	.08	**	.05	.06	**
Tenured	-.47	-.06	**	-.15	-.04	**	-.04	-.03	**	-.00	-.00	
Discipline: Hard-Applied	-.24	-.02		-.73	-.13	**	-.25	-.11	**	-.09	-.03	**
Discipline: Hard-Pure	-1.97	-.19	**	-.92	-.21	**	-.31	-.17	**	-.18	-.09	**
Discipline: Soft-Applied	.59	.06	**	-.11	-.03	**	-.07	-.04	**	.01	.00	
Discipline: Soft-Pure	-.32	-.04	**	.53	.16	**	.21	.15	**	-.00	-.00	
	$R^2 = .127$** $R^2Ch = .061$**			$R^2 = .264$** $R^2Ch = .120$**			$R^2 = .218$** $R^2Ch = .094$**			$R^2 = .095$** $R^2Ch = .015$**		
Job Activity												
Primary Interest: Research	-.03	-.01		.06	.03	**	.09	.11	**	-.05	-.06	**
Research: Collaborative	.35	.05	**	.00	.00		.00	.00		.06	.05	**
	$R^2 = .132$** $R^2Ch = .005$**			$R^2 = .265$** $R^2Ch = .001$**			$R^2 = .228$** $R^2Ch = .010$**			$R^2 = .101$** $R^2Ch = .006$**		
Institutional Characteristics												
Structural Diversity	-.02	-.05	**	-.00	-.01	*	.00	.01		-.00	-.03	**
	$R^2 = .135$** $R^2Ch = .003$**			$R^2 = .265$** $R^2Ch = .000$			$R^2 = .228$** $R^2Ch = .000$			$R^2 = .102$** $R^2Ch = .001$**		

TABLE 3 Results of Blocked Hierarchical Regression for all Institutions in the Sample (N=26775) (continued)

Unstandardized and Standardized Coefficients for Regression Predicting

Variable	Active Learning			Curriculum Inclusion			Research on Diversity			Attendance at Diversity Workshops		
	b	Beta	Sig	b	Beta	Sig	b	Beta	Sig	b	Beta	Sig
Institutional Climate												
Civic Responsibility Orientation	.15	.13	**	.03	.05	**	.01	.05	**	.02	.07	**
Student-Centered Emphasis	.04	.03	**	.01	.02	*	.00	.01		.01	.03	**
Structural Diversity Emphasis	.03	.02	*	.03	.05	**	.01	.03	**	.03	.14	**
Active Multicultural Support	-.10	-.07	**	-.09	-.15	**	-.03	-.13	**	-.04	-.15	**
Curricular Inclusion Emphasis	.18	.07	**	.16	.13	**	.04	.07	**	.04	.07	**
Collegial Relationships Emphasis	-.11	-.07	**	-.01	-.02		-.01	-.02	*	.00	.00	
Institutional Prestige Orientation	.05	.03	**	.00	.00		.00	.00		-.01	-.02	*
Academically Able Students	.28	.09	**	.02	.02	**	.01	.03	**	.02	.03	**
	$R^2 = .173$** $R^2Ch = .038$**			$R^2 = .297$** $R^2Ch = .032$**			$R^2 = .246$** $R^2Ch = .018$**			$R^2 = .143$** $R^2Ch = .041$**		

Asian American faculty (ß = –.05), tenured faculty (ß = –.04), and faculty in soft-applied disciplines (ß = –.03).

Factors predicting involvement in research on diversity. The following factors are associated with a significantly higher likelihood of engaging in research addressing issues of race, ethnicity, or gender: faculty in the soft-pure disciplines (ß = .15), women faculty (ß = .15), faculty whose interests lean toward research rather than teaching (ß = .11), faculty at higher ranks (ß = .08), faculty who perceive their institutions as emphasizing curricular diversity (ß = .07), civic responsibility (ß = .05) and student diversity (ß = .03), and as having highly able students (ß = .03), faculty at comprehensive and liberal arts institutions (ß = .03), African American faculty (ß = .03), American Indian faculty (ß = .03), and Mexican American/Chicano faculty (ß = .03).

These factors are associated with a significantly lower likelihood of engaging in research addressing issues of race, ethnicity, or gender: faculty in the hard-pure disciplines (ß = –.17), faculty who perceive their institutions to have high levels of multicultural support (ß = –.13), faculty in the hard-applied disciplines (ß = –.11), white faculty (ß = –.08), Asian American faculty (ß = –.07), tenured faculty (ß = –03), and faculty in the soft-applied disciplines (ß = –.03).

Factors predicting attendance at racial awareness workshops. The following factors are associated with a significantly higher likelihood of having attended a racial or cultural awareness workshop: faculty who perceive their institutions to value student diversity (ß = .14), women faculty (ß = .12), faculty who perceive their institutions to emphasize civic responsibility (ß = .07) and curricular diversity (ß = .07), faculty at higher ranks (ß = .06), faculty who tend to do collaborative research (ß = .05), faculty who perceive their institutions to be student centered (ß = .03) and have able students (ß = .03), African American faculty (ß = .03), Mexican American/Chicano faculty (ß = .03), and American Indian faculty (ß = .02).

These factors are associated with a significantly lower likelihood of having attended a racial or cultural awareness workshop: faculty from all four types of institutions (research, ß = –.17; doctoral, ß = –.09; comprehensive, ß = –.08; liberal arts, ß = –.05) when compared with faculty at two-year colleges, faculty who perceive their institution to have high levels of multicultural support (ß = –.15), faculty in the hard-pure disciplines (ß = –.09), white faculty (ß = –.06), faculty who report a greater relative interest in research than in teaching (ß = –.06), Asian American faculty (ß = –.04), faculty at more diverse institutions (ß = –.03), and faculty in the hard-applied disciplines (ß = –.03).

Conclusions

Note that the highest proportions of students of color in the data sample are enrolled at research and doctoral institutions, because it is these universities that have generally pursued affirmative action in admissions most aggressively. Yet the faculty at these institutions are the least likely to use active learning techniques or curriculum inclusion or to have attended racial-awareness workshops. Similarly, higher levels of student diversity on campus are found in these analyses to be associated with less use of active learning methods by faculty and lower likelihood of attendance at racial-awareness workshops.

Across all of the regression analyses, women faculty are more likely to be involved in teaching and learning activities supporting a diverse student body. African American, American Indian, or Mexican American/ Chicano faculty are also more likely to use these methods. Yet the institutions that have pursued affirmative action in college admissions most aggressively have made relatively little progress in hiring and promoting women and minority faculty.

We know from earlier research on school desegregation that increased diversity in education is no guarantee of academic success for students of color, but that success depends on the adaptability of the institution to the needs of those students. Moreover, research on campus racial climate indicates that the institutional climate for diversity is important to the success of all college students, regardless of racial/ethnic background (Hurtado et al., 1998. 1999). The findings from this study suggest that much remains to be done in understanding and assessing institutional responses to increased diversity. Clearly, arguments that ignore the institutional context and declare affirmative action a failure are misguided and inappropriate. It is imperative that institutional responses to increased diversity also be considered and that institutions be examined for the roles that they play in either enhancing or inhibiting the achievement of all students.

Notes

1. See Janet Ward Schofield, "Maximizing the Benefits of Student Diversity: Lessons from School Desegregation Research," in this volume.
2. The final response rate to this survey was 61 percent.

References

Altschuler, T., & Richter, S. (1985). Maintaining faculty vitality. *New Directions for Community Colleges, 13*(4), 49–62.

Astin, A. W. (1993). *What matters in college? Four critical years revisited.* San Francisco: Jossey-Bass.

Astin, A. W., & Chang, M. (1995). Colleges that emphasize research and teaching: Can you have your cake and eat it too? *Change, 27*(5), 45–49.

Baldwin, R., & Krotseng, M. (1985). Incentives in the academy: Issues and options. *New Directions for Community Colleges, 13*(3), 5–20.

Bayer, A. (1973). *Teaching faculty in academe: 1972–73* (ACE Research Reports, vol. 8, no. 2). Washington, DC: American Council on Education.

Blalock, J. M. (1967). *Toward a theory of minority-group relations.* New York: Wiley.

Bowen, H. (1977). *Investment in learning.* San Francisco: Jossey-Bass.

Bowen, W. G., & Bok, D. (1998). *The shape of the river: Long-term consequences of considering race in college and university admissions.* Princeton, NJ: Princeton University Press.

Chickering, A. (1971). Research for action. In P. L. Dressel (Ed.), *The new colleges: Toward an appraisal* (pp. 25—52). Iowa City, IA: American College Testing Program.

Easton, J., & Guskey, T. (1983). Estimating the effects of college, department, course, and teacher on course completion rates. *Research in Higher Education, 19*, 153–158.

Feldman, K. A., & Newcomb, T. M. (1969). *The impact of college on students.* San Francisco: Jossey-Bass.

Guskin, S., & Bassis, M. (1985). Leadership style and institutional renewal. *New Directions for Higher Education, 13*(1), 13—22.

Hurtado, S., Milem, J., Clayton-Pedersen, A., & Allen, W. (1999). *Enacting diverse learning environments: Improving the campus climate for racial/ethnic diversity* (ASHE/ERIC Higher Education Reports Series, 26, no. 8). Washington, DC: George Washington University/ERIC Clearinghouse on Higher Education.

Hurtado, S., Milem, J. F., Clayton-Pedersen, A. R., & Allen, W. R. (1998). Enhancing campus climates for racial/ethnic diversity through educational policy and practice. *Review of Higher Education, 21*, 279–302.

Johnson, D. W., & Johnson, R. T. (1985). Classroom conflict: Controversy versus debate in learning groups. *American Educational Research Journal, 22*, 237–256.

Johnson, D. W., & Johnson, R. T. (1986a). Computer-assisted cooperative learning. *Educational Technologies, 26*, 12–18.

Johnson, D. W., & Johnson, R. T. (1986b). Mainstreaming and cooperative learning strategies. *Exceptional Children, 52*, 553–561.

Johnson, D. W., Johnson, R. T., & Smith, K. A. (1988). *Cooperative learning: An active learning strategy for the college classroom.* Minneapolis: University of Minnesota Press.

Kozma, R., Belle, L., & William, G. (1978). *Instructional techniques in higher education.* Englewood Cliffs, NJ: Educational Technology.

Ladd, E. (1979). The work experience of American college professors: Some data and an argument. In *Current issues in higher education.* Washington, DC: American Association for Higher Education.

Merton, R. (1973). *The sociology of science: Theoretical and empirical investigations.* Chicago: University of Chicago Press.

Milem, J., & Astin, H. (1992, April). *Science faculty: Culture, roles and pedagogy.* Paper presented at the annual meeting of the American Educational Research Association, New York.

Milem, J., & Wakai, S. (1996a, April). *Student centered approaches to teaching and learning: Lessons to be learned from faculty at historically black colleges and women's colleges.* Paper presented at the annual meeting of the American Educational Research Association, New York.

Milem, J., & Wakai, S. (1996b, November). *Understanding how faculty teach: Facilitators and inhibitors of student-centered pedagogy.* Paper presented at the annual meeting of the Association for the Study of Higher Education, Memphis.

Palmer, P. J. (1987). Community, conflict, and ways of knowing. *Change, 19,* 20–25.

Statham, A., Richardson, L., & Cook, J. (1991). *Gender and university teaching: A negotiated difference.* Albany: State University of New York Press.

Slavin, R. E. (1987). *Cooperative learning: Student teams* (2nd ed.). Washington, DC: National Education Association.

Slavin, R. E. (1988). *Student team learning: An overview and practical guide* (2nd ed.). Washington, DC: National Education Association.

CHAPTER 12

Faculty Experience with Diversity: A Case Study of Macalester College

ROXANE HARVEY GUDEMAN

Introduction

A central mission of traditional American liberal arts colleges is to prepare students for civic responsibility, teaching them to test their beliefs against the perspectives of others in vigorous debate. The more diverse the experience of scholars within the community, the more likely it is that ostensibly objective knowledge and universal truths will be challenged. One argument for racial and ethnic diversity in the academy is that it brings representation and perspectives of groups that have traditionally been excluded from the marketplace of ideas (Dworkin, 1996). Increasingly, policymakers and academics alike recognize that a homogeneous academic environment cannot adequately prepare students for responsible citizenship. Beyond its impact on the individual classroom, diversity, or the lack thereof, affects the rigor and integrity of disciplinary scholarship. Historians of science and other scholars note that the problems, methods, and findings of academic disciplines may deeply reflect the traditions and interests of the cultural groups within which the disciplines arose. Scholars increasingly recognize that the academy must venture outside its traditional social boundaries to expand knowledge and discourse. Martha Nussbaum (1997) expresses this imperative in her suggested agenda for liberal arts education:

> Three capacities above all are essential to the cultivation of humanity in today's world. First is the critical examination of oneself and one's

251

traditions. . . . This means a life that accepts no belief as authoritative simply because it has been handed down by tradition . . .

Citizens who cultivate their humanity need, further, an ability to see themselves not simply as citizens of some local region or group but also, and above all, as human beings bound to all other human beings by ties of recognition and concern.

The third ability of the citizen . . . can be called narrative imagination. This means the ability to think what it might be like to be in the shoes of a person different from oneself, to be an intelligent reader of that person's story, and to understand the emotions and wishes and desires that someone so placed might have. (pp. 9–11)

A laudable central goal, according to this vision, is to provide students (and faculty) the opportunity to move beyond their taken-for-granted or "commonsense" frames of reference through introduction to the experiences and theories of others. The research described here tests the belief that domestic racial/ethnic diversity in the classroom contributes to achieving the educational goals and understandings described above. Results indicate that the faculty of Macalester College, a small, selective liberal arts college in Saint Paul, Minnesota, find that the presence of U.S. citizens of different races and ethnicities in the classroom contributes to stretching all students beyond their assumed world of beliefs and social practices. These findings, and the specific comments of faculty surveyed, speak to the need for diversity throughout academe and begin to dispel some of the concerns raised by opponents of campus diversity initiatives.

Macalester Faculty Assess the Effects of Diversity: Background

Macalester has had a sizable European American majority since its founding over one hundred years ago. However, since at least the late 1950s, the college has viewed multiculturalism as a valued tool in educating its students for the intellectual, social, and civic challenges of contemporary society. In May 1992, Macalester adopted its current mission: "Macalester is committed to being a preeminent liberal arts college with an educational program known for its high standards for scholarship and its special emphasis on internationalism, multiculturalism, and service to society." President Michael McPherson (1998), a strong advocate of the value of diversity, recently commented that the four "pillars" of the college's mission—academic excellence, multiculturalism, internationalism, and service—are complementary, not competitive:

We affirm that excellence in our teaching and learning, in part, de-
rives from our commitment to these [four] values. . . . In the world we
are aiming to prepare our students for, a claim of academic excellence
that ignores or downplays the realms of internationalism, multiculturalism, and service can only ring hollow.

The college has committed significant resources to fulfilling its goals
of multicultural recruitment and support of talented students, faculty,
and staff of color, and to establishing classes that reflect the range of social, artistic, scientific, and philosophical experiences of peoples in the
United States. Macalester is appropriately self-critical about not having realized the full promise of diversity, but the college surely must be ranked
among those sincerely working to achieve that promise. The chartering
hypothesis of this research was that, given the college's broad, multifac-
eted support of multiculturalism, the classroom experience of faculty
would be a good test of whether domestic racial/ethnic diversity contributes to fulfilling Macalester's educational mission (Chang, n.d.).

All continuing Macalester faculty in residence in the spring 1998 semester received a Faculty Diversity Questionnaire in the final week of
class. The American Council on Education (ACE) and the American Association of University Professors jointly sponsored development of the 11-
page questionnaire by a research consortium that used Macalester as a
pretest site for a national survey concerning faculty experience with diversity.[1] It contained ninety-six short-answer or rating questions, and six
questions requesting a brief written response. In their responses, faculty
evaluated their experiences with diversity in the classroom and provided
a wide variety of background information about themselves. Two cover
letters, one from the ACE and one from a Macalester faculty task force,[2]
explained the survey and requested cooperation. All faculty were assured
that their responses were confidential and that results would be reported
by division (humanities, social sciences, natural sciences), not by department, in order to protect anonymity and confidentiality. Although the
questionnaire was designed for faculty in the humanities and social sciences, the Macalester faculty task force sent the questionnaire to natural
scientists as well.[3] In all, 132 faculty received the questionnaire; 81 responded. Respondents to the questionnaire represented a cross-section of
the Macalester community, including diversity across key dimensions
such as gender, race, discipline, tenure, and political orientation.[4] The
task force was satisfied with response rates, therefore researchers opted
not to pursue follow-up solicitation in the fall.

Macalester Faculty Assess the Effects of Diversity: Results

Results of the questionnaire are divided into three short and two long sections, reporting in order (a) faculty perception of the college's commitment to diversity, (b) faculty views about whether diversity has lowered the quality of the institution or student body, (c) an overview of the collective faculty experience with diversity, (d) analysis of faculty differences concerning the value of diversity in the class, and (e) faculty definitions of racial/ethnic diversity in the classroom. In the results reported below, the details of statistical tests are found in footnotes in order to improve readability. The principal tests used are one-way t-tests, analyses of variance followed by detailed comparisons via t-tests, correlations, Chi Square tests, and the Sign Test. The conventions used as a shorthand to indicate these tests are as follows: (a) F = ANOVA F test, (b) T1 = one sample t-test, (c) T2 = two sample t-test, (d) χ^2 = Chi Square test, and (e) ST = Sign Test.[5] The significance level of the test is indicated as follows: (a) $p <$ .05 = *; (b) $p < .01$ = **; (c) $p < .005$ = ***; (d) $p < .001$ = ****; (e) $p < .0005$ = *****; and (f) $p < .0001$ = ******.[6] For readers not trained in statistics, the significance level indicates the probability that a given outcome might occur merely by chance.[7]

A. Do Faculty View the Institution as Committed to Diversity?

Given Macalester's high-profile commitment to diversity, one goal of this research was to ascertain the extent to which faculty's experience and the college's stated policies are in alignment. Diversity and multiculturalism have become buzzwords of modern society that reinforce the need to evaluate not only policy intentions, but also policy implementation. Several questions addressed this issue of faculty's "on the ground" experience of Macalester's diversity initiatives.

The majority of faculty respondents (58%) reported that diversity is a high priority of the college, while 18 percent reported diversity as the college's highest priority. Viewed in comparison to the 20 percent and 4 percent, respectively, who described diversity as a medium or low priority, faculty responses suggest that Macalester's stated commitment to diversity permeates the academic environment[8] (see Figure 1). This finding is further supported by the faculty response regarding diversity in relation to Macalester's educational mission. In this instance, a combined 92 percent of respondents judged diversity to be either essential or very important to the institution's mission, as compared to only 8 percent who concluded it is either somewhat important or not important[9] (see Figure 2). One respondent commented, "We've already agreed in principle since our

FIGURE 1   *"How high a priority do you believe it is at your current institution to create a diverse campus environment?"*

Mean = 2.1; Standard Deviation = .7; N = 74

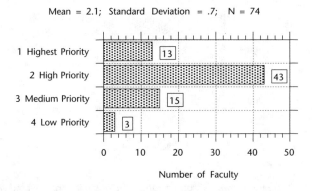

Number of Faculty

FIGURE 2   *"How important is having racially/ethnically diverse student bodies to your institution's mission?"*

Mean = 1.7; Standard Deviation = .7; N = 78

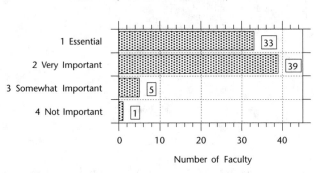

Number of Faculty

mission statement includes multiculturalism. We agreed that preparing students for the future must include preparing them to live in a racially/ethnically diverse community."

B. Has Domestic Diversity Negatively Affected the Quality of the Institution or Student Body?

One argument against diversity, usually made by opponents of affirmative action, is that an institution's quality will somehow decline as a result of diversity initiatives. This argument is based upon the assumption

FIGURE 3   *"Too much emphasis on racial/ethnic diversity has lowered the quality of the institution."*

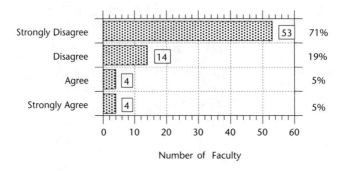

FIGURE 4   *"Too much emphasis on racial/ethnic diversity has lowered the quality of the students who are admitted."*

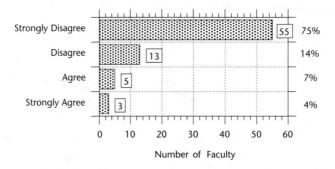

that minority applicants are necessarily less qualified than their white peers, or less able to succeed as college students. We asked Macalester faculty whether they thought the quality of instruction at the college or the quality of the student body has suffered as a result of diversity (see Figure 3). The vast majority (71%) strongly disagreed or disagreed (19%) with the questionnaire statement, "Too much emphasis on racial/ethnic diversity has lowered the quality of the institution."[10] Only 5 percent agreed with this statement, and another 5 percent strongly agreed. Similarly, 75 percent of faculty strongly disagreed with the statement that an emphasis on diversity has lowered student quality, while only 4 percent strongly agreed with that statement[11] (see Figure 4). Obviously, from the faculty viewpoint, increasing racial diversity does not compromise educational excellence. In fact, most faculty indicated that access and diversity are prerequisites for excellent education.

C. The Faculty as a Whole: Effects of Diversity in the Classroom

In this section, the collective responses of all faculty are reported in order to illustrate the overall tenor of attitudes about diversity at Macalester. A later section of this chapter disaggregates faculty response according to personal and professional characteristics.

Kinds of Diversity Valued by Faculty. Historically, colleges and universities have held a variety of positions regarding the forms of diversity in the student body and faculty that contribute to fulfilling their educational missions. The Macalester faculty judged whether ten different kinds of diversity contribute "to the quality of learning" in their classrooms on a scale ranging from "Very Important" to "Very Unimportant."[12] Of the options provided, faculty judged "diverse U.S. races/ethnicities," "gender balance," and "international diversity" to be "important" contributors to the quality of education in the classroom.[13] Of the remaining seven forms of diversity indexed, three were judged to be helpful; however, they were only marginally significant (see footnote 11).

Faculty Experience with the Effect of Diversity in the Classroom. Another argument made in opposition to diversity in the classroom is that the introduction of diverse racial/ethnic student composition has a chilling effect on students' willingness to engage in discussion and debate around issues of race and ethnicity. In an effort to ascertain whether this "chilling effect" is observed at Macalester, faculty were asked to judge whether specific educational outcomes were more frequent, more positive, or different in a class with greater racial/ethnic diversity. The educational outcomes indexed all pertain to Nussbaum's three imperatives for a liberal arts education, the examination of one's own beliefs, the introduction to a range of alternate belief systems and lifeways, and the acquisition of a contextual understanding of the lives of others. The response rate varies because some faculty responded "not applicable" or "don't know" to some questions, and hence were not included in the statistical analysis. These latter two responses were chosen most frequently by faculty who had taught in classes with little diversity and/or in classes in which there was no content related to race/ethnicity.

Findings from this line of questioning are summarized in Figure 5. In each case, a t-test was performed comparing the mean of the observed responses to the hypothetical mean that would be expected if faculty were responding by chance. In addition, so that summary percentages could be reported, each person's response was categorized either as indicating that diversity contributes to the educational outcome, or that it does not contribute.

Working from the general to the specific, findings indicate that faculty deem diversity to be an asset to teaching and learning. Ninety-one percent of faculty reported that racial-ethnic diversity in the classroom "allows for a broader variety of experiences to be shared."[14] More specifically, a large majority of faculty responded that minority students "sometimes" through "very often" raise issues/perspectives not raised by nonminority students.[15] Similarly, 75 percent said that "race/ethnic issues are discussed more substantively in [my] . . . diverse classroom" and 76 percent reported that students in diverse classrooms are more likely to incorporate racial/ethnic issues into their assignments.[16,17] When asked what type of learning occurs in a more diverse class, one faculty member replied, "More complex, nuanced, perspectivist—less absolutist." This latter topic, the type of discussions that take place in a diverse classroom, is an example of one that some faculty judged that they could not answer either because they did not teach diverse classes, or their classes did not include content about race or ethnicity. Of seventy-three faculty responding to this question, 27 percent selected "not applicable" and 4 percent chose "don't know."

Questions that probed for more detail about the nature of interaction in a diverse classroom elicited similarly positive responses regarding the value of diversity to discourse depth and quality. The majority of faculty (69%) reported that in racially/ethnically diverse classrooms, the stereotypes that students bring with them to the classroom are more likely to be confronted, including[18] stereotypes about social/political issues[19] and stereotypes about substantive issues in the field.[20] Going directly to the question of whether diversity has a chilling or otherwise negative effect on classroom discourse, faculty were asked explicitly whether diversity impedes discussion of substantive issues or creates tensions along racial/ethnic lines. To the former, 79 percent responded that substantive discussion is NEVER impeded by diversity[21] and 63 percent reported that interactions among students of different races/ethnicities NEVER "create tensions or arguments." This result is marginally significant.[22] One shortcoming of the latter indicator is that the question is worded in such a way that faculty must report the existence or absence of tension. It is unclear, taking this question in isolation, whether "tension" was interpreted by faculty to mean, for example, unproductive hostility, or whether they

FIGURE 5   *Frequency with Which Hypothesized Outcomes of Diversity Occur*

	Positive Difference	No Difference	Hypothesis Supported. 1 Sample T-test.
FACULTY AGREE *Racial/ethnic diversity in your classroom allows for a broader variety of experiences to be shared.*	91%	7%	p < .0001
FACULTY AGREE *Minority students have raised issues/perspectives in your classroom that have not been raised by nonminority students.*	80%	20%	p < .0001
FACULTY AGREE *Race/ethnic issues are discussed more substantively in your diverse classroom than your homogeneous classroom.*	75%	25%	p < .0001
FACULTY AGREE *Students in your racially/ ethnically diverse classroom are more likely to incorporate relevant racial and ethnic issues in their assignments.*	76%	24%	p < .0001
FACULTY AGREE *Students in diverse classes are more likely . . . to confront their stereotypes concerning SOCIAL/POLITICAL ISSUES.*	69%	31%	p < .0001
FACULTY AGREE *Students in diverse classes are more likely . . . to confront their stereotypes concerning SUBSTANTIVE ISSUES IN THE FIELD.*	70%	30%	p < .0005
FACULTY DO NOT AGREE *Racial/ethnic diversity in your classroom impedes discussion of substantive issues.*	80%	20%	p < .0001
FACULTY DO NOT AGREE *Interactions between students from different racial/ethnic backgrounds in your classroom create tensions and arguments along racial/ethnic lines.*	63%	37%	p < .05

Note: All of the items in this table can be coded as either supporting or not supporting the hypothesis that diversity brings positive benefit in the classroom. The questions all asked faculty to judge whether the presence of a diverse student body in the classroom increased the frequency of the positive or negative outcomes listed on a scale ranging from "all the time" through "never."

might characterize "tension" as a productive challenge to students' assumptions and values.

Elsewhere on the questionnaire, and in focus groups, faculty were given the opportunity to clarify their experience and definition of tension in the classroom, thereby helping to put this finding into perspective. In the proper context, some faculty described feeling that intense, passionate debate lies at the heart of perspective-sharing in academia and that, therefore, if handled properly, tension is beneficial so long as all feel empowered to participate in the debate. Handling controversy constructively is one of the skills that gifted teachers hope to maximize. One respondent commented, "Even though the atmosphere may be more charged [in diverse classes], the experiential learning is outstanding, as is the potential for intellectual inquiry." Another said, "There's tension sometimes, but I don't think that's bad. It's important to name and negotiate the discomforts, for everyone."

Some questions that assess whether diversity in classes has positive educational benefits were structured so that responses could be classified as (a) supporting the hypothesis, (b) neutral with respect to the hypothesis, or (c) not supporting the hypothesis. These findings are shown in Figure 6.

Overall, the findings speak to the effect of diversity on the breadth of student perspectives. For example, 62 percent of faculty reported that "interaction between students of different racial/ethnic backgrounds" is important or very important in "helping students develop a willingness to examine their own perspectives and values," as compared with 19 percent who judged this interaction unimportant.[23] One respondent commented: "Students need to have experience working with difference. Generally, we need to know about each other in order to take the first steps at creating a multicultural community that has members that can effectively engage the issues of the day."

Again, a central purpose of this line of questioning was to ascertain whether Macalester faculty agreed or disagreed with the opposition argument that diversity initiatives have a negative effect on the educational environment and, more specifically, whether they negatively affect the education received by the European American majority at historically white institutions. The findings illustrated in Figures 5 and 6 suggest that Macalester faculty judge the effects to be either positive or neutral. The two findings below summarize this point and eliminate any doubt that, overall, faculty believe that the challenges created by a diverse student body stimulate positive intellectual and social growth.

Sixty-seven percent of faculty reported that "having students of other racial/ethnic groups in . . . the classroom affect[s] white students" POSITIVELY in "the issues they consider."[24] Faculty also reported that white students read course materials more critically when students of color are in the class, which they viewed as a POSITIVE outcome.[25] For example,

FIGURE 6   *Faculty Judge Diversity's Positive, Neutral, or Negative Effect on Desired Outcomes*

	Positive Difference	No Difference	Negative Difference	Hypothesis Supported. 1 Sample T-test.
FACULTY AGREE Diversity in classes helps students *"develop a willingness to examine their own perspectives and values."*	62%	19%	19%	p < .0001
FACULTY AGREE Diversity in classes exposes *"students to perspectives with which they disagree or do not understand."*	65%	15%	20%	p < .0001
FACULTY AGREE *"Having students of o ther racially ethnic group in your classroom [POSITIVELY] affect white student in the issues they consider."*	67%	33%	0%	P < .0005
FACULTY AGREE *"Having students of other racially ethnic group in your classroom [POSITIVELY] affect white student in the critical reading of course materials."*	60%	38%	2%	p < .005
FACULTY AGREE that their own *"views about racial/ethnic diversity have been [POSITIVELY] affected by racially/ethnically diverse classrooms."*	75%	23%	2%	p < .0001

Note: The results summarized in this table include survey items that had three outcomes: diversity brings positive change or is important, diversity makes no difference in the classroom or has both positive and negative effects, or diversity brings negative change or is unimportant. Thus the three categories, on balance, are that diversity brings positive benefits, diversity is neutral, or diversity is irrelevant or negative.

one respondent commented, "I feel sure that the white students, particularly, learn from peers of color about perspectives on power and the formations of society." Another said, "The students of color often bring new learning and teaching styles to the table. It is a richer experience for all students."

Also indicative of faculty perceptions of the effect of diversity in the classroom is whether the faculty themselves feel they have benefited from a more heterogeneous student body. To this question, the large majority of faculty, 75 percent, responded that their own "views about racial/ethnic diversity have been POSITIVELY affected by" the diversification of the student body.[26]

A survey of the outcome variables suggests that, on balance, the Macalester faculty have found that diversity in the classroom positively contributes to achieving valued educational outcomes. There were two key exceptions, however: (a) whether a diverse class contributes to helping all students think critically, and (b) whether a diverse class helps students develop leadership skills. These two indices are discussed in the next section.

D. Individual Differences among Faculty

Faculty come to teaching with many differences, both personal and professional. Factors that the ACE/AAUP research team hypothesized might be related to diverging educational experiences with diversity in the classroom included (among many others): academic division (humanities, social sciences, natural sciences), academic rank (professor, associate professor, assistant professor, instructor/lecturer), gender, race/ethnicity, country of birth, political affiliation (radical, liberal, conservative, moderate, far right), and whether the individual had experience teaching in more diverse classes or taught courses with racial/ethnic content. Of these variables, political affiliation is of particular interest because it tests what might be considered a reasonable assumption: that politically conservative faculty are likely to oppose diversity initiatives since it is largely conservatives in the nonacademic sector who oppose affirmative action. As the findings indicate, however, Macalester's politically conservative faculty were more positive about diversity than this assumption would predict.

At Macalester, some of the individual characteristic variables were correlated with each other—for example, academic rank, gender, and politics. Of the respondents, men were more likely to have higher rank (78% professor, 48% associate professor, 35% assistant professor, 14% lecturer/instructor)[27] and to be more politically conservative (100% of conservatives, 81% of moderates, 47% of liberals, and 30% of radicals are men).[28] (Overall, approximately 53.5% of the faculty responding to these two items were male.) Faculty of higher rank were likely to be more politically conservative; the most frequently selected political category chosen by full professors was "moderate"; the most frequently chosen by all other faculty was "liberal."[29] Gender was also associated with academic division; 53 percent of the humanities respondents were female, compared to 42 percent of the social science faculty and 40 percent of the natural science faculty.

A variable one might expect to be related to the perceived value of diversity is whether faculty included race/ethnicity-relevant content in one or more classes. The researcher hypothesized that those who taught race/ethnicity-relevant content would rate the contribution of domestic diversity in the classroom as more important to achieving educational goals than would those who did not teach the content. Preliminary analyses investigated whether being a faculty member who included race/ethnicity-relevant content in a class was correlated with the other background variables reviewed. Academic rank, race/ethnicity, gender, and national origin were *not* significantly associated with having taught classes with content relevant to diversity.[30] Having taught such content was, however, related to both academic division and political self-description. Humanities and social science faculty were more likely than natural science faculty to include racial/ethnic content and also to consider diversity to have pedagogical value. Politically conservative and moderate faculty were found to be less likely to teach diversity-relevant content,[31] and also less likely to report great benefit from diversity in the classroom.[32] On balance, however, conservative faculty concurred with their more liberal colleagues that diversity in the classroom is either beneficial or neutral, not detrimental. In other words, politically conservative faculty, on the average, do not view diversity as negative although they are more likely to view it as less important or even as irrelevant. This is an important finding, as it suggests that even those whose politics may place them in opposition to affirmative action generally may recognize the value of diversity in the academic setting.

Faculty who teach classes that include racial/ethnic content include individuals from a surprising range of academic disciplines. Of 77 faculty responding to this question, 50 (65%) reported teaching classes with racial or ethnic content. They came from 23 of the 27 academic departments or programs whose faculty returned questionnaires: anthropology, art, biology, communications studies, comparative North American studies, computer science, dramatic arts, economics, education, English, geography, history, other languages, linguistics, mathematics, music, philosophy, political science, psychology, religious studies, sociology, Spanish, and women's studies. Collectively, only four departments—French, geology, chemistry, and physics—had all respondents report that they taught no classes with racial/ethnic content.

One hypothesis of this research was that the perceived value of racial/ethnic content would decline according to faculty experience teaching such content. In other words, researchers predicted that 1) the twelve faculty who taught an ethnic studies class would find diversity the most beneficial in the classroom; 2) the 38 faculty who taught a class that included racial ethnic content (and who did not teach an ethnic studies class) would find diversity next most beneficial; and 3) the 27 faculty who taught *no* classes with ethnic content would find race/ethnicity the least beneficial. The three groups will be referred to as *CLASS, CONTENT, NONE* in reporting the statistical results.

This general hypothesis is strongly supported by faculty responses. When statistically significant differences occurred among the three groups, they exhibited a consistent pattern in which those who taught a class focused on diversity reported the greatest educational benefits for diversity; those who included content about diversity reported the next greatest benefits; and those who did neither reported the least benefits. In no case did faculty who taught no diversity-related content report (significantly or not) greater educational benefits from teaching in diverse classrooms than those who did teach such classes.

In Section C, above, a number of results reported overall faculty perception that diversity has positive educational effects. Not surprisingly, more detailed analyses of some of these variables show that faculty who teach about race/ethnicity view diversity as contributing more than those who do not teach the subject. In the findings reported below, similar highly correlated items have been averaged together to create a single index. Figures 7 and 8 demonstrate the variation found.

Of faculty who teach racial/ethnic content, 100 percent agree that diversity in the classroom increases the range of issues/perspectives and experiences discussed in class, including some not typically raised by nonminority students. Those who teach classes focused on diversity rate the contribution as more important than those who only include some diversity content. In contrast, only 74 percent of those who do not teach racial/ethnic content agree that this outcome occurs in more diverse classes.[33] When asked to consider the value of a "critical mass of same race/ethnicity students" to the success of classroom discussions, 80 percent of faculty who teach a class focused on ethnicity, and 46 percent of faculty who include diversity-relevant content viewed the presence of other students from the same racial/ethnic group as enhancing student participation, whereas only 8 percent of those who teach neither a class nor content on the subject made this judgment.[34] Further, 83 percent of faculty who teach a class focused on race/ethnicity, and 76 percent of those who include racial/ethnic content (in contrast to only 38% of those who do not) judge that it is important to have students of different racial/ethnic backgrounds in classes in order to have students examine their own perspectives and values[35] (see Figure 7). One faculty member re-

FIGURE 7   *Percent of Faculty Who Report That the Presence of Other Students/ a Critical Mass Enhances the Beneficial Effects of Diversity by Teaching Content*

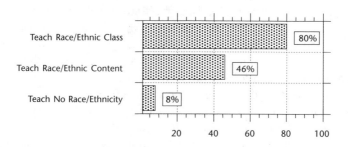

FIGURE 8   *Faculty Rating of the Importance of Diversity in the Classroom to Developing Student Ability to Think Critically by Teaching Content*

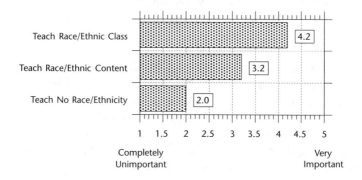

ported that, in a diverse classroom, students are more likely to consider "questions of identity," to show "curiosity for learning about others (culture, background [ethnic, etc.])," and to engage in "personal exploration at a philosophical level."

Each of these findings speaks volumes about the potency of racial/ethnic content—its effect on teaching and learning, and in convincing faculty of its value. It is not surprising that those who teach the content recognize its value. The significance of this finding, however, is in its implications for encouraging faculty who resist diversity policies to alter their views. The findings reported here suggest that the experience of teaching the content, perhaps even once, is likely to affect faculty willingness to incorporate that content into future curricula.

The questionnaire also asked faculty whether they believe diversity contributes to a particular educational goal. Again, looking at responses according to faculty experience teaching racial/ethnic content, several interesting findings emerge. The faculty did not unanimously agree that a diverse classroom contributes to a *particular* educational goal. However, detailed analyses indicated that those who taught a class focused on race/ethnicity, or who included some content relevant to race, found diversity to be of specific educational value, whereas those who did not found diversity to be neutral in specified educational effects. The two findings reported below concern traditional core educational goals in liberal arts colleges—the development of critical thinking and of the ability to lead.

Faculty with more experience teaching diversity-relevant content judged diversity in the classroom to be important in helping "students develop their abilities to think critically (see Figure 8)."[36] Similarly, faculty with more experience teaching diversity related content were more likely to agree that diversity in the classroom is important in developing "student's leadership abilities."[37]

E. What Is Diversity in the Classroom?

Given the extent to which this research relies on faculty response to questions about experience with diversity, it was necessary to incorporate inquiry into faculty definitions of diversity, i.e., who comprises a diverse student body, and what qualifies as a diverse class? When the Macalester faculty answered the diversity questionnaire, about 11 percent of the students enrolled at Macalester College were U.S. students of color, and about the same percentage were international students. Faculty were asked to indicate the percentage of minority students in the most diverse class that they had taught, and also in a class that they would judge "diverse" in their department.

The most frequently chosen response selected by faculty reporting the highest percent of U.S. students of color in any of their classes was "6–10 percent"; the range varied from 0–5 percent through over 40 percent.[38] They judged that 11–15 percent would constitute a diverse class in their department; 72 percent chose this range or higher.[39] The faculty, on average, defined a "diverse" class as one with a minority representation that was larger than their own most diverse class. Researchers also ran an additional test to see if a significant number of faculty agreed that a class defined as diverse should have a higher proportion of minority students than they personally had experienced. They found that over half (51%) of the faculty chose a description of a "diverse class" that was HIGHER than

FIGURE 9   *SECTION E Results: Faculty Assess Importance of a Critical Mass*

	Positive Difference	No Difference	Hypothesis Supported. 1 Sample T-test.
FACULTY AGREE *Participation in classroom discussion by students of a particular racial/ethnic group is increased by the presence of other students from the same racial/ethnic group.*	83%	17%	p < .0001
FACULTY AGREE *A critical mass of students of a particular racial/ethnic group is important to their participation in your classroom.*	70%	30%	p < .0001

that which they indicated described their own most diverse class (in comparison to 30% who chose the SAME range, and 19% who chose a lower range).[40] When evaluating classroom experiences, faculty reported that diversity enhanced desired educational outcomes more successfully when the representation of diverse groups went beyond that of a solo or token presence. This reinforces findings reported earlier regarding a "critical mass" of students representing races and ethnicities. Responses suggest that faculty find, when the ratio of minority to majority is too imbalanced, the educational benefits of diversity are reduced, especially for the minority. For example, 83 percent of faculty agreed that students participate more frequently in classroom discussions when others of their race/ethnicity are present[41] (see Figure 9). And again, 70 percent of faculty agreed that "a critical mass of students of a particular racial/ethnic group is important to their participation in your classroom"[42] (see Figure 9).

This latter finding is confirmed by faculty descriptions in the supplementary questionnaire of "what constitutes a critical mass," and by faculty focus groups concerning the importance of having multiple representatives of different groups. To these questions, faculty commented, "When the critical mass is reached, students of color are empowered and participate more fully" and "Racially diverse students are often less likely to participate if they are in the minority or don't have a critical mass." Asked to clarify what they meant by "critical mass," faculty focused on the need for students to feel safe and comfortable, and, by implication, the lack of safety or comfort felt when one finds oneself a "solo" or "minority of one." One respondent elaborated, saying, "Enough students to overcome the silencing effect of being isolated in the classroom by ethnicity/race/gender. Enough students to provide safety for expressing views." Another said "critical mass" means "a minimum number to provide a 'safe' environment for open discussion."

In focus group discussions, faculty also discussed the pedagogical value for all students of having multiple representatives of domestic racial/ethnic groups. They commented that both minority and majority students learn about the breadth of experiences within U.S. categories of race/ethnicity, which broadens their understanding of these communities. They added that multiple representation helps reduce the stereotyping that may occur when only one person represents a group. Faculty also commented that students who are "solo" members of a conversation voice frustration about being perceived as a category rather than as an individual. One respondent punctuated this discussion, saying, "I'd be thrilled to have a critical mass of students of color. I've never had one. This is a serious concern for us as a discipline."

Two Views of Classroom Equality: Treating All Alike versus Treating All Differently

While the majority of Macalester faculty reported positive opinions about diversity on campus and, by extension, voiced support for educational equity, their responses were less cohesive around how to implement diversity initiatives and bring about equity. Written comments and supplementary focus groups brought these divisions to light. Faculty all reported being opposed to racism and in support of equity, but they did not agree about how to enact equity.

Some faculty believe that race (and gender) should be irrelevant in the classroom; others believed that race (and gender) are important factors that need to be addressed on many different levels by the academy. These differences are reflective of the "color blind" v. proactive positions we see elsewhere in the debate over racial/ethnic equality initiatives.

Faculty in disciplines that typically do not address social life, hence race/ethnicity, were more likely than their peers to affirm positively that the academy should be race- and gender-neutral, and to try to run their classrooms and research groups without consideration of social variables. Faculty whose disciplines did incorporate a consideration of humans in social groupings were much more likely to argue that research and classroom experience would be strengthened by acknowledging and embracing difference. One faculty advocate of the race-neutral point of view stated:

I do not make race a factor in my classes if at all possible. When a student answers a question I do not think "That is a black student's answer." I do not calculate how many of my students are in which U.S. Census designation. I don't use U.S. Census designations to classify my students. I do not even use skin color. I get lots of skin color. I'm not going to assume a color denotes "black" or "Indian" or "Hispanic." Sometimes it does, but that has to be determined on an individual basis.

This faculty person's point of view is an important caveat to the overall response of faculty regarding race and the educational drawbacks of perpetuating homogeneity in the academy. It reminds us that there is some danger in focusing too exclusively on racial/ethnic difference, pointing out that such tunnel vision may inadvertently essentialize and prioritize the racial or ethnic identity of students over other aspects of their identity. On the other hand, we must exercise caution not to overstate this risk. The view that all must be treated the same springs, at least in part, from the assumption that all the standards for judging appropriate conduct and excellence are necessary and socially neutral, rather than "natural" only to a subgroup of the whole. Faculty adherents of this position may unquestioningly impose inappropriate social and cognitive expectations specific to their subgroup that are irrelevant to the development of intellectual excellence and civic responsibility. The value of vigorous debate is that it corrects the tendency to view the world (of theory or of social life) only through one's own cultural lens.

Because the preponderance of data strongly support the position that Macalester faculty view diversity in the classroom as beneficial or, at worst, neutral, the author has focused on these positions and has drawn supporting quotations that illuminate these views. But it should be reported that a few faculty voiced some concerns about diversity as enacted at Macalester and as represented in the questionnaire. For example, one faculty member noted that they taught about Native Americans, and stated that, because they were neither a race nor an ethnicity, they found the questionnaire unanswerable.

A social fact at Macalester that can make it difficult to fulfill the promise of diversity is the distribution of students and faculty among racial/ethnic groups. Despite the institution's efforts, the population of minority students at Macalester is still relatively small. As documented above, those Macalester faculty who find that diversity is of value report that a critical mass of students of relevant racial/ethnic categories enhances the benefits of diversity. Faculty report that in the absence of a critical mass, those in the minority may feel shy, uncomfortable—silenced. Several Macalester faculty characterized their classes as falling short of this critical mass. When too much in the minority, the educational experience of U.S. students of color may be less than optimal.

Another difficulty can be a lack of academic and social support for bright minority students whose academic preparation may be unequal to that of their majority classmates because of unequal access to quality education at the elementary and high school levels. Though the problem of poor college preparation is by no means limited to minority students, students of color are disproportionately represented in this group. Preparatory differences, especially if racially/ethnically "biased," contribute to the complexity of fulfilling the promise of diversity. These differences in initial educational endowments create classroom challenges that faculty may not be trained to address.

Finally, some faculty expressed concern about whether majority students ever felt "silenced" in diverse classes: "Students, white students in particular, can be tense and defensive in a racially diverse classroom." These comments do not cancel out the responses of those who viewed lively debate or tension in a positive light. They do, however, point to an understandable anxiety felt by many individuals when faced with conflict that they perceive as potentially inflammatory. Facilitating productive, charged discourse is a skill that can be learned. Presumably faculty expertise and mentoring could play a significant role in teaching other faculty to create safe climates for the discussion of students' divergent ideas and experiences.

Conclusion

The hypotheses tested in this research have been strongly supported by the Macalester data. Faculty at a small, selective, historically European American liberal arts college that now has a commitment to diversity have found that the presence of students from many domestic racial/ethnic groups benefits all students. Specific findings include, first, that faculty judge that domestic racial and ethnic diversity in the classroom is important in fulfilling the college's educational mission.

A second important finding is that, on balance, faculty report that the following educational outcomes are positively affected by the presence of multiple racial/ethnic groups in the classroom: (a) broader sharing of experiences, (b) raising new issues/perspectives, c) substantive discussion of racial/ethnic issues, (d) incorporation of relevant racial and ethnic issues in assignments, (e) confrontation of stereotypes relevant to social/political issues, (f) confrontation of stereotypes concerning substantive issues in the faculty member's discipline, (g) development of a willingness to examine one's own perspectives and values, and (h) exposure to perspectives with which students disagree or which they do not understand. Faculty also agree that the majority of European American students benefit from racial diversity, as evidenced by their consideration of new issues and their more critical reading of course materials. Further, faculty report that they themselves view diversity more positively as a result of their classroom experiences.

Third, faculty who taught classes focused on race/ethnicity reported greater or equal benefit from classroom diversity than did those who only included content relevant to diversity. In turn, those who only included content relevant to diversity reported greater or equal benefit than did those who did not teach about diversity on several of the measures that the faculty as a whole had judged diversity to facilitate. These include the following valued outcomes: (a) the inclusion of [new] perspectives and experiences, (b) the examination of one's own perspectives and values and exposure to contradictory ones, and (c) the importance of having a "critical mass" of representatives from the racial/ethnic groups present.

Fourth, faculty who taught about race/ethnicity viewed classroom diversity as a more valued tool in achieving some educational goals than did those who did not teach about diversity, including (a) improvement in the students' ability to think critically and (b) development of students' leadership abilities.

And, finally, faculty report the importance of moving beyond the "solo" or "token" presence of students (and faculty) of color to ensure that a "critical mass" is achieved in which all feel supported by others, and in which diversity *within* groups also may be explored.

Notes

1. The American Council on Education's (ACE) Minority Concerns division and the American Association of University Professors' (AAUP) Committee L for the Status of Minorities in the Profession have collaborated in building a research consortium that would conduct and advise on research concerning the educational impact of diversity in the classroom. The core research group consists (in alphabetical order) of Jonathan Alger, formerly of the AAUP, now with the University of Michigan; Jorge Chapa, Michigan State University; Roxane Gudeman, Macalester College; Patricia Marin, ACE; Geoff Maruyama, University of Minnesota; Jeff Milem, University of Maryland; Jose Moreno, Harvard University; and Deborah Wilds, formerly with ACE, now with the Gates Foundation. A number of other people also participated in discussing the research. Roxane Gudeman pilot-tested the questionnaire at Macalester College, then analyzed and wrote up the results which are reported in this paper.

Funding for this project has been provided by the Spencer Foundation, the American Council on Education, the American Association of University Professors, The Civil Rights Project at Harvard University, the Julian Samorra Research Institute, Michigan State University, and the Law School Admissions Council.

2. Several Macalester College faculty members (Anna Meigs, Clay Steinman, Janet Carlson, Jim Stewart) led the process of applying to the Bush Foundation for funds to support enhancing the ability of Macalester faculty to be effective classroom teachers and advisers with all students, however different their cultural experiences were from those of the faculty. The Bush Foundation awarded Macalester a planning grant to be used in developing a major grant proposal. A group of approximately twenty faculty collaborated with the organizers in working on this proposal. Activities that occurred during the planning process included holding focus groups, visiting other institutions, and collecting information from faculty via the Faculty Diversity Questionnaire.

3. The questionnaire used was developed by a research team working under the auspices of the American Council on Education and the American Association of University Professors. The goal of the team was to design a questionnaire that would be sent to a random sample of several thousand higher education faculty at a cross-section of institutional types across the United States. Target faculty were to be faculty in the social sciences and humanities.

4. Of the respondents, 54 percent were male; 46 percent, female; 87 percent were white/Caucasian (domestic and international); 13 percent, another race/ethnicity (domestic and international); 42 percent were humanities faculty; 26 percent, social scientists; and 32 percent, natural scientists. Forty percent of the sample were full professors; 26 percent, associate professors; 25 percent, assistant professors; and 9 percent, lecturers or instructors. Politically, 25 percent of the faculty described themselves as "radical," 48 percent as "liberal," 20 percent as "moderate," and 6 percent as "conservative." No one described her/himself as "far right." Eleven of the sample faculty were born outside the United States—seven in the humanities division, and 2 each in the social sciences and humanities. Continents of origin included Asia (Southeast and South), Europe, South America, and North America. Finally, 65 percent reported including racial/ethnic content in one or more of their classes; 35 percent did not.

5. Analyses of variance, t-tests, and Sign Tests all assess the probability of whether a difference in average scores or proportional frequencies among two or more groups or two sets of data might merely represent random fluctuations in sample averages drawn from sets which have the SAME underlying average or frequency, in which case any difference observed would be judged "not significant," or whether the difference, given the frequency or range of scores, is large enough that we may conclude that it did not occur by chance. The accepted "standard" for drawing this conclusion in psychology is that a finding of the given magnitude would be predicted to occur only five or less times in 100 samples. When multiple tests are done, as in this study, one must use a more rigorous standard because the assessment of multiple tests raises the probability that any one of them will be "significant" by chance.

Correlations and Chi Square tests show whether or not two variables either vary in value together (correlations) or vary in frequency together (Chi Square). Two variables are significantly correlated IF knowledge of the value of one helps predict the value of the other. The relationship may be positive, in which case higher values on one variable predict higher values on the other, or negative, in which case higher values on one predict lower values on the other. Chi Square tests measure whether knowledge of one non-numerical characteristic of an individual helps predict their characteristic on another variable. For example, we might ask how many faculty in the social sciences and natural sciences teach content relevant to diversity. If the proportion of natural sciences faculty teaching about diversity is sufficiently lower than the proportion of social sciences faculty teaching about diversity, then we may conclude that there is a "real" difference, not just a randomly observed difference, between the likelihood that natural scientists and social scientists will teach about diversity.

6. Psychologists judge that a significance level of .05 or less is a "significant" result that supports a conclusion that an outcome consistent with the hypothesized outcome is not just a chance finding.

7. All of the probability levels described in the text are, by convention, labeled "statistically significant" in most cases. When a researcher makes many statistical comparisons, as in this case, a "lower" probability should be used before judging a result significant because the collective probability of any of the results occurring by chance must be considered.

    The LOWER the probability level, the LESS LIKELY it is that the result is merely a chance one, and the more likely it is that the result reflects an hypothesized outcome.

8. T1******. The faculty were found to be more supportive of diversity than expected by chance. (One sample, one sided t-test = –4.361, df = 75, p < .0001.)

9. T1******. The faculty were significantly more likely to see diversity as essential to fulfilling the college's mission than expected by chance. (One sample, one sided t-test = –9.748, df = 79, p < .0001.)

10. T1******. The faculty significantly disagree with the statement that an emphasis on diversity has lowered the quality of the institution. (One sample, one-tail t-test = 10.96; df = 74; p < .0001)

11. T1******. The faculty significantly disagree with the statement that an emphasis on diversity has lowered the quality of the student body (One sample, one-tail t-test = 11.86; df = 72; p < .0001).

12. (F******; T1*****)

13. A repeated measures ANOVA indicated that the forms of diversity differed significantly from one another (F9,56 [504] = 6.99; p < .0001). Detailed comparisons indicated that faculty judged racial and ethnic diversity to be more important in contributing to the quality of learning than was a "range of ages," "differing academic majors," and geographic diversity. Our sample t-tests were performed using the scale midpoint, 3, as the hypothesized mean. "Racial/ethnic diversity," "gender balance," and "international diversity" had t values of 3.7 or greater with associated individual probabilities of less than .0005 (one-tailed), which is an acceptable criterion of significance given the 10 comparisons that were made [to be collectively significant at the .05 level, each comparison had to reach a probability of occurrence under the assumption of chance of .005 or less]. The three forms of diversity judged to be marginally important to the faculty had t values with probabilities of occurrence ranging between .02 and .01 (one-tailed), which did not meet the standard for significance necessary in the context of multiple comparisons. The final four comparisons were not significantly judged to be important.

14. T1******. The faculty significantly agree that "racial-ethnic diversity in your classroom allows for a broader variety of experiences to be shared" sometimes through very often. One sample, one-tail t-test, t = 9.32, df = 68, p < .0001.

15. T1******. The faculty significantly agree that minority students sometimes through very often raises issues/perspectives not raised by non-minority students. One sample, one-tail t-test, t = 6.73, df = 69, p < .0001.

16. T1******. The faculty significantly agree that race/ethnic issues are sometimes through always discussed more substantively in a diverse classroom than in a homogeneous classroom. One sample, one-tail t-test, t = 5.293, df = 50, p < .0001.

17. T1******. The faculty significantly agree that students in their racially/ethnically diverse classroom are sometimes through always more likely to incorporate relevant racial and ethnic issues in their assignments. One sample, one-tail t-test = 5.95; df = 53; p < .0001.

18. In addition to the two forms of stereotypes reported in the main body of the paper and in Figure 5, faculty agreed that two other types of stereotypes were significantly more likely to be confronted in diverse than in homogeneous classes, those about "racial/ethnic issues" (t = 5.23; df = 49; p < .0001) and those about "personal experiences." (t = 4.85; df = 44; p < .0001). Because the content overlapped somewhat with other questions, these two results have been relegated to this footnote.

19. T1******. Faculty significantly find that students in diverse classrooms are sometimes through always more likely to have stereotypes confronted concerning social/political issues. One sample, one-tail t-test = 4.39; df = 48; p < .0001.

20. T1*****. Faculty significantly find that students in diverse classrooms are sometimes through always more likely to have stereotypes confronted concerning substantive issues in their field. One sample, one-tail t-test = 4.39; df = 48; p < .0001.

21. T1******. The faculty agree that diversity never "impedes the discussion of substantive issues." One sample, one-tail t-test = –5.35, df = 72; p < .0001. *[No–never = 58; sometimes through very often = 15.]*

22. T1*. On average, faculty agree that diversity NEVER "create[s] tensions and arguments along racial/ethnic lines." One sample, one-tail t-test = –2.21; df = 69; p < .02. Note that this result must be judged as marginal at best since the associated probability is rather high in this context of multiple comparisons.

23. T1******. Faculty significantly agree that "interaction between students of different racial/ethnic backgrounds" is important or very important in "helping students develop a willingness to examine their own perspectives and values." One sample, one-tail t-test = 3.97, df = 67, p < .0001.

24. T1*****. Faculty significantly agree that white students are positively affected in the issues they consider by the presence of students of other racial/ethnic groups in the classroom. One sample, one-tail t-test = –3.82; df = 60; p < .0002.

25. T1***. Faculty significantly agree that white students are positively affected in the issues they consider by the presence of students of other racial/ethnic groups in the classroom. One sample, one-tail t-test = –2.86; df = 62; p < .005.

26. T1******. Faculty significantly agree that their "views about racial/ethnic diversity" have been POSITIVELY "affected by racially/ethnically diverse classrooms." One sample, one-tail t-test = –5.75; df = 67; p < .0001.

27. Rank and gender are significantly related to each other. (Chi Square between rank and gender χ^2 = 15.18, df = 3, p < .005.)

28. Gender and political choice are significantly related. (Chi Square between gender and political choice χ^2 = 14.30, df = 3, p < .005.)

29. Rank and political choice were significantly related. Chi Square between academic rank and political choice χ^2 = 19.20, df = 9, p < .05.

30. Within the faculty, we would expect those whose disciplines also have incorporated a commitment to diversity to value diversity more highly. Historians, sociologists, psychologists, and anthropologists are examples of disciplines in which the

principal professional association has affirmed the pedagogical and professional value of diversity. But within each discipline lie a range of topical foci that may or may not include racial/ethnic diversity as part of the content. Of the traditional liberal arts disciplines, we could expect those in the humanities and social sciences and perhaps some of those in the biological sciences to be most likely to include diversity as a focal topic. And we might also expect that preprofessional programs such as education, those disciplines that have many preparing for medical, business, law, theological, social work, public service, etc., to be concerned about social diversity in the populations served.

Indeed, we find that those in the humanities and social sciences do report higher benefit from diversity in the classroom than those in the social sciences. Indeed, some faculty responded "not relevant" to questions concerning the effect of diversity even though these same faculty had agreed that diversity was an important institutional value.

31. The Chi Square test was used to compare Political Choice with Inclusion of ethnic content. $\chi^2 = 12.67$; df = 6; p < .05. Comparing the two political anchors in this population, "far left" and "conservative," we find that 25% of those who describe themselves as "far left" teach a class focused on racial/ethnic diversity in comparison to none of those describing themselves as "conservative." On contrast, only 5% of the "far left" include no racial ethnic content, in contrast to 40% of "conservatives."

32. Faculty were divided into two categories, liberal (far left and liberal) and conservative (moderate, conservative). The average score of the two groups was compared on their judgments about whether diversity in the classroom had positively affected their views about racial and ethnic diversity. Both groups judged diversity to have had a positive effect on their views, but liberal faculty rated the effect as significantly more positive than did conservative faculty. (Unpaired, 1-tail t-test = − 2.65; df = 65; p < .005.)

33. F******; CLASS > CONTENT, T2*****; CONTENT > NONE, T2******. In a one-way analysis of variance, the extent to which faculty taught about diversity was found to be related significantly to extent to which they endorsed the statement that a diverse classroom "increases the range of issues/perspectives . . . discussed" in the predicted direction. F = 12.53, df(2,64); p < .0001. Planned comparisons: Class v. Content: t = 3.97, df = 46, p < .0005; Content v. None: t = 4.71, df = 53, p < .0001.

34. F******; CLASS > CONTENT T2*; CONTENT > NONE, T2***. Two items concern whether "a critical mass" of students of a particular racial or ethnic group is important in determining if students will participate in the class, and whether participation in class discussions is increased by the presence of others of the same race/ethnicity. The two items were highly correlated (r = .726) and were combined. A one-way analysis of variance using Teach Diversity as a grouping variable revealed that the more faculty taught about diversity, the more they judged the presence of more than a token number of students to be important in whether students participated. F = 8.43; df(2,43); p < .001. Planned Comparisons: Class v. Content: t = 2.04; df = 32; p < .02; Content v. None: t = 2.65; df = 34; p < .006.

35. In a one-way analysis of variance, the extent to which faculty taught about diversity was found to be related significantly to the extent to which they endorsed the statements "it is important to have diversity both to encourage students to examine their own views", and also to "expose them to perspectives with which they disagree or which they do not understand" in the predicted direction. F = 8.51; df = (2,62); p < .0005. Planned comparisons: Class v. Content: t = 2.16, df = 47, p < .03; Content v. None: t = 2.81, df = 51, p < .01. Please note that two similar items were

summed in this comparison in order to simplify reporting. The correlation between the two items was very high (r = .889).

36. F******; CLASS > CONTENT, T2*, CONTENT > NONE, T2****. In a one-way analysis of variance, the extent to which faculty taught about diversity was found to be related significantly to extent to which they endorsed the statement that diversity in the classroom is important in "helping students develop their ability to think critically." One-way ANOVA df(2,65) F = 12.243, p < .0001. One-tail planned comparisons: Class v. Content: t = –2.36, df = 45, p < .01; Content v. None: t = –3.45, df = 54, p < .0005.

37. F*; CLASS > CONTENT, T2*, CONTENT > NONE, T2 NS. In a one-way analysis of variance, the extent to which faculty taught about diversity was found to be related significantly to the extent to which they endorsed the statement that diversity in the classroom is important in "helping students develop their ability to think critically." One-way ANOVA df(2,61) F = 3.74, p < .05. One-tail planned comparisons: Class vs. Content: t = –1.81, df = 43, p < .05; Content vs. None: t = –1.46, df = 50, p = NS.

38. Eighteen faculty said 0–5 percent; 24 said 6–10 percent; nine said 11–15 percent; 12 said 16–25%; and four said over 40 percent. No one selected 26–40 percent.

39. The median response was 11–15 percent with 72 percent (n = 48) of the faculty choosing this category or higher.

40. ST, ****. One sample sign test, p < .005.

41. T1, ******. Faculty agree that participation in class discussions is enhanced by the presence of other students from the same racial/ethnic group. One sample, one-tail t-test = 6.92; df = 57; p < .0001.

42. T1******. Faculty significantly agree that "a critical mass of students of a particular racial/ethnic group is important to their participation." One-sample, one-tail t-test = 4.87; df = 49; p < .0001.

References

American Council on Education and American Association of University Professors. (2000). *Does diversity make a difference? Three research studies on diversity in college classrooms*. Washinton, DC: American Council on Education.

Chang, M. (1999, January). *An examination of conceptual and empirical linkages between diversity initiatives and student learning in higher education*. Paper presented at the American Council on Education Working Conference and Research Symposium on Diversity and Affirmative Action, Washington, DC.

Dworkin, R. (1996). We need a new interpretation of academic freedom. In L. Menand (Ed.), *The future of academic freedom* (pp. 187–198). Chicago: University of Chicago Press.

Haskell, T. (1996). Justifying the rights of academic freedom in the era of "power/knowledge." In L. Menand (Ed.), *The future of academic freedom* (pp. 43–94). Chicago: University of Chicago Press.

McPherson, M. (1998, October). *A meditation on our values*. Macalester Web page. Available: www.macalester.edu

Nussbaum, M. (1997). *Cultivating humanity: A classical defense of reform in liberal education*. Cambridge, MA: Harvard University Press.

CHAPTER 13

Reflections on Affirmative Action: Its Origins, Virtues, Enemies, Champions, and Prospects

PAUL M. GASTON

Thirty years ago—it was the spring of 1969—University of Virginia students brought to a climax a new movement of positive action to acknowledge and confront the scourge of racism that tainted their university and denied justice and respect to their fellow citizens. Memories of that season of marches, midnight meetings, speeches, demands and counterdemands, victories and compromises, came flooding in on me as I sat in a jammed-to-the-edges auditorium in the spring of 1999.[1] The out-of-town speaker condemned the university for what she called its practice of racial discrimination. "I don't think you end discrimination by discriminating against new groups of people," Linda Chavez said. "Our admissions policy," she claimed, "smacks of the kind of racism that has long plagued this nation." Then she told us that we must not "continue to judge people based on the color of their skin." Like other speakers across the nation at her end of the political spectrum, she told us that the legacy of Martin Luther King Jr. was on her side.[2]

I sank despondently in my seat, wondering how it was that this Orwellian *Newspeak* had spread viruslike through our culture.[3] Looking about the room I wondered how many here had been infected by it, how many battles would have to be fought all over again. I wished for a time machine that would bring to the stage the young heroes of 1969. Their courage, clarity of moral purpose, and honest engagement with their past had broken the log jam of our common history.

The movement of 1969 was more than a decade in the making. When I joined the faculty in 1957, the burden of the university's history weighed heavily, and was everywhere in plain sight for any who wished to look. Three years earlier the U.S. Supreme Court had unanimously and eloquently condemned the Virginia law requiring that blacks and whites attend separate (and everywhere unequal) public schools. The state's leaders responded with defiance, vowing to shut down schools before they would let black and white children enter them together. In the fall of 1958 they made good on their word, padlocking school doors in Charlottesville, Norfolk, and Warren County. One Virginia county, Prince Edward, was the only community in the South that actually ended public education completely, shutting down its entire school system to avoid integration. The university's president, Colgate Darden, a decent and humane man, knew the folly and understood the mean-spiritedness of this "massive resistance" program, but he could not bring himself to mobilize opposition to it.[4]

The president and the Board of Visitors also opposed the racial integration of the university. They accepted the inevitability of it reluctantly, forcing blacks seeking admission to sue or take advantage of previous court orders. It was not until 1961 that the first African American entered the college, the last bastion in the university of "separate but equal" segregation. Edgar Shannon, who succeeded Darden in 1959, apparently persuaded the Board of Visitors to allow an engineering student to transfer—in the middle of the academic year—thus heading off an inevitable defeat in the courts. All through the late 1950s and well into the 1960s the administration's cautious resistance was unchallenged by influential student opinion. Undergraduates in particular opposed and often venomously condemned each new crack in their culture of segregation. The *Cavalier Daily* denounced a student-faculty boycott of the nearby movie theater that admitted whites only as an affront to the university's tradition of honor. The Student Council refused to allow a newly formed interracial group to exist on campus until it promised it would never foster "demonstrations." Only then would the council, in its own words, deem the group "worthy of the university and of Student Council approval."[5]

By 1963, civil rights groups and discussions were a small but conspicuous part of the UVA scene. Dr. King came to speak in March of that year. The first sit-in took place at a nearby restaurant two months later.[6] Student opposition to the segregation spirit of the past showed itself more forcibly with each new academic season. The administration, however, remained cautious and aloof. Admissions dean Marvin Perry later quietly provided a student interracial group with helpful information on admissions procedures. Thus armed, students became unofficial recruiters of black applicants, traveling to a few black high schools with application forms and a message of welcome. These students were the first "affirmative action" agents at their university.

By 1965, the balance of opinion among student leaders and opinion-makers, as well as in the student body generally, was moving away from the die-hard segregationists. Determined blacks were now making their way into the student body; the national mood was shifting dramatically; far-reaching civil rights laws were passed; the national civil rights movement seemed to have washed away myths that had undergirded segregation; and the cadre of progressive students and faculty grew to the point where a movement for change could be sustained. By 1967 and 1968, *Cavalier Daily* editors blasted the university for its "tolerance of prejudice" and the "furtherance of a sick heritage." And the Student Council, instead of harassing and harnessing interracial and progressive groups, now launched investigations of racial discrimination within the university and churned out resolutions demanding positive action on many fronts.[7]

During the 1968–1969 academic year, the student movement reached the peak of its moral and political persuasiveness. Fifty-two full-time black students were now in residence. A student coalition comprising the newly formed Black Student Union, radical groups like the Southern Student Organizing Committee and the Students for a Democratic Society, and the larger "moderate" group of more traditional leaders set the agenda for university change and charted the course to the future. After one all-night meeting, the coalition issued a bold call for action:

> In times like these rational and compassionate men cannot afford to tolerate bigotry. . . . Thus we of the University community feel it to be our moral obligation to press the Board of Visitors, the Governor of the State of Virginia, the Legislature, as well as citizens of the state, for immediate action in the area of race relations. The days are gone in which progress can be measured by minute degrees. The days are gone when apologies are sufficient.[8]

The governor—a massive resistance leader named Mills Godwin who said that even the slightest integration of public schools would be "a cancer eating at the very life blood of our public school system"[9]—dismissed the students rudely when they called on him, making it clear that the culture of segregation would not be dismantled by the state's elected leaders. On the university grounds, however, the coalition shaped Student Council action, set the tone for editorial writing and news reporting, and won critical support from the Inter Fraternity Council. Drawn into this heady ferment, President Shannon became a partner in the movement for change. Before the year was out, he accepted most of the coalition's demands. The governor and the legislature were bypassed and the Board of Visitors did not rein in the president. The university would never be the same again.

President Shannon made commitments that year to begin to recruit black undergraduates. As a modest move in that direction he gave a young black graduate student the job of traveling about the state to encourage African Americans to apply for admission. The days when blacks could be recruited only unofficially and secretly were over. The president and the faculty also promised to seek black faculty members, to teach a course in black studies, and to inaugurate an interdisciplinary Afro-American Studies program. It was a small beginning, but it was a beginning.

* * *

A generation has come and gone since then. A lot of history has been built on the achievements of the students of the 1960s. Building on these accomplishments, the university began to attract the kind of talented and worthy student body that any self-respecting university should admire. Now, as you walk into any classroom or about the grounds, you will see students from every state in the Union and 108 foreign countries, along with a few (too few) Native Americans and "hyphenated-Americans" of both ancient and recent origin.[10] In addition to African Americans you will see Mexican- Chinese- Japanese- Korean- and Vietnamese-Americans, all virtually absent from the landscape thirty years ago. The revolutionized configuration of the student body has brought with it an inescapable demonstration of the old aphorism that student learning is not limited to the classroom and the library. We understand better than before the importance of what students learn from each other. The broadening of the student body has created a wider range of learning opportunities, quickened and sharpened intellectual discourse, reduced parochialism, and encouraged students to question assumptions and better understand their own inherited values and beliefs.

The presence of black students—they constitute about 10 percent of the student body—works in both obvious and subtle ways to improve the quality and validate the mission of the university. For one thing, it acts as a potent check on previously unchallenged expressions of bigotry and mean-spiritedness. Racial slights and slurs persist, but the presence of real people in place of the demeaning stereotypes born of innocence and ignorance is a powerful educative force for white students and faculty alike;

and, in ways hard to document, that presence helps to relieve them of the hubris Thomas Jefferson long ago identified as one of the unspoken penalties of white power and privilege. For their part, black students in large numbers have become loyal alums, the number of them making financial contributions to the university slightly exceeding the alumni average. This is but one of many validations of the courage, sacrifice, and wisdom of their predecessors who made their admission possible. Their predecessors knew, and they now find, that opportunities once denied are there to be seized. Their lives are better materially, intellectually, and spiritually because they have been here. Finally, the mission of the university to serve the Commonwealth and the nation is forwarded by their presence and perseverance. It is hard to think of a greater asset for social stability and wise public policy than a racially integrated citizenry, loyal to the nation and state but vigilantly watchful and constructively critical of its actions.

The university is a better place because of both diversity and affirmative action, but they are not the same thing. They are entwined in a symbiotic relationship, but positive actions to recruit and enroll black students, although they result in a racially diverse student body, stem from unique origins and their continuation is justified because of ongoing special circumstances. The origins lie in the 300 years of exclusion and exploitation prescribed by the white supremacy culture. In this sense, affirmative action is rooted in America's deepest moral dilemma and goes to the heart of who we are as a people. Justification of its continuation—and, indeed, expansion and improvement—lies in the many structural and personal barriers that have yet to be removed, as well as new ones society condones.

As it has become an integrated and more broadly diverse institution, UVA has simultaneously vaulted to the position of number one (some, especially Californians, would say number two) public university in the country. The commonly offered reasons for our excellence are our internationally acclaimed faculty and the rising competitiveness of the quest for admission. Faculty members decline offers from Harvard, Yale, Princeton, Johns Hopkins, and other famous centers of learning to come or stay here. The best students in the country often decline admission offers from once more-favored colleges and universities to enroll here. One could hardly have imagined this in 1969. Most of us who have been here for all these years, however, know that top faculty and bright students are not the whole story. The deeper explanation is that our excellence is organically related to the very opening up of the university that began with the student movements of the 1960s. Our excellence could not have been achieved by keeping our doors closed. It has been made possible by opening them. Continued excellence depends not only on keeping them open, but, in fact, on opening them wider. These are needs and ambitions no court should be allowed to repudiate.[11]

How Affirmative Action Changed My Classes

When I joined the faculty at the University of Virginia in 1957, I hoped that my teaching of Virginian and southern history might challenge young men of the state and region to reevaluate the beliefs that made them feel morally secure at the top of the racial privilege pyramid.

Some of them accepted the challenge. The books they read and the discussions we held led them to concede that slavery was not benign; that segregation was instituted to protect white privilege; and that their own good fortune was rooted in the long history of exploitation of blacks by whites. (Virginia public schools had a history textbook, *Cavalier Commonwealth*, that informed students that many blacks had been happy under the old system.) A few students even came to question the sainthood of General Lee.

These students, however, were a small minority. For the majority, books, lectures, and discussions were weak opponents of the received wisdom handed down from generation to generation by trusted family guardians of historical truth. My notes from the late 1950s and early 1960s are filled with examples of tradition thwarting scholarship. Confronted by *The Strange Career of Jim Crow*, C. Vann Woodward's powerful brief history of segregation, students rejected its findings because father and mother said they were false. More than one cited the authority of the family servant as proof that the "colored people" preferred to be separate from the whites.

One year I worked particularly closely with a tall, handsome, self-assured son of one of the First Families of Virginia. We had friendly, spirited exchanges in my office and agreed to read each other's favorite books. I was cheered by an essay in his final examination paper that acknowledged humane features of the New Deal, including some of its racial policies. A few days later he strolled into my office to ask to change what he had written. He told me: "My father says I was wrong." I countered: "Do you mean that your father can wipe out in one conversation what I have been trying to establish for a year?" "That's about it," he replied, with a broad grin.

Students like this one dominated the classrooms in those days. With their inherited racial beliefs, sometimes questioned by the few dissenting white students, they were never embarrassed by the presence of the people whose history and nature they spoke of with confidence. Before the decade was out the voices of the dissenters grew stronger, but it was not until the 1970s that black students appeared regularly in my classes. Then the old hubris of race and class was confronted in new and effective ways.

Sometimes the simple presence of blacks in the room undermined it. The central problem with most of the racist whites I taught was not flawed character but the ignorance and inexperience born of their inheritance. Reared to be decent people by the narrow standards of their forebears, they usually applied that decency to their new classmates. In the process they learned to question their own generalizations. I watched many of these students in those early days work on more measured, thoughtful responses to the questions I posed, wondering how they would sound to the new students. I also watched them listen carefully to their black classmates whose views of the history we were studying differed so markedly from theirs. They began to ask themselves why this was so.

These things happened without any planning on my part; they flowed from the mere fact of the integrated classroom, building on the contrasting backgrounds and assumptions of the students. I added to this natural dynamic by structuring assignments that required black and white students to work together cooperatively, collaborating on interviews, research, and writing. There were never enough African Americans in my large lecture class to make this exercise as fruitful as I would have liked, but it worked wonders for those involved as they experienced the real nature of historical inquiry and analysis, freed as much as possible from the warping authority of inherited beliefs.

In the 1980s and 1990s the African American enrollment moved up to about 10 percent of the college population while the self-confident racism of a generation earlier dissipated. My teaching experiences, however, continued to underscore the dangers of an all-white classroom and strengthened my commitment to affirmative action.

The most striking example I recall started in the late 1980s and continued until I retired in 1997. During those years my students viewed and discussed *Eyes on the Prize*, the brilliant six-part television documentary history of the civil rights movement. Both white and black students agreed that the segregation regime shown in the film was appalling. Overwhelmingly, however, the white students coupled their expressions of horror with a sigh of relief that, as they believed, those days were gone. The movement and the government had ended white supremacy. I could have told them about the flaws in their understanding of history, but, as in my early teaching days, the authority they needed was that of the affected people. And they received it. The African Americans linked past and present in ways that startled and enlightened them. They were better educated students because of the presence, patience, and persistence of their black colleagues.

Affirmative action of the kind I have described here is essential to higher education for many reasons, the pursuit of justice and the good health of our society high among them. My own experience as a teacher tells me it is also essential to the quest for truth and the dissipation of prejudice, as valuable to whites as it is to blacks.

The Attack on Affirmative Action

Until very recently, the university community generally applauded its growing diversity, especially including the 10 percent of the student body that is African American. Isolated complaints and challenges seemed quirky holdovers from the past. Now that has begun to change. Linda Chavez's organization (strategically named The Center for Equal Opportunity) recently issued a well-publicized study charging that our university, along with others, practices a new form of racial discrimination in its admissions process. Blacks—as blacks—are favored over whites—as whites.[12] Following immediately on the release of her study, the Center for Individual Rights named the university as a possible target of a lawsuit. In these new and unsettled conditions, a vigorous student debate over affirmative action emerged, revealing many more supporters than enemies. Critics, however, were more vocal than at any time in the recent past. Concern for the future caused the university rector to appoint a three-person committee from the Board of Visitors to gather information to be ready for a lawsuit should one be entered.

The attack on affirmative action is national in scope. At the close of the 1960s, a powerful reactionary movement began to take shape. We need to understand the history of that movement in order fully to understand the deeper implications and real objectives of the current anti-affirmative action assault.

It began to appear most clearly with Richard Nixon's battle in the 1970s against urban school integration, and then continued with the broad effort in the Reagan years to roll back the progressive racial legislation of the previous generation. Those years also saw the rise of an aggressive, confident conservative movement grappling for the moral high ground. Its crusade was funded and shaped by an ever-increasing number of well-financed and astutely run think-tanks, which churned out a cascading flow of ideologically charged reports on the failures of the liberal past and the promise of the conservative future. With each new pronouncement serving as a catalyst for the next and with the cast of spokesmen broadening to include regulars on the television and talk-show circuits, the nation's confidence in affirmative action as a means of countering the damage done by three centuries of race-based policies of negative action began to waver. Responding to the public mood, a new majority of conservative jurists, appointed by Presidents Nixon, Reagan, and Bush, began to reinterpret the Constitution, finding less and less justification for affirmative action generally.

Radiating from the core of the assault on affirmative action in university admissions policies is a hauntingly *1984*-like claim about the nature and legacy of the civil rights movement. With few exceptions, affirmative action critics are hostile to the basic aims of the civil rights movement and are alienated from all but a handful of black leaders today. They claim, however, that their objection to affirmative action is rooted in their loyalty to Martin Luther King Jr. and the authentic aims of the civil rights movement. The civil rights "establishment," as they call it, earns only their scorn. It is, in their catechism, the great betrayer, not the champion, of African Americans and of the American Dream. Rush Limbaugh wonders how "the vision that Dr. Martin Luther King Jr. had for a color-blind society has been perverted by modern liberalism." Newt Gingrich and Ward Connerly, blasting "the failure of racial preferences," begin their broadside by recalling what they call King's "heartfelt voice" that envisioned a society in which people would be judged by "the content of their character rather than the color of their skin."[13]

The "content of their character rather than the color of their skin" excerpt from King's 1963 "I Have a Dream" speech has become the incantation of choice for the foes of affirmative action. It provides moral cover by draping the King mantle over the most unlikely partisans of the civil rights movement and uses the most famous voice of that movement to condemn policies to which he and it gave birth. Ward Connerly, the Sacramento businessman and University of California regent, became the spokesman of a crusade to win votes for the California anti-affirmative action referendum on King's birthday with the announcement that "Dr. King personifies the quest for a color-blind society." Dr. King's family had to request the advocates of this measure to remove their television commercial, which they claimed was distorting King's views. Conservatives claimed that understanding the King legacy should help stop the terrible "drift" from King's ideal. That drift, as conservative Arch Puddington puts it, widened into a powerful rush "to the current environment of quotas, goals, timetables, race-norming, set-asides, diversity training, and the like." No champion of King pledging fealty to civil rights history could possibly support such things.[14]

Except, of course, that the King that these people enlist in their cause is a figment of their imagination. The shrewd manipulation of the King myth by "color-blind conservatives" began almost as soon as he died, when his nonviolent philosophy was enlisted in the war against the Black Power movement and the outbreaks of urban violence. When the school busing controversy began in the early 1970s, King's words were misused to contain the spread of school integration. By the 1990s his words were routinely exploited as justification for rolling back integration in the colleges and universities achieved through affirmative action.

The "dream" speech is the primary text for "color-blind conservatives." King did say that his dream was deeply rooted in the American dream. But his nightmare, as he said repeatedly, was deeply rooted in the everyday reality of American racism. The promise of the American dream was a promise only; it was, he said, a promissory note to black Americans that was returned by the bank of justice marked "insufficient funds." And to hope for a time when people would be judged "by the content of their character rather than the color of their skin" was not to endorse "race-neutral" public policies. Before the dream of a "color-blind" society could ever become reality, America would have to give up on its color-conscious practice of racial discrimination. King saw few signs of that happening in the country responsible for his nightmares.

It is true that King's comments on affirmative action, a policy not much out of its infancy when he was murdered, generally included approval of a color-blind approach, but never for the same reasons championed by today's reactionary opponents of affirmative action—a fact the Newspeakers work hard to disguise. For one thing, he knew that race-conscious policies in the 1960s would offend large segments of the white population. For another, the debate over how to counteract the damage done by racism was relatively new, and many reasonable people believed that simply opening doors was the critical first step. Moreover, affirmative action in education was hardly on the agenda at all in those days when the first significant numbers of blacks were making their way into previously segregated colleges and universities. Most of the discussion centered on employment and economic inequality. Compensatory policies there were much on King's mind. Testifying before the Kerner Commission, for example, he spoke approvingly of Prime Minister Nehru's "preferential" policies for the Untouchables caste as India's way of "atoning for the centuries of injustice." Instead of proposing a similar policy for America, however, he urged a sweeping new bill of rights for the disadvantaged. Slavery and segregation had impoverished many whites as well as blacks, he believed, and they should be included in any plan to bring economic justice to the country.[15]

It was during these last three years of his life, after the passage of the Civil Rights Act of 1964 and the Voting Rights Act of 1965, that King advocated radical measures that were and are carefully ignored by "color-blind conservatives." Among other things, success would require facing the truth that "the dominant ideology" of America was not "freedom and equality," with racism "just an occasional departure from the norm." To the contrary, he believed that racism was woven into the fabric of the country, intimately linked to its economic system, social structure, and materialistic values. They were all "tied together," he wrote; racism was not an independent variable, standing there on its own. What was really needed was "a radical restructuring of the architecture of American society."[16]

So much for Martin Luther King as the moral partner of the "color-blind conservatives."

* * *

It was against this background that Linda Chavez brought the anti-affirmative action message to Charlottesville. She came as the guest of a new conservative student group called, without embarrassment or irony, the Jefferson Leadership Foundation. In the wake of Chavez's UVA appearance, one *Cavalier Daily* columnist, a third-year college student, leapt to second her indictment of the university. he saw no irony in castigating admissions dean Jack Blackburn, who had shared the platform with Chavez although he was a beneficiary of the university's quota system giving preferential admissions to Virginia residents.[17] The dean's policy, he said, made it easier for blacks, because they are black, than for whites, because they are white, to win admission to the university. "The admissions office should not admit minority students under a different standard than white students," the columnist wrote. He then added his coup de grace: "This is racial discrimination, plain and simple."[18]

Of course it is not "racial discrimination," plain or simple. Newspeak again. One wants to believe that the author meant no offense, but it is hard not to find something grotesque in the claim of a moral equivalency between two diametrically opposed realities. It strains credulity to believe anyone can actually believe that affirmative action and white supremacy are occupants of a common bed of evil. The same is true for the use of such popular terms as "reverse discrimination," suggesting a turning of the tables by blacks on whites. Such assertions raise troubling questions about motives and values, to say nothing of logic and knowledge of history. They need to be swept away before they are allowed to be used as justifications for the end of affirmative action. Gearing up for the struggles ahead of us, I sat down to see if I could fashion a metaphorical broom. This is what I came up with.

Racial discrimination, in its historic sense, meant that black people, not individually but as a race, could not

- attend schools attended by white people;
- attend schools equal to those of white people;
- drink from the same water fountains, relieve themselves in the same toilets, or wash their hands in the same basins used by white people;
- eat in the same restaurants as white people;
- sleep in the same motels and hotels as white people;
- swim in the same pools or from the same beaches as white people;
- sit next to white people in lecture halls, at concerts, or in other public auditoriums;
- sit next to white people on buses or streetcars or other means of public transportation;
- be born or seen by a doctor in the same hospitals or buried in the same graveyards as white people;
- vote or hold public office;
- expect to live in the same neighborhoods, hold the same jobs, or attain the same standards of living as white people.

These are particular forms of historic racial discrimination. They are well known for their place in law and as the manifestations of white supremacy that the civil rights movement sought to end. But we need also to recall the values and beliefs of the white supremacy culture that gave rise to and justified this racial discrimination, its ultimate reason for being. These included the belief that black people, not individually but as a race, were genetically inferior to white people and that this genetic deficiency was responsible for the fact that black people were

- less intelligent than white people
- more prone to crime than white people
- diseased
- unclean
- untruthful
- unreliable

- immoral
- violent
- sexually promiscuous
- sexually threatening, through their men, to white women

The list could go on. These beliefs, even internalized by some blacks, allowed too many white people to condone lynch mobs, poverty, malnutrition, and sickness; and to invent means beyond counting of handing out insult and injury.

Affirmative action means none of these things. It bears no generic, historic, analogous, or constitutional relationship to racial discrimination and the white supremacy myths that created it. What affirmative action in education does mean is

- making a broad effort to identify potential black applicants and to encourage them to apply for admission, often in the face of institutional and emotional barriers;
- judging each applicant holistically as an individual, not as a member of a race;
- offering admission to black students whose application materials are predictive of their success in the university;
- offering admission to some black students whose SAT scores and high school grades are lower than those of some white or Asian or Hispanic applicants who are not offered admission;
- instituting a systematic program of encouraging successful black applicants to accept their offers of admission;
- creating an objective measure of the success of these actions in achieving their goals.

Misconceptions about the admissions process often spring from an unexamined assumption that universities base their admissions offers on estimates of the candidates' academic promise. Such estimates, according to this assumption, can be based objectively on standardized tests and high school grades, with perhaps letters of recommendation thrown in. Such estimates of academic ability are obviously important. But their importance is blown completely out of proportion and their relevance skewed when critics claim discrimination because Applicant A was denied admission while Applicant B, with a lower SAT score, was not. In fact, this must be a normal part of the admissions process, essential to the university's mission. No respectable university bases its offers of admission on estimates of academic ability alone. That would be to repudiate the fundamental goals and aspirations of higher education in America. Harvard, for example, could probably fill up its freshman class with high achievers from one or two states, most from similar upper- and upper-middle-class backgrounds—with the ironic result that they would stop going to Harvard because it did not have the cosmopolitan student body they wanted and expected.[19]

As Dean Blackburn patiently explains, he and his associates try to take a holistic approach, judging each applicant as a whole person, taking into account, in addition to academic ability, the peculiar interests, needs, talents, skills, sex, race, nationality, and place of residence—all these and probably more. The result is that some students from every applying category are rejected: white, black, Hispanic, Asian—as well as male and female, brilliant and not brilliant, rich and poor, athlete and nonathlete, the musician and the tone deaf, leaders and followers, Virginians and non-Virginians. To say that one of these whose application for admission is not successful is a victim of "discrimination" is to empty the word totally of its derogatory meaning—*making choices on the basis of class or race or category without regard for individual merit; to show prejudice*—and return it to its literal meaning—*to make clear distinctions; to make sensible decisions; to judge wisely; to show careful judgment*. Understanding the word this way would be a good thing, but it is not likely that an opponent of affirmative action would agree, or would concede that we have to make choices and that our discriminating judgment should be trusted. And yet that is precisely what a moral and fair university must do to meet its obligations to the citizenry, the national interest, and students. There is no magic formula, no fixed scale for assigning points for each human characteristic. There is discrimination, good faith, a sense of history, and the vision of a future made better by our colleges and universities.

*   *   *

So Linda Chavez was wrong when she told her audience here that we are "discriminating against new groups of people." She was wrong when she said that our admissions policy "smacks of the kind of racism that has long plagued this nation." She was wrong when she charged that we "continue to judge people based on the color of their skin." And she was wrong when she told us that Dr. King's legacy was on her side. She was wrong, but she and her views continue to gain influence.

Affirmative action exists in contemporary America because of the *Bakke* Supreme Court ruling, with the deciding vote case by Justice Lewis Powell of Virginia, who tried to head off a categorical, mechanical formula that would prohibit race from ever being considered in admissions deliberations. He laid out the principle that has not been repudiated by the high court. The principle is this: Race may legitimately be considered where it is "simply one element—to be weighed fairly against other elements—in the selection process." J. Harvie Wilkinson, Powell's one-time law clerk, later a UVA law professor, and now a member of the Fourth Circuit, praised the justice for insisting "that race, *qua* race," could be used by university admissions officers. The irony of a southern conservative saving affirmative action is easy to understand, Wilkinson writes, because Powell believed that law "had to serve the cause of social stability."[20]

It is not only social stability that is at stake today, although that continues to be a major factor. Now, as it prepares for its defense against a possible lawsuit, one hopes that the University of Virginia will take a firm stand not just in defense, but in proud affirmation of what it has achieved in its quest to build a remarkable student body meeting the burden of history and serving the present and future needs of the Commonwealth and the nation.

Twice in its history Virginia has had to choose whether to be the South of the nation or the north of the South. Both times it chose the latter. In 1861 it overcame principled opposition from many of its citizens to secede from the Union. Its prestige emboldened the Confederacy; its manpower, leadership, and resources lengthened and made bloodier the fratricidal war; and its fight for the preservation of slavery became an indelible part of its legacy. Nearly a century later it once again overcame the principled opposition of fellow Virginians to lead the South in a crusade of "massive resistance" against the supreme law of the land, which now called for an end to segregation in its public schools. That decision, like the first one a century earlier, emboldened fellow white southerners and helped to plunge the South and the nation into a long nightmare of hatred and recrimination from which they have not yet recovered.

The Board of Visitors examined the issue after the threat of litigation and criticized the affirmative action plan. University president John Casteen quietly ended the university's affirmative rating process for black applicants in the fall of 1999, following a high-level review. There was, however, an angry response from students and faculty, and the university announced that it was reconsidering the policy change. Who would have thought, when I first came to the university grounds, that our students and our faculty would have to fight against a threat from the federal courts to return us to much greater segregation. After three decades as an interracial university, many wanted to hold onto the changes. Ironically, the threat was from the federal courts which had been transformed by national politics, with little awareness of the history of the issue or what has been accomplished, lacking the wisdom of Justice Powell, whose hopes have been abundantly realized at Mr. Jefferson's university.

Notes

1. I was not actually at the university during the 1968–1969 academic year; on a research leave elsewhere, I kept in touch through letters from students, including the leaders of the student protests, as well as through colleagues, the *Cavalier Daily*, and occasional visits to Charlottesville.
2. *Cavalier Daily*, March 3, 1999.
3. George Orwell coined the term *Newspeak* to stand for the way in which a totalitarian society manipulated and subdued the populace by deliberately using words in ambiguous and contradictory ways—telling lies by appearing to tell the truth. See his classic *Nineteen-Eighty-Four, a Novel* (New York: Harcourt, Brace, 1949). Traces of Newspeak have always appeared in American political discourse, but perhaps never quite so pervasively as in the consultant-driven smooth rhetoric to which we are subjected today. The case of Dr. King as the enemy of affirmative action and the enemies of affirmative action as the friends of Dr. King is one of many such examples, albeit one of the most insidious.
4. Colgate W. Darden to George S. Mitchell, July 25, 1953. Southern Regional Council Archives; copy in author's possession. For a superb study of Darden's racial views, see Mark N. Hamer, "Colgate W. Darden and the School Desegregation Crisis," Honors thesis, University of Virginia, 1988.
5. Bryan Kay, "The History of Desegregation at the University of Virginia: 1950–1969," Unpublished manuscript, University of Virginia, 1979, pp. 66–77; *Cavalier Daily*, April 20, 1961.
6. Paul M. Gaston, "'Sitting in' in the 'Sixties: A Public Lecture Sponsored by the University Union on Life in the 1960s," Unpublished speech, 1985; copy in author's possession. Copies are sometimes available on the Web for courses in American history.
7. *Cavalier Daily*, December 10, 1978.
8. Quoted in Kay, "History of Desegregation," p. 144.
9. Benjamin Muse, *Virginia's Massive Resistance* (Bloomington: Indiana University Press), 1961, p. 30.
10. The figure for foreign countries represented in the student body comes from the academic year 1997–1998.
11. For the most part, affirmative action has worked to enlarge and strengthen a black middle class, here as well as elsewhere. The 10 percent African American enrollment at the university is far below the percentage of blacks in the state. Among the many needs of the state and the nation that universities must help to meet in the future is the opening up of educational opportunity to the poor, blacks especially, but whites also.
12. Robert Lerner and Althea K. Nagai, *Preferences in Virginia Higher Education* (Washington, DC: Center for Equal Opportunity, 1999).
13. Rush H. Limbaugh III, *See: I Told You So* (New York: Pocket Books, 1993), p. 244; Newt Gingrich and Ward Connerly, "Face the Failure of Racial Preferences," *New York Times*, June 15, 1997.
14. Jack E. White, "I Have a Scheme: Ward Connerly's Effort to Hijack Dr. King's Legacy Is Full of Black Humor," *Time*, February 3, 1997, p. 46; Arch Puddington, "What to Do about Affirmative Action," *Commentary*, June 1995.

15. On the origins of affirmative action and King's role in the discussion, see John David Skrentny, *The Ironies of Affirmative Action: Politics, Culture, and Justice in America* (Chicago: University of Chicago Press, 1996), esp. p. 96.

16. David J. Garrow, *Bearing the Cross: Martin Luther King, Jr., and the Southern Christian Leadership Conference* (New York: William Morrow, 1986), pp. 536–539; "Federal Role in Urban Affairs," Hearings before the Subcommittee on Executive Reorganization of the Committee on Government Options, U.S. Senate, 89th Cong., pt. 14, p. 2981.

17. The 65 percent quota for Virginia residents raises a revealing insight into the thinking of anti-affirmative action advocates. Several students over the past few years have remarked to me that they oppose affirmative action because it stigmatizes black students as inferior, unable to gain admission without the affirmative action crutch. Yet I have never met a white Virginian who felt that the quota system that benefited him or her could be similarly regarded as a crutch without which admission would have been denied. Nor have I ever met a Virginian who felt "stigmatized" by the quota system even though out-of-state students had to meet higher standards, on average, than in-state students.

18. Peter Brownfield, "Eliminating the Race Question," *Cavalier Daily*, March 8, 1999. Most of the students at the Chavez-Blackburn "debate" seemed to me to support affirmative action and their dean. That is evidently true of student opinion in general, although no polls have been taken. Student support for affirmative action emerged even before the threat of a lawsuit appeared on the scene, most clearly with the formation of a group called Advocates of Diversity in Education.

19. These points, and many others, are made with particular authority in William G. Bowen and Derek Bok, *The Shape of the River: Long-Term Consequences of Considering Race in College and University Admissions* (Princeton, NJ: Princeton University Press, 1998). The Bowen and Bok work, unique in its empirical study of the actual effects of affirmative action, is based on the records and experiences of 45,000 students over twenty years at twenty-eight elite institutions. It concludes that affirmative action has been a major factor in the creation of a stable black middle class and that it has taught whites to value integration. The University of Michigan lawyers, building on this study, plan to make their own empirical case for affirmative action. See Steven A. Holmes, "Diverse U. of Michigan Tries New Legal Tack," *New York Times*, May 11, 1999.

20. J. Harvie Wilkinson, *From Brown to Bakke: The Supreme Court and School Integration: 1954–1978* (New York: Oxford University Press, 1979), pp. 301–303.

About the Contributors

Dan A. Black is Professor of Economics and Senior Research Associate of the Center for Policy Research at Syracuse University, and a Senior Fellow at the Carnegie Mellon University Regional Census Data Center in Pittsburgh. His research focuses on labor economics and transfer programs. He is author of "Discrimination in an Equilibrium Search Model" in *Journal of Labor Economics* (1995), and coauthor, with J. Barron and M. Loewenstein, of "Gender Differences in Training, Capital, and Wages" in *Journal of Human Resources* (1993).

Mitchell J. Chang is an Assistant Professor in the Graduate School of Education and Information Studies at the University of California, Los Angeles. His areas of interest are the educational effects of diversity in higher education, racial representation and identity, and Asian American studies. His recent publications include "Improving Racial Diversity: A Balancing Act among Competing Interests" in *Review of Higher Education* (2000) and "Expansion and Its Discontents: The Formation of Asian American Studies Programs in the 1990s" in *Journal of Asian American Studies* (1999).

Kermit Daniel is a Consultant with Monitor Group in New York City. Previously he was an Assistant Professor at the Wharton School of the University of Pennsylvania. He is author of "The Marriage Premium" in *The New Economics of Human Behavior,* edited by M. Tommasi and K. Ierulli (1995), and coauthor, with J. Lott, of "Should Criminal Penalties Include Third-Party Avoidance Costs?" in *Journal of Legal Studies* (1995).

Paul M. Gaston is Professor Emeritus of History at the University of Virginia in Charlottesville, where his subjects included Southern and civil rights history. His principal works include *Man and Mission: E. B. Gaston and the Origins of the Fairhope Single Tax Colony* (1993), *Women of Fair Hope* (1984), and *The New South Creed* (1970).

Roxane Harvey Gudeman is a Lecturer at Macalester College in St. Paul, Minnesota. She is a member of the American Association of University Professors' Committee on Historically Black Institutions and the Status of Minorities in the Profession. She is coauthor, with J. Bergquist, of "Academic Freedom and Tenure: Mount Marty College" in *Academe* (1999) and, with S. Gudeman, of "Competition/Cooperation: Revisiting the May 1994 Femecon Debates" in *Feminist Economics* (1997).

Sylvia Hurtado is Associate Professor and Director of the Center for the Study of Higher and Postsecondary Education at the University of Michigan–Ann Arbor. Her major research interests include the ways colleges promote student learning and development for participation in a diverse democracy. She is coauthor, with D. Schoem, of *Intergroup Dialogue: Deliberative Democracy in Schools, Colleges, Workplace, and Community* (forthcoming) and, with J. F. Milem, A. Clayton-Pederson, and W. R. Allen, of *Enacting Diverse Learning Environments: Improving the Campus Climate for Racial/Ethnic Diversity* (1999).

Michal Kurlaender is a doctoral student at the Harvard Graduate School of Education. She has worked as a researcher at The Civil Rights Project at Harvard University for the past four years. Her research interests center around educational stratification and mobility, and on the civil rights implications of education reform efforts.

Jeffrey F. Milem is Associate Professor in the College of Education at the University of Maryland. He is interested in racial dynamics in higher education, the educational outcomes of diversity, and the impact of college on students. He is coauthor, with K. Hakuta, of "The Benefits of Racial and Ethnic Diversity in Higher Education" in *Minorities in Higher Education, 1999–2000: Seventeenth Annual Status Report from the American Council on Education* and, with S. Hurtado, A. Clayton-Pedersen, and W. R. Allen, of *Enacting Diverse Learning Environments: Improving the Campus Climate for Racial/Ethnic Diversity* (1999).

Gary Orfield is Professor of Education and Social Policy at Harvard University. He is also founding codirector of The Civil Rights Project at Harvard University and director of the Harvard Project on School Desegregation. His central interest is the development and implementation of social policy, with a focus on the impact of policy on equal opportunity for success in U.S. society. His recent books are *Religion, Race, and Justice in a Changing America*, with H. J. Lebowitz (1999), and *Chilling Admissions: The Affirmative Action Crisis and the Search for Alternatives*, with E. Miller (1999).

Scott R. Palmer is former Deputy Assistant Secretary in the Office for Civil Rights of the U.S. Department of Education, and Adjunct Professor at the University of Maryland, College Park. In the former capacity he was responsible for legal policy development, including the promulgation of regulations and policy guidance related to the enforcement of federal civil rights laws in education.

Timothy Ready is a Senior Program Officer in the Commission on Behavioral and Social Sciences and Education of the National Research Council in Washington, DC. He is working on a program to promote collaboration between researchers and educators for the purpose of increasing the use of research to enhance student learning. Ready is also an anthropologist who has conducted research on the education and health of Hispanic Americans. His publications include "A Strategy to Tame the Savage Inequalities" (1999) and "Affirmative Action and Project 2000 by 2000" (1996); both appeared in *Academic Medicine* and were coauthored with H. W. Nickens.

Neil L. Rudenstine is President of Harvard University, a position he assumed in 1991. He served previously as Executive Vice President of The Andrew W. Mellon Foundation and was a Professor of English and Senior Administrator at Princeton University. A scholar of Renaissance literature, Rudenstine is an honorary Fellow of New College, Oxford University, and Emmanuel College, Cambridge University, as well as the American Academy of Arts and Sciences.

Janet Ward Schofield is a Professor of Psychology and a Senior Scientist at the Learning Research and Development Center at the University of Pittsburgh. Her main research interests are race relations in K–12 schools and the impact of computer technology on classroom social processes. She is author of "Causes and Consequences of the Colorblind Perspective" in *Multicultural Education,* edited by J. A. Banks and C. A. McGee Banks (2000), and *Black and White in School: Trust, Tension, or Tolerance* (1982).

Jeffrey Smith is Associate Professor of Economics at the University of Western Ontario in London, Ontario. His research centers on the evaluation of social programs, such as job training for the disadvantaged. He is coauthor, with J. Heckman, N. Hohmann, and M. Khoo, of "Substitution and Dropout Bias in Social Experiments: A Study of an Influential Social Experiment" in *Quarterly Journal of Economics* (2000) and, with J. Heckman and R. LaLonde, of "The Economics and Econometrics of Active Labor Market Programmes" in the *Handbook of Labor Economics,* edited by O. Ashenfelter and D. Card (1999).

Dean Whitla is Lecturer on Eduation and Director of the Counseling and Consulting Psychology Program at Harvard Graduate School of Education. A psychologist and psychometrist, his current major research projects include a national study of racial and ethnic diversity programs, faculty development in United Negro College Fund colleges, and improving health care in rural communities through medical informatics.

John T. Yun is a doctoral candidate in education policy research at the Harvard Graduate School of Education. His research focuses on issues of economic equity in education, specifically patterns of school segregation during the past ten years, educational differences between private and public schools, and the effect of school funding on education outcomes. He is coeditor, with E. Mintz, of *The Complex World of Teaching: Perspectives from Theory and Practice* (1999).

Author Index

Subject Index